7/13/10
$27.95
B&T
A5
14 day
7/10

NECESSARY SECRETS

NECESSARY SECRETS

NATIONAL SECURITY, THE MEDIA, AND THE RULE OF LAW

GABRIEL SCHOENFELD

W. W. NORTON & COMPANY

NEW YORK | LONDON

For information about permission to reproduce selections from
this book, write to Permissions, W. W. Norton & Company, Inc.,
500 Fifth Avenue, New York, NY 10110

For information about special discounts for bulk purchases, please contact
W. W. Norton Special Sales at specialsales@wwnorton.com or 800-233-4830

Manufacturing by Courier Westford
Book design by Marysarah Quinn
Production manager: Julia Druskin

Library of Congress Cataloging-in-Publication Data

Schoenfeld, Gabriel.
Necessary secrets : national security, the media, and the rule of law
/ Gabriel Schoenfeld. — 1st ed.
p. cm.
Includes bibliographical references and index.
ISBN 978-0-393-07648-6 (hardcover)
1. Freedom of information—United States. 2. Freedom of the press—
United States. 3. Security classification (Government documents)—
United States. 4. Official secrets—United States. 5. National security—
United States. 6. Rule of law—United States. I. Title.

JC598.S36 2010
323.44'50973—dc22

2010003506

W. W. Norton & Company, Inc.
500 Fifth Avenue, New York, N.Y. 10110
www.wwnorton.com

W. W. Norton & Company Ltd.
Castle House, 75/76 Wells Street, London W1T 3QT

1 2 3 4 5 6 7 8 9 0

To Esther, Shoshana, and Ruth

There are some secrets, on the keeping of which so depends, oftentimes, the salvation of an Army. Secrets which cannot, at least ought not to, be intrusted to paper; nay which none but the Commander in Chief at the time, should be acquainted.

—George Washington letter to Patrick Henry
Morristown, New Jersey
February 24, 1777

I do ask every publisher, every editor, and every newsman in the nation to reexamine his own standards, and to recognize the nature of our country's peril. In time of war, the government and the press have customarily joined in an effort based largely on self-discipline, to prevent unauthorized disclosures to the enemy. In time of "clear and present danger," the courts have held that even the privileged rights of the First Amendment must yield to the public's need for national security.

—President John F. Kennedy
Address before the American Newspaper Publishers Association
Waldorf-Astoria Hotel
New York City, April 27, 1961

CONTENTS

PREFACE

I AM A NEW YORKER who was in Manhattan on the morning of September 11, 2001. Like millions of others here, I saw the destruction wrought by al Qaeda firsthand, saw the dust-covered survivors trudging northward, breathed the smoke from the smoldering rubble and felt it sting my eyes. That afternoon, after the trek home to my family in Brooklyn, seven miles from ground zero, I found a layer of ash on my car. What was in the ash? Along with pulverized concrete, glass, and steel, did it contain the remains of firefighters and office workers turned to dust? That was just one of the many questions coursing through my brain on the evening of the day that war came to my city. I was again in Manhattan on March 11, 2004, the day that Islamic terrorists bombed the Madrid transit system, killing 191 people and maiming more than 1,700. And I was in Manhattan once again on July 7, 2005, when suicide bombers struck the London transit system, killing 52 and wounding hundreds. Like millions of others, I ride the New York City subways daily. So do two of my three daughters.

It was in light of this history and these circumstances, a personal history and personal circumstances in no way unique to me, that I was incensed by the publication in the *New York Times* of a series of stories in 2005 and 2006 compromising some of the secret counterterrorism programs that the U.S. government had initiated to avert a repetition of such terrible catastrophes. But along with outrage, I was intensely curious about the legal regime that permitted, or appeared to permit, this kind of tell-all-and-damn-the-consequences journalism. This book, which began as an essay that originally appeared in *Commentary* in March 2006—"Has the *New York Times* Violated the Espionage Act?"—is an outgrowth of my impassioned curiosity.

In my *Commentary* essay I had called upon the Justice Department to prosecute the *Times* under a 1950 statute making it a crime to publish certain kinds of classified information. The controversy engendered by my article led to invitations to testify before the Senate Judiciary Committee and the House Select Committee on Intelligence, where my views were given a respectful hearing by representatives from both parties. However, in some quarters my analysis invited reprobation and worse, with the editor of the *New York Times Book Review*—a section of the newspaper that had until that point frequently published my writing—accusing me of McCarthyism.[1]

The charge of McCarthyism was, of course, nothing more than an attempt to foreclose debate about a subject some are unwilling to discuss: namely, the appropriate role of the press in wartime. But not all the journalists at the paper were inclined to hurl epithets. And certainly the attorneys of the newspaper were not. Indeed, George Freeman, the assistant general counsel of the *Times*, in the best traditions of the newspaper, invited me to participate in a number of discussions of the subject at forums provided by the New York State and American Bar Associations. Those sessions brought me into public interchange with, among other notable figures in the controversy, Jill Abramson, managing editor of the *Times*; Dean Baquet, the paper's Washington bureau chief and formerly the top editor at the *Los Angeles Times*; Daniel Ellsberg, the central protagonist of the Pentagon Papers drama of 1971; James Goodale, who had been general counsel of the paper at that watershed moment; and Floyd Abrams, the country's premier First Amendment lawyer, who had represented the *Times* in the Pentagon Papers case.

The presence of such heavy guns in the discussion was fully warranted, for wartime secrets and the role of the press in protecting or disclosing them is a subject both important and complex, pitting our most cherished values against one another and bringing key institutions of democratic governance into collision. In exploring this terrain I have been drawn into the broader task of constructing a counternarrative to the standard history of free expression in America. As I have discovered, that standard history has ossified into orthodoxy. Its adherents have fallen into the trap described by Herbert Butterfield in *The Whig Interpretation of History*, in which the historian stands on the summit of the present and peers down upon the past to affirm and reaffirm his own political convictions, a mode of mountaineering that obscures a proper view of history's slopes.[2]

Butterfield's characterization applies with uncanny precision to our own whig school of legal history—legal history as the unfolding story of unfettered freedom. Major histories of First Amendment law prefer overwhelmingly to argue by omission, with the result that they often conceal as much as they reveal. Geoffrey Stone's much-celebrated *Perilous Times: Free Speech in Wartime: From the Sedition Act of 1798 to the War on Terrorism*[3] has been hailed as a "masterpiece of constitutional history" by no less a figure than Elena Kagan, the former dean of the Harvard Law School who was appointed solicitor general of the United States in 2009. Yet this "comprehensive" tome fails even to mention major episodes that cut against its thesis, such as the so-called Black Chamber affair in the 1930s, the nearly catastrophic *Chicago Tribune* leaks during World War II, and an array of cases from *Marchetti* to *Snepp* in which the federal government has gone to court, successfully, to rein in the printing presses to protect national security secrecy in times of both war and peace.

Although my attempt at historical correction leaves me sharply critical of the recent conduct of the *New York Times* and the First Amendment absolutism that underpins it, this book is not intended as a prosecutor's brief. The problem of governmental secrecy has become a burning issue in American political life and cries out for historically informed analysis. It is my hope that a fuller understanding of our past can help us skirt some self-imposed perils and return us to a proper balance between the exigencies of national defense and the blessings of our cherished liberty.

NECESSARY SECRETS

INTRODUCTION

O N DECEMBER 5, 2005, the White House was the scene of an extraordinary confrontation. In a sitting room off to the side of the Oval Office were the top officers of the *New York Times*: Philip Taubman, the paper's Washington bureau chief, Bill Keller, the paper's executive editor, and Arthur Sulzberger, Jr., its publisher, along with Eric Lichtblau, a reporter covering the Justice Department beat. Arrayed across from them in the hushed chamber were President Bush and a number of his most senior subordinates: John Negroponte, Director of National Intelligence, the White House counsel Harriet Miers, national security adviser Stephen Hadley, and Gen. Michael Hayden, director of the National Security Agency (NSA).

The newspapermen had been summoned to the meeting; days earlier, they had informed the administration that the paper was preparing to publish an article revealing the existence of a highly classified NSA program designed to tap al-Qaeda phone calls and e-mails. President Bush and his aides wanted to deliver a last warning—they had been pleading with the *Times* to spike the story for more than a year—about the grave harm to the nation that would follow. America's paper of record had to exercise responsibility, said the president; if the paper went ahead with the story and another al-Qaeda attack ensued, "there'll be blood on your hands."[1] The warning fell on deaf ears. Upon leaving the White House, Keller told

Sulzberger, "Nothing I heard in there changed my mind."[2] Eleven days later the story appeared on page 1 of the *New York Times*.

The consequences of the *Times*'s decision were far reaching and, even now, with the Bush administration receding into history, continue to ripple through our politics. Was the newspaper right to do what it did? Was it, as its editors proclaimed, fulfilling its fundamental mission of keeping the public informed about a matter of vital interest? Or was it, as its critics contended, breaking the public trust and putting a journalistic coup ahead of national security, thereby endangering the country? Should journalists like Lichtblau and James Risen, the two *Times* reporters who broke the story, be showered with prizes (as they were), including the Pulitzer, for uncovering the truth? Or should they have faced prosecution for contravening statutes forbidding the publication of classified information and been fined or even sentenced to jail? Can the U.S. government lawfully step in to block publication of stories that will severely damage national security? Should it ever? Such questions are part and parcel of an unresolved and perhaps irresolvable conundrum of government by popular consent.

On the one hand, as is perfectly obvious, openness is an essential prerequisite of self-governance. "The basis of our governments being the opinion of the people, the very first object should be to keep that right," wrote Thomas Jefferson two centuries ago.[3] The electorate in a democracy depends upon the free flow of information, particularly information about the workings of government, to make considered choices about policies and the political leaders who will carry them out. Secrecy about the workings of government impedes the marketplace of ideas and distorts the electorate's understanding of the alternatives before it.

Over the last five decades of American life, preserving Jefferson's "very first object" has been the locus of perpetual struggle. *The Torment of Secrecy* was the apt title of Edward Shils's classic examination of our secrecy dilemmas in the midst of the McCarthy era as the country veered between "the enraged demand for a rigid security policy" and "the evasive denial that there is any need for any security policy at all."[4] The same theme was picked up by Daniel Patrick Moynihan a few decades later in his *Secrecy: The American Experience*, in which he bemoaned the Cold War legacy of a "vast secrecy system that shows no sign of receding" despite the end of the Soviet-American conflict.[5]

More recently we have been inundated by a flood of warnings that our government is concealing its activities from the American people in untoward ways for untoward purposes. Barack Obama came into office pledging to make his administration the most transparent of all time. Though he has taken significant steps in that direction, he has been contending with an intensifying drumroll of criticism from both Left and Right for the way in which his administration is controlling information. The candidate who on one day was lashing the Bush administration for its excessive secrecy was on the next, as president, invoking the state secrets privilege in court cases, appointing policy "czars" so as to dodge congressional vetting, and declaring, "I have fought for the principle that the United States must carry out covert activities and hold information that is classified for the purposes of national security and will do so again."[6] Only months into his presidency, the American Civil Liberties Union (ACLU), which had welcomed Obama's call as a candidate for greater openness, had reversed field and was lambasting his "adoption of the stonewalling tactics and opaque policies of the Bush administration [which] flies in the face of the president's stated desire to restore the rule of law, to revive our moral standing in the world and to lead a transparent government."[7]

With the problem of governmental secrecy unresolved, a bevy of lobbying organizations like the ACLU, OpenTheGovernment.org, and the Reporters Committee for Freedom of the Press remains on the offensive. At the same time the press continues to be heralded, largely by voices in the press itself, as the heroic force standing in opposition to the clandestine doings of the national security state. Alarm over excessive secrecy, sounded during Democratic and Republican administrations alike, has over a period of decades thoroughly congealed into conventional wisdom. But much of the conventional wisdom—as is so often the case—is wrong.

The fact is that we continue to live in the most open society in the history of the world. Our Founding Fathers constructed a political system based upon a high degree of transparency. In the two-plus centuries of American history that have elapsed since the drafting of the Declaration of Independence, we have moved steadily toward even greater openness. In the last half century, if we look at the broad sweep of things, the trend has only accelerated.

Lyndon Johnson signed the Freedom of Information Act into law in 1966. It mandates the full disclosure of government records on demand. A decade later Congress passed the Sunshine Act, which guarantees that the meetings of government agencies be open to the public. The Presidential Records Act, enacted in 1978, grants public access to all official documents of former presidents after no more than twelve years. All these laws come complete with exceptions to protect things like privacy, trade secrets, and national security deliberations, but they nonetheless reflect the intensity of our national commitment to keeping the public informed about what government is doing in its name. Recent decades have also witnessed revolutionary changes in technology—including especially the rise of the Internet—that have greatly facilitated the cause of open government and given new tools to both the media and private citizens to explore in great depth the workings of our public institutions.

Our country continues to operate under a broad consensus that secrecy is antithetical to democratic rule and can encourage a variety of political deformations. The potential for excessive concealment has grown more acute as the American national security apparatus expanded massively in the decades since World War II, bringing with it a commensurately large extension of secrecy.* With huge vol-

---

*In 2008 alone, there were a staggering 23,217,557 "derivative classification" decisions, the government's term for any step "incorporating, paraphrasing, restating, or generating in a new form information that is already classified." See Information Security Oversight Office, *Report to the President* (2008), 6, http://www.archives.gov/isoo/reports/2008-annual-report .pdf.

umes of information pertaining to national defense walled off from the public, secrecy almost inevitably has become haphazard.[8] Arresting glimpses of mis- and overclassification are not hard to uncover. With evident caprice, the CIA has disclosed, for example, the total government-wide intelligence budget for 1997, 1998, 2007, and 2008, while similar numbers for both earlier and later years remain a state secret.

Secrecy can facilitate renegade governmental activity, as we saw in the Watergate and the Iran-Contra affairs. It can also be a breeding ground for corruption. Egregious recent cases are easy to tick off: Randy "Duke" Cunningham, a senior Republican member of the House Defense Appropriations Committee, used classified earmarks to a military-spending bill to funnel funds to cronies in a scheme that landed him in jail on bribery charges; Kyle Dustin "Dusty" Foggo, the CIA's executive director—the number-three position in the agency—used the cloak of secrecy to conclude sweetheart deals with a longtime personal friend, also landing himself in jail.

But the obvious pitfalls are not the end of the story. A long list of abuses notwithstanding, secrecy, like openness, remains an essential prerequisite of self-governance. To be effective, even many of the most mundane aspects of democratic rule, from the development of policy alternatives to the selection of personnel, must often take place behind closed doors. To proceed always under the glare of the public would cripple deliberation and render government impotent. And when one turns to the most fundamental business of democratic governance, namely, self-preservation—carried out through conduct of foreign policy and the waging of war—the imperative of secrecy becomes critical, often a matter of survival. Even in times of peace, the formulation of foreign and defense policies is necessarily conducted in secret.

BUT THIS IS NOT a time of peace. Ever since September 11, the country has been at war. And we are not only at war, we are engaged in a particular kind of war—an intelligence war against a shadowy and determined adversary. The effectiveness of the tools of intelligence—from the recruitment of agents to the operation of satellite reconnaissance systems—remains overwhelmingly dependent on their clandestine nature. It is not an overstatement to say that secrecy today, as we engage in a struggle without a discernible end point, is one of the most critical tools of national defense.

In the midst of this intelligence war, advocates of ever-greater openness, primarily located in the press but also in a host of interest groups, have been waging a war of their own against secrecy in government, often focusing on the most sensitive areas of foreign, defense, and intelligence policy. The major fronts in this war are in Congress, the courts, and the media. One cannot quarrel with most of the tactics and stratagems of the antisecrecy advocates. Whatever position one might take in the underlying policy and legal disputes, the particular methods they employ—petitioning Congress for changes in the law or filing suits in court to compel the disclosure of closely held information—are part of the normal push and pull of our governmental system.

But there is another facet of the war against secrecy that often falls *outside* the normal push and pull of our political life and raises profound problems both for our security and our system of democratic self-governance, namely, unauthorized disclosures—"leaks," in common parlance—of secret information to the press.

Here it is necessary to draw a crucial distinction. As any American government official or journalist will readily attest, leaking is part and parcel of our system of rule. Not a day goes by in Washington without government officials sharing inside information with journalists and lobbyists in off-the-record briefings and in private discussions over lunch. Some of the material changing hands in this fashion winds up getting published. A study by the Senate Intelligence Committee counted 147 separate disclosures of classified information that made their way into the nation's eight leading newspapers in a six-month period alone.[9] As these startlingly high numbers indicate, leaks to the press are a well-established informal practice. They enable policy makers to carry out any one of a number of objectives: to get out a message to domestic and foreign audiences, to gauge public reaction in advance of some contemplated policy initiative, to curry favor with journalists, and to wage inter- or intra-bureaucratic warfare. For better or worse, leaking has become part of the normal functioning of the U.S. government.

Yet there is also leaking of a very different character: the disclosure of highly sensitive national security secrets to the press. The two forms of leaking are not always readily distinguishable. Government secrets dwell on a continuum from the innocuous to the ultrasensitive. Journalists, eager to break news, have a vested interest in collapsing the spectrum.* In recent years the problem has bedeviled Democratic and Republican presidents alike. "Unauthorized disclosures can be extraordinarily harmful to the United States national-security interests and . . . far too many such disclosures occur," complained President Clinton in 2000.[10] The Bush administration, facing an unprecedented set of foreign-policy challenges, struggled to clamp down on leaking, to no avail. President Obama is now wrestling with precisely the same dilemmas, with the CIA

---

*A prime example of this collapsing is an oft-cited passage in the affidavit filed in the Pentagon Papers case by Max Frankel, then the Washington bureau chief of the *New York Times*:

> Presidents make "secret" decisions only to reveal them for the purposes
> of frightening an adversary nation, wooing a friendly electorate,
> protecting their reputations. The military services conduct "secret"
> research in weaponry only to reveal it for the purpose of enhancing
> their budgets, appearing superior or inferior to a foreign army, gaining
> the vote of a congressman or the favor of a contractor. The Navy uses
> secret information to run down the weaponry of the Air Force. The
> Army passes on secret information to prove its superiority to the Marine
> Corps. High officials of the Government reveal secrets in the search for
> support of their policies, or to help sabotage the plans and policies of
> rival departments. Middle-rank officials of government reveal secrets so
> as to attract the attention of their superiors or to lobby against the orders
> of those superiors.

The practices Frankel describes are indeed widespread. But the picture is nonetheless overdrawn, making it appear as if secrecy is *always* illegitimate, a device employed solely in the struggle for bureaucratic and political advantage and never for the legitimate purpose of protecting our security.

pressing the Justice Department to investigate leaks of top-secret information.

But there is nothing new under the sun. Secrecy has been a chronic neuralgic point in our democracy. Writing in 1961, the political scientist Edward Longaker complained that the executive branch of the U.S. government had "become a storehouse of hidden fact." Exploiting the legitimate claims of secrecy, it "habitually overclassifies documents, absurdly segments scientific research, and maintains convenient shields to protect administrators from the curiosity of the public and the press."[11] As we shall see, battles over the control of classified information have flared up at many junctures extending all the way back to the First Continental Congress in the eighteenth century, and have punctuated our politics ever since.

Careless handling of information was to cost both the Confederacy and the Union untold lives during the Civil War. During World War I the dangers posed by leaks were one factor that prompted Congress to enact the Espionage Act of 1917, which stands today as our fundamental law governing secrets. On the eve of and during World War II, leaks were dearly paid for in treasure and blood. In the Cold War we responded to the experience of World War II—and to the new existential danger posed by nuclear weapons—by initiating unprecedentedly tight controls on information. It was only as the Cold War waned that we began to unwind from that crisis-driven approach and embrace maximum transparency, at least in our rhetoric if not always in reality. Then came September 11, and the default position of openness had to be flipped once again to its reverse.

Today, nearly a decade after September 11, and notwithstanding bows in the direction of transparency, government officials, very much including those in the Obama administration, almost invariably come to regard it as a distracting impediment to deliberation and policy making. The great German sociologist Max Weber was right when he observed that "every bureaucracy seeks to increase the superiority of the professionally informed by keeping their knowledge and intentions secret."[12] An illustrative trifle was on display in June 2009, when the Obama administration initiated a battle to keep the press and the public from gaining access to the log of White House visitors. In seeking to conceal this seemingly harmless information, they were precisely embracing a stance put forward by the Bush administration—and all previous administrations—that Obama had deplored as a candidate.[13] Campaign rhetoric is the variable in the equation; the imperatives of power are the constants.

Journalists operate by a different calculus. Standing outside the bureaucracies and peering in, they see it as their hallowed calling to scrutinize all the workings of government and then convey their findings to the public for it to make judgments of its own. Our system of rule, it often seems, consists of a perpetual pitched battle between the keepers of secrets in the government and the sworn enemies of secrecy in the press. The tension between these two camps has as of late erupted in an unprecedented series of conflicts and collisions. In recent years we have witnessed a host of journalists, including James Risen of the *Times* and Bill Gertz of the *Washington Times*, facing court proceedings involving their publication of secret information. We have also seen the dramatic spectacle of a reporter, Judith Miller of the *New York Times*, imprisoned for eighty-five days on a contempt citation for refusing to reveal her confidential sources.

An extraordinary development of a different sort but having no less bearing on our subject was the indictment in 2005 of two employees of the American-Israel Public Affairs Committee (AIPAC), a pro-Israel lobbying organization, on charges of unauthorized receipt and transmittal of classified information under the Espionage Act of 1917—the first time this statute has ever been employed against civilians for doing nothing more, or so the defendants claimed, than what other lobbyists (and journalists) do in the normal course of business virtually every day of the year.

With such battles on the rise, the temperature of the national debate over secrecy has risen to a fever pitch. Old story or not, what is clear—and novel—is that in our own era national security leaking occurs with abandon. We find ourselves, in confronting this state of affairs, sharply divided. Some members of Congress and officials of the executive branch—sometimes in the name of truth, sometimes in the quest for partisan advantage—are pressing for the release of ever more secrets, a phenomenon we have witnessed most recently in the debate over interrogation practices. Others continue to express dismay over the fact that our government is seemingly unable to safeguard information vital to the effective conduct of American foreign policy. The press, for its part, continues to bemoan excessive secrecy.

We did not arrive at this juncture by happenstance.

CHAPTER I

WITHOUT FEAR OR FAVOR?

W AR IS ONE of the great engines of governmental secrecy. It
should therefore come as no revelation that this most recent
chapter of a much longer story has its genesis in the surprise attack
of September 11. In the weeks and months after that catastrophe,
the entire country was gripped by the fear of an even more terrible
follow-on attack, perhaps one employing weapons of mass destruction. Inside government, especially its higher echelons, the fear was
even more intense, radically augmented by a document received
daily, known as the "threat matrix."

Prepared for the president and ranking policy makers by the
sixteen agencies that compose the U.S. intelligence community,
and often dozens of pages long, the threat matrix, in one official's
description of it, includes "warnings extracted from the tens of billions of foreign phone calls and e-mail messages that fly around the
world each day, from scores of human informants, satellite photographs, and other sources. It summarizes every known new threat,
ranging from obviously false accusations to credible warnings about
catastrophic weapons of mass destruction and conventional attacks
in the United States and allied countries around the globe. For each
threat the matrix lists possible targets, information on the group

planning the attack, an analysis of the threat's credibility, and notes about actions taken in response."[1]

The daily reporting of danger induced an overpowering sense of vulnerability. To policymakers, September 11 made it plain that a highly imaginative grand-scale attack on our homeland could be planned and successfully executed. It also drove home the fact that even as thousands of people were laboring in Washington cubbyholes, in embassy posts abroad, and in electronic eavesdropping stations around the globe to discern the plans and intentions of al Qaeda, patterns of danger might often be missed in the vast array of dots.

And indeed, despite the billions spent on intelligence and huge investments of time and manpower, the government had few if any clues about where or when or how we might be struck again. Stamped on the consciousness of everyone in the security sphere of the U.S. government was not only the carnage of September 11 but the memory of our innocence on September 10, when those charged with safeguarding the country were serenely going about their business, not knowing what they would learn the following day.

George W. Bush responded to the unseen menace of a second wave of attacks as presumably any president would. Returning to the White House after a harrowing day zigzagging across the skies on *Air Force One*, his command to his subordinates was: "Don't let this happen again." But how best to carry out that directive? Overnight, secret intelligence, sharply cut back in the decade following the end of the Cold War, became a critical defensive instrument.

Getting accurate information about al Qaeda and affiliated radical Islamic movements, and getting it rapidly enough to act upon, now became a supreme national imperative. A number of clandestine intelligence programs—programs that we now know a great deal about thanks only to leaks—were set in motion. Among the more significant of these was the NSA program to intercept the communications of al-Qaeda suspects here and abroad.

Communication is the lifeblood of terrorist planning and execution. To carry out even a relatively modest terrorist attack requires an extensive exchange of information. Only a moment's reflection is enough to make it obvious that there are few available channels in which such exchanges can occur. Couriers are slow and run a great risk of detection when crossing international borders. They might suffice when dispatched from cave to mountaintop in the tribal badlands of Pakistan, where the leadership of al Qaeda is currently believed to be constituted, but they would hardly serve well in planning an operation from there to hit a faraway target like Madrid or New York City.

The global postal system is not an attractive alternative. It too is slow, unreliable, and vulnerable to interception. In terms of speed, clarity, dependability, and security, telephone and e-mail simply cannot be surpassed. What we learned from the 9/11 Commission Report—the fact that the al-Qaeda plotters made extensive use of e-mail and telephones as they pushed forward their scheme—was not exactly a revelation.

Given the premium on gaining access to terrorist communication, it is unsurprising that the White House urgently began ramping up the role played by the National Security Agency in the fight against al Qaeda. Founded in 1952 in the midst of the Korean War, the NSA is the body within the intelligence community responsible for intercepting and deciphering the communications of America's adversaries (and those of friends, too). Making use of a global network of listening stations bristling with antennas, satellite collection systems in outer space, and a vast staff of computer scientists, mathematicians, linguists, and cryptographers, the NSA was long wrapped in the deepest secrecy. Its workers were forbidden to reveal even the name of their employer, dubbed "No Such Agency" in the trade.

The NSA has gradually come into public view over the past two decades, but it has still remained a largely clandestine governmental arm, its communications-intelligence product (known as Comint) deemed uniquely valuable and, along with two other categories of ultrasensitive secrets (the design of nuclear weapons and the identities of CIA agents), guarded by a special statute punishing its disclosure.

As the 9/11 plot was being organized in the late 1990s through the first half of 2001, the NSA picked up some of the signal traffic generated by al Qaeda, but agency analysts failed to investigate the locations of the operatives on whom they were eavesdropping. It also almost obsessively resisted tracking, even with lawfully granted warrants, those Americans who were communicating with al-Qaeda operatives abroad. Its leadership believed that such domestic surveillance was a function properly left to the FBI.

This laxity ended with 9/11. Some months after the attack Bush signed off on the NSA's Terrorist Surveillance Program. The program aimed to uncover and tap into the flow of terrorist communications, with the primary goal of uncovering al-Qaeda sleeper cells here in the United States. Using the "vacuum cleaner" listening capacity of the NSA, it evidently scooped up a vast array of "international" calls—that is, calls going into and out of the United States. Purely domestic calls were not included. Using address information— e-mail addresses and telephone numbers, and also by searching for "trigger words" inside the content of these communications—the data were electronically sorted and, when matched with known or suspected al-Qaeda operatives, the communications made available for closer inspection by counterterrorism analysts.

The NSA program was humming along silently until the *Times* brought it into public view on December 16, 2005, in the sensational front-page story headlined "Bush Lets U.S. Spy on Callers Without Courts," with which we began.[2] Crediting the information to "nearly a dozen current and former officials who were granted anonymity because of the classified nature of the program," Risen and Lichtblau laid out the basic details.

They reported that the NSA was eavesdropping on as many as five hundred people in the United States at any given moment, with a revolving list of targets so that, as names were dropped and added from the list, "the number monitored in this country may have reached into the thousands." Overseas, the article stated, "about 5,000 to 7,000 people suspected of terrorist ties are monitored at one time." But these intelligence attainments, the newspaper suggested, came at a price in American liberty. The most striking fact about the program, reported the *Times*, was that in a departure from previous practice, and causing controversy within the government itself, NSA surveillance of Americans was being conducted without warrants.

Reaction to the story was swift and severe and came from all political directions. Risen and Lichtblau had noted in their article that the *Times* had learned of the NSA program more than a year earlier and had opted to withhold the story. This infuriated many on the Left. If the paper had the story in-house before the historically close 2004 November presidential election, then it had protected Bush from the (supposedly) damaging political effects of the revelation, quite possibly costing John Kerry the White House.*

On the other side of the coin, from within the government and other quarters came charges that the paper had recklessly injured national security and compromised one of the country's most vital counterterrorism tools. According to Porter Goss, the then-CIA director, the harm wrought to his agency's "capabilities to carry out our mission" was "very severe."[3] A host of senators and congressmen, Republicans and Democrats alike, chimed in to condemn the leak. Jane Harman, the ranking Democratic member of the House Intelligence Committee, declared that the *Times*'s disclosure of the "essential" program had "damaged critical intelligence capabilities."[4]

A story by the *Times* eight days later laid out even more classified details about the NSA program, provoking further indignation. It described how the NSA was monitoring "the main arteries for moving voice and some Internet traffic into and out of the United States."

---

*The claim that the paper inadvertently protected Bush by holding the story is debatable. As Bill Keller has pointed out, "Judging from the public reaction to the NSA eavesdropping reflected in various polls, one could ask whether earlier disclosure might have helped President Bush more than hurt." "Talk to the Newsroom: Executive Editor Bill Keller," April 14, 2006, http://www.nytimes.com/2006/04/14/business/media/14asktheeditors .html?pagewanted=all.

Broaching intelligence sources and methods, it described how the NSA was collaborating with the private telecommunications companies that operate the switches through which international calls are routed.

Goss and other officials have never spelled out in a precise way the nature of the harm caused by the breach. Indeed they have complained that they are at a grave disadvantage in such discussions; any attempt to demonstrate the damage would entail further disclosures of top-secret operations. But their claims about damage seem plausible enough, and it is not difficult to imagine that a highly publicized report indicating that the NSA could readily tap into calls from, say, Islamabad to Detroit might cause some al-Qaeda communications to dry up.

According to more than a few credible testaments, the program, until it was compromised, had been a notable success. "Crucial for protecting the nation against its most menacing threat," was how Director of National Intelligence John Negroponte described it.[5] Gen. Hayden credited it with making it "far more likely that [the] NSA will be able to detect, grab, and intercept al-Qaeda communications that are most important." He continued, "If we had had this program in place [before 9/11], we would have identified some of the al-Qaeda operatives in the United States."[6]

It is easy, of course, to dismiss the assertions of government officials as self-serving and/or exaggerated. And NSA surveillance was clearly not a silver bullet. But even Risen and Lichtblau's own story had highlighted the program's achievement in disrupting our adversaries. It was particularly successful, they reported, in exploiting material seized from ranking al-Qaeda operatives captured abroad. When Abu Zubaydah, Osama bin Laden's deputy, was apprehended in Pakistan in March 2002, the CIA obtained his computers, cell phone, and personal phone directory. NSA analysts were then able to monitor the phone numbers it had obtained, providing an invaluable instrument for tracking terrorists, some of whom were in the United States. The program, the two *Times* reporters also noted, contributed to an investigation leading to the arrest in 2003 of Iyman Faris, an al-Qaeda operative who had been casing targets in New York. It had also helped to expose another plot in 2004 seeking to use fertilizer bombs to blow up British pubs and subway stations.

No doubt with these and other accomplishments in mind, President Bush called the publication of the leaked material "a shameful act." He spoke of the stakes involved in covert interception of terrorist communications. The failure to intercept something as brief, he said, as "a two-minute phone conversation between somebody linked to al Qaeda here and an operative overseas could lead directly to the loss of thousands of lives."[7]

In short order the Justice Department empaneled a grand jury to investigate the source of the leak. Alberto Gonzales, Bush's attorney general, appeared on national television to raise the possibility that not only would the leakers within government be sought out and punished but that the *Times* itself might be vulnerable to prosecution. "There are some statutes on the book," he said, "which, if you read the language carefully, would seem to indicate that that is a possibility. . . . We have an obligation to enforce the law and to prosecute those who engage in criminal activity."[8]

CLEARLY THE EDITORS of the *Times* did not wander into an epic confrontation with the U.S. government on a lark. What prompted them—in the teeth of warnings from President Bush and his national security team—to drop highly sensitive counterterrorism secrets into the public domain? We rarely know as much about the backstory of a leak as we do about this one.

Working their sources in the Justice Department, the CIA, and other intelligence bureaucracies, by the summer of 2004, Risen and Lichtblau had pieced together elements of the NSA surveillance program and had written up a story for publication. At this juncture Risen, reporting for the *Times* but also at work on his own book about the war on terrorism, placed a call to Gen. Hayden, asking him about a program (in Lichtblau's paraphrase of the conversation) "to eavesdrop on Americans without a warrant." He then read the general the lead paragraph of his draft.

Hayden's reaction?

> The usually unflappable Hayden was clearly jolted, and a bit flustered. An Air Force general, accustomed to carefully scripted briefings on classified material in bug-free, secure facilities, was now being asked on an open phone line about perhaps the most classified program in the government. Whatever the NSA was doing, Hayden told Jim [Risen], was "intensely operational." And, he added quickly, it was "legal, appropriate, and effective." Jim tried to ask him a few more questions. Hayden refused to say anything more.[9]

Risen's call provoked intense distress in the intelligence community and in the White House. The *Times*, as officials saw it, was poised to compromise one of its most important counterterrorism initiatives. Among the lawyers in the NSA there was consideration of the nuclear option: petitioning the courts to issue a restraining order enjoining publication, a step fatefully taken by Richard Nixon in the Pentagon Papers case in 1971. The White House, equally alarmed by the leak but sensitive to the political costs of reenacting a drama that had ended badly for Nixon, opted for a tempered approach. It decided to do something that it and previous administrations had done on rare occasion: ask a news organization to spike a story.

First, Philip Taubman, the paper's Washington bureau chief, was invited to meet with Hayden at the NSA to hear the case. Then Bill Keller was asked to come down to Washington to hear the same warning from Hayden, with national security adviser Condoleezza Rice and other high-ranking officials at his side. "They were shocked," Keller later recalled, that "they were having to share this with journalists."[10]

These fraught encounters were but the first in a series. The message being delivered by the White House in all of them, in Lichtblau's summary, was consistent and unequivocal: "If we published what we knew, we would be handing al Qaeda an advantage that it would exploit to attack the United States again, and the *New York Times*—by disclosing the program in the country's most prominent newspaper—would bear responsibility for the consequences."[11]

With as many as ten different senior officials imploring him not to publish, Keller initially opted to comply with the administration's plea. "It's rare that the government makes a concerted, top-level appeal to hold a story (I can think of only four or five instances in my nineteen years as an editor)," wrote Keller later, "and it's even more rare that we agree. . . . They laid out a detailed argument that publishing what we then knew would compromise ongoing anti-terror operations. . . . Their arguments were compelling enough that we felt the responsible course was to hold the story."[12]

Risen, eager to get his scoop before the public, was outraged by what he saw as his superiors' pusillanimity; "beyond furious," he pleaded with his editors to change their minds.[13] To no avail. It was more than a year later that the paper decided to move forward, leading to the fierce confrontation in the Oval Office of early December 2005, followed by the paper's publication of the story two weeks later.

The initial December 16 story said nothing about any internal debates at the *Times*. Neither did it offer much detail about the aggressive behind-the-scenes contest of wills between the White House and the paper. It only noted tersely that "the White House [had] asked the *New York Times* not to publish this article, arguing that it could jeopardize continuing investigations and alert would-be terrorists that they might be under scrutiny. After meeting with senior administration officials to hear their concerns, the newspaper delayed publication for a year to conduct additional reporting."[14]

On the same day that the story appeared, Bill Keller posted his own explanation of the delay on the *Times*'s Web site. He pointed to the existence of a debate within the government about the propriety of the NSA operation. He explained that, in the course of its reporting, the paper had developed "a fuller picture of the concerns and misgivings that had been expressed during the life of the program."[15] Though "it is not our place to pass judgment on the legal or civil liberties questions involved in such a program," wrote Keller, "it became clear those questions loomed larger within the government than we had previously understood. . . . We published the story when we did because after much hard work it was fully reported, checked and ready, and because, after listening respectfully to the administration's objections, we were convinced there was no good reason not to publish it."[16]

Every word Keller wrote may have been true, but as later would become clear, his statement was disingenuous. Even at the time it was widely regarded as incomplete, lacking a narrative that would make sense of exactly what had happened inside the paper over the course of more than a year in which the newspaper had been sitting on the leak. "Woefully inadequate," were the words used by the *Times*'s own ombudsman, Byron Calame, to characterize Keller's explanation of the postponement and the decision finally to publish.[17] And Calame's intensive efforts to reconstruct the story behind the story came to naught. The *Times*'s editors were—in his own word—"stonewalling" him. Notwithstanding the paper's oft-reiterated commitment to "greater transparency," Calame wrote, "I have had unusual difficulty getting a better explanation for readers."[18]

CALAME'S DIFFICULTIES in obtaining information from his own newspaper point to a series of mysteries. Why exactly did the *Times* hold the story for more than a year? Why did it then reverse course? And why did its editors then "stonewall" about the real considerations?

These mysteries can all be unraveled. As fragments from various accounts make plain, at least initially Taubman and Keller did take the administration's warnings with genuine seriousness. And as Keller maintained, the paper did indeed choose to dig deeper into the NSA surveillance program. What it eventually found was the existence of a debate within the government about the program's legal foundations. The nature of that debate bears vitally on any appraisal of what the *Times* did. If the NSA was engaged in a runaway clandestine program, undertaken outside the law, the *Times*'s actions in revealing it must be regarded one way. If it was unequivocally lawful, the picture would look very different. If the answer is ambiguous—which happens to be the case—then any verdict on the *Times* would also, inevitably, have shades of gray.

We must begin with the backdrop. Amid the domestic turbulence of the sixties and seventies the NSA had been drawn into the fray. In 1967, at the direction of President Johnson, it embarked on a project code-named MINARET that focused the agency's eavesdropping capacity on a watch list comprising some six hundred individuals involved in the antiwar and civil rights movements. The objective was to determine if any were subject to influence or control by foreign agents. Richard Nixon then expanded this surveillance and exploited it for partisan political ends, enlisting other agencies, including the IRS, the FBI, and the CIA in the effort, until there were secret dossiers detailing the activities of some three hundred thousand Americans.

After these and other abuses came to light in the Church and Pike committee hearings in the mid-1970s, Congress passed legislation, the Foreign Intelligence Surveillance Act (FISA), designed to safeguard against a repetition of such transgressions. This 1978 statute established special tribunals, the Foreign Intelligence Surveillance Court and an appeals court sitting over it, to approve orders for wiretaps on particular targets. Most significantly, for our purposes, the act contained a provision stating that FISA and the criminal wiretap laws "shall be the *exclusive means* by which electronic surveillance [of] . . . communications may be conducted." It also made it a crime for government officials to engage in eavesdropping "other than pursuant to statute."

In the aftermath of 9/11 the Bush administration found its counterterrorism efforts hamstrung by FISA. For one thing, obtaining a court order to initiate surveillance under its provisions was a time- and labor-consuming endeavor that required, in each individual case, the production of an extensive dossier outlining the reasons for the order, the nature of the information being sought, the methods by which it would be obtained, and the review of the dossier by the attorney general or his top deputy prior to their obligatory signature.

Such cumbersome procedures were workable for the traditional law-enforcement approach to counterespionage and counterterrorism. If FISA's purpose was to facilitate evidence gathering for the prosecution of individuals whom the authorities *already* had "probable cause" to suspect of engaging in illegal activities, it worked tolerably well, balancing investigative purposes with civil liberties.

But in contending with the menace posed by al-Qaeda sleeper cells, when the goal was no longer the relatively leisurely task of prosecution but the urgent one of detection before an act of terrorism had been committed, FISA no longer sufficed. The case of Zacarias Moussaoui, the al-Qaeda operative who had enrolled in a Minnesota flight school where he was learning how to fly—but not to land—a Boeing 747, was a devastating illustration of the act's limitations. After Moussaoui's arrest on immigration charges three weeks before 9/11, the local FBI was unable to examine his laptop without a warrant, and their supervisors in Washington were reluctant to go to the FISA courts, believing that establishing probable cause would be a stretch.

For another thing, there had been major advances in telecommunications technology over the two and a half decades since FISA was enacted, rendering it unsuitable for the new war in which we were now engaged. From the outset FISA had drawn a distinction between calls routed by radio waves through satellites and those carried by cable. The act had not been intended to bar the NSA from the warrantless interception of calls carried by radio waves, and it contained a provision explicitly exempting them from its provisions.[19] Court orders would be necessary only in the case of a tap into a call or message carried via cable.

This distinction made sense when the law was passed in the late 1970s. A significant fraction of international calls at that juncture were routed by radio waves, while calls within the United States were carried largely by cable. Permitting the warrantless interception of wireless communication and requiring court orders for tapping cable calls thus matched the purpose of the act reasonably well, accommodating NSA's mission of harvesting foreign intelligence while discouraging the unauthorized surveillance of Americans.

BUT AS THE COMMUNICATIONS revolution progressed over the eighties and nineties, a technological reversal took place. Many local calls, particularly those made on cell phones, began to be carried via radio waves, while many overseas calls—those of most interest to counterterrorism investigators—began to be transmitted via fiber-optic cable.[20] Complicating the picture even further, as American companies assumed ever-greater predominance of the global telecommunications market, even foreign-to-foreign calls, as noted earlier, came to be routed both via cable and satellite through switches on American soil.

Thus not only had the distinction between means of transmission —wireless or cable—become irrelevant, but so too had the geographic location of callers. Precisely the same problem cropped up with regard to foreign-to-foreign e-mail communications, which were often now routed through U.S.-based servers. Requiring a court order to intercept such communications was a preposterous barrier to U.S. intelligence gathering. But this was exactly what FISA—a law passed long before there was an Internet—seemed to demand.

The Bush administration was thus confronted with a dilemma. On the one hand FISA interfered with the speed and agility needed to uncover and apprehend al-Qaeda sleeper cells in the United States. On the other hand the statute's exclusive means provision seemed, at least on the surface, to rule out any program not operating under its ambit.

One path out of the dead end was to turn to Congress for a solution. In the period after 9/11, there can be little doubt that Congress, had it been asked, would have acted to adjust FISA to better suit the NSA's proposed new role. After all, five weeks after the attack, by wide margins in both houses and with support from both parties, Congress approved the Patriot Act, which contained some other significant alterations in the FISA statute. At the time there were even some senators who were wondering aloud, and even asking the administration, if Congress needed to expand the NSA's authority to conduct surveillance. The Bush administration nonetheless rejected this idea.

The overriding reason was doctrinal: the conviction in the White House, advocated most forcefully by David Addington, Vice President Cheney's chief counsel, that the wartime powers of the presidency had eroded in the post-Watergate era and the perils of this erosion had come home to roost. To ask Congress for its approval of a program properly in the executive branch's purview was to cede it even more power and further impair the president's ability to perform his most central function of keeping the nation safe.

A more practical reason to shun congressional action was the need to cloak the program in secrecy; it would not do to broadcast to our enemies, via congressional debate, a picture of what the NSA could do. More significant, it would not do to broadcast what the NSA could *not* do. Even if Congress were to have gone into executive session to deliberate, informing all 535 members of the House and Senate of the critical details of such a sensitive matter would have virtually guaranteed leaks and dangerous publicity.

The White House thus opted to circumvent the statute and its exclusive-means provision. Was this a violation of the law? Let us assume for the moment that it was. Even so, it can be argued, there were ample precedents for a president to bend or break the law when facing a supreme national emergency like the one the United States was facing after 9/11.

As England battled for its survival in 1940, FDR provided destroyers to the British in an unadorned violation of the Neutrality Act. In the midst of the Civil War, Lincoln suspended the ancient writ of habeas corpus, usurping Congress's powers under the Constitution.* History has judged neither president particularly harshly. In words that speak directly to the situation confronting the White House after 2001, Thomas Jefferson had long ago put the pertinent principle on paper in a letter he titled "A Law Beyond the Constitution":

> A strict observance of the written laws is doubtless *one* of the highest virtues of a good citizen, but it is not *the highest*. The laws of necessity, of self-preservation, of saving our country when in danger, are of higher obligation. To lose our country by a scrupulous adherence to written law would be to lose the law itself, with life, liberty, property and all those who are enjoying them with us; thus absurdly sacrificing the end to the means.[21]

But in fact breaking the law was scarcely necessary to deal with the obstacles posed by FISA. And considering how events unfolded, the decision to disregard it was, at a minimum, a costly political mistake. A respectable set of arguments could have been marshaled to bypass the statute while remaining *within* the law. Indeed, a set eventually was marshaled and put forward publicly in a Justice Department white paper but only *after* the program was leaked.

Trumping the FISA statute, argued the white paper, was nothing less than the "President's well-recognized inherent constitutional authority as Commander in Chief and sole organ for the Nation in foreign affairs." It was this authority that extended to the conduct of "warrantless surveillance of enemy forces for intelligence purposes to detect and disrupt armed attacks on the United States."[22] Historical

---

*Arthur Sylvester, the Pentagon spokesman under John F. Kennedy, speaking to the New York chapter of the journalism fraternity, Sigma Delta Chi, shortly after the Cuban missile crisis, offered a variant. It was not only lawbreaking that was permissible in a crisis: "I think the inherent right of the government to lie—to lie to save itself when faced with nuclear disaster—is basic, basic." Cited in Martin Gershen, "The 'Right to Lie,'" *Columbia Journalism Review* (Winter 1966–67), 14–16.

precedents and the history of the act itself made plain that presidents of both parties had consistently asserted the constitutionally derived prerogative of conducting foreign intelligence surveillance without a warrant. Indeed, at the time FISA was under consideration, President Carter's attorney general, Griffin Bell, noted that while the bill recognized "no inherent power of the President to conduct electronic surveillance," this lacuna "does not take away the power of the President under the Constitution."[23] And President Clinton's deputy attorney general, Jamie Gorelick, had explained to the House Intelligence Committee that "the Department of Justice believes, and the case law supports, that the President has inherent authority to conduct warrantless *physical* searches for foreign intelligence purposes."[24] When it comes to electronic surveillance, the same principal would obtain.

It is true that some portions of the white paper, particularly its arguments maintaining that the post-9/11 Congressional Authorization to Use Military Force was an explicit override of the FISA statute, were far less compelling. It is also true that reputable constitutional scholars can be found on both sides of the continuing controversy. After all, to say that the president retains an "inherent" power to conduct warrantless surveillance does not necessarily mean that he possesses an "exclusive" power in this realm. This issue is still up for grabs.

But whatever the lingering debate, the significant point is that *none* of the arguments for the lawful nature of the program was put forward by the Bush administration at the outset. Instead, inside Justice in the period immediately following 9/11, in part owing to the pressure of events, in part owing to the White House's expansive notion of executive power, a sustainable case was not made in a timely fashion. Indeed, the initial legal memorandums produced by the Justice Department to authorize the program in the early days after 9/11 were severely defective.

The NSA program had been championed by Addington, working in close coordination with White House counsel Alberto Gonzales, and its legal architecture elaborated by John Yoo, a deputy in the Justice Department's Office of Legal Counsel (OLC), the critical bureaucratic unit that determines whether actions undertaken by the executive branch conform to the law. Yoo's memorandums, intellectually in harmony with Addington's views about executive power, set forth sweeping assertions about the president's power to disregard statutes in the face of danger to the country. Congress, one such memorandum argued, cannot "place any limits on the President's determinations as to any terrorist threat, the amount of military force to be used in response, or the method, timing, and nature of the response. These decisions, under our Constitution, are for the President alone to make."[25]

In a White House bound by a thick skein of restrictive statutes thrown over the executive branch in the wake of Watergate, and now contending with an unprecedented threat to American security, Yoo's memo was greeted with enthusiasm and relief. It was also, however, a legal land mine, resting on no citations, in conflict with settled law, and set to detonate when subjected to scrutiny.[26] Almost immediately murmurs of alarm began to be heard from various corners. In the FISA court, Colleen Kollar-Kotelly, the federal judge then overseeing the proceedings, is reported to have questioned whether information obtained from the NSA program had been improperly used as a basis to apply for FISA warrants, making them forbidden fruit.[27] This complaint appears to have led the Bush administration briefly to suspend the program while the Justice Department reviewed it and suggested new managerial guidelines.

At the same time sharp divisions over the program were forming at the Justice Department itself. John Yoo's close collaboration with the White House, often bypassing officials outranking him, thrust him into conflict with his colleagues, including his ultimate boss at Justice, Attorney General John Ashcroft. In early 2003, when the head of OLC left to take a federal judgeship, Yoo's candidacy for the top slot was quashed. Shortly thereafter he resigned. Into the OLC directorship came Jack Goldsmith, a Harvard law professor of conservative bent then working in the Pentagon general counsel's office. What Goldsmith found as he familiarized himself with his predecessor's work shook him profoundly. The legal basis of one essential counterterrorism measure after another was flawed. The NSA program was among them.

Goldsmith communicated his reservations to others in the department, including James Comey, the number-two man at Justice, and also to Ashcroft. With the NSA program coming up for renewal in mid-March 2004 (a step built into its initial structure and requiring the signature of the attorney general every forty-five days), the three officials were intending to press the White House to alter the program—the precise nature of the proposed changes remains classified to this day—and erase all doubts about its lawfulness. This plan, however, was waylaid by a chance happening.

Ashcroft was incapacitated by an acute case of pancreatitis. Comey then stepped in to become acting attorney general. In the flurry of events caused by the transition, time for negotiating changes with the White House elapsed. On March 10, the very day before his signature was due on the reauthorization, Comey informed the White House that he would not be signing the reauthorization unless the program was altered. White House officials, fearing that the NSA surveillance machinery would be shut down entirely, summoned ranking congressional leaders from Capitol Hill—the so-called Gang of Eight—for an emergency consultation.

This in turn led to a White House decision to approach Ashcroft in the hospital to ask him to overrule Comey. Comey learned of the impending visit and raced to the hospital, aides and FBI director Robert S. Mueller III in tow. They arrived just before Gonzales and White House chief of staff Andrew Card could make their plea. With the clashing officials assembled by his bedside, Ashcroft, though appearing deathly ill, lucidly defended Comey's decision and refused to sign the authorization.

The March 10 hospital-room convocation was unquestionably one of the most shocking departures from the norms of White House–Justice Department communication since the department's founding in the nineteenth century. It was followed by an equally bizarre chapter, which began with a White House decision to continue the NSA program without Justice Department approval. This in turn prompted Comey, Goldsmith, and other top officials to prepare to resign en masse. But then yet another unforeseeable happening intervened. On March 11, as the White House and the Justice Department were on the verge of an immensely damaging rift, Islamic suicide bombers set off ten explosions in Madrid's mass-transit system at the height of rush hour, killing 191 and wounding 1,755.

There could have been no more powerful reminder of what was at stake. Within hours a consensus emerged that the NSA program should continue. Bush, meeting with Comey that morning, gave his full backing to have Justice alter the program as it deemed fit: "Do what the Department thinks is right," the president told him. Shortly thereafter the NSA program was adjusted to put it on a more solid legal foundation.

IF IN DECEMBER 2005, while Keller and his colleagues at the *Times* were considering their next step, they had known about this fantastic chain of events, secrecy or no secrecy, the story of the NSA wiretapping program would no doubt have been impossible to resist. But they had not known. The record of the clash over the program was itself classified at a very high level—it bore the designation SCI (for "sensitive compartmented information") and did not leak out until 2007.* The *Times* did have wind of disagreements within the government, but it scarcely knew their scale.

---

* Gonzales was instructed by President Bush to take notes of the White House meeting with the Gang of Eight. He did, producing notes bearing the ultrasensitive SCI marking. Ironically, Gonzales then mishandled these documents, bringing them to his home and then moving them to a safe in his office that lacked proper safeguards for storing classified material. He became subject to a Justice Department inquiry and was ultimately cleared of any criminal charges, although he acknowledged carelessness as a custodian of classified materials. See Office of the Inspector General, Oversight and Review Division, "Report of Investigation Regarding Allegations of Mishandling Classified Documents by Attorney General Alberto Gonzales," Department of Justice, September 2, 2008, http://www.usdoj .gov/oig//special/50809/final.pdf.

What the newspaper *did* know about the program was that if the NSA program was a runaway presidential abuse of power, as its reporting was later to suggest, it was running away in a most peculiar fashion. Although the newspaper strenuously downplayed it, both the judicial and legislative branches of government had been regularly apprised of the program's operations and, in light of the circumstances and the danger to the country, both had given their assent.

As Lichtblau himself was to report, in October 2001, the month in which the NSA surveillance was launched, Ashcroft gave a full briefing on the program's workings to Royce Lamberth, the chief judge on the FISA court. Although later, after the program was exposed, Lamberth was to criticize it as "unwise," at that moment of crisis he did not demur. Indeed, over the following months, Lamberth worked with the Justice Department to craft a system that would avoid intermingling information garnered from investigations conducted under orders issued by his court with information derived from NSA intercepts.[28]

When doubts about that system were voiced by Judge Kollar-Kotelly, the program, as I have already noted, was halted for review and adjustments were made. The system, in short, was functioning with the normal give-and-take of our constitutional system: The judiciary and the executive branch were collaborating in the midst of a crisis to make a classified program succeed within the confines of law.

So too was Congress kept in the loop. From the outset, leaders of the House and Senate were kept informed about the program, albeit in a manner limited by Congress's own rules for dealing with highly sensitive information. The Gang of Eight was briefed about the NSA surveillance on more than a dozen occasions by Vice President Cheney himself. Although controversy was to erupt after the leak over whether the full intelligence committees of both houses should have been read into the program, not one member of the Gang of Eight expressed any reservations on that score at the time. And only one member, Senator Jay Rockefeller, expressed concerns about the NSA surveillance itself *before* it leaked. Other members—no profiles in courage here—were to chime in with outrage only afterward.

Rockefeller, for his part, had sent a handwritten letter to Vice President Cheney that, while not directly challenging the legality of the program, expressed concern that "without more information and the ability to draw on any independent legal or technical expertise, I simply cannot satisfy lingering concerns raised by the briefing we received," and that "I feel unable to evaluate, much less endorse these activities."[29] Cheney did not reply to Rockefeller's missive, and the senator took no further action other than to place a copy of his own letter in his office safe, where it remained unread by anyone else until after the leak. This action, the epitome of caution, was hardly the behavior of a passionate objector.

In any event, by December 2005 doubts about the program like those entertained by Rockefeller were not the main thing on the mind of the editors of the *Times*. Other factors having nothing to do with the legal debate and everything to do with internal pressures at the newspaper were impelling them forward. By this point the *Times* editors were themselves concealing something from their readers. Indeed, just as there had been a land mine buried in the Justice Department by John Yoo, there was a very different sort of land mine in the editorial offices at W. 43rd Street, and it had been planted in the very same drawer where the NSA story had been filed.

The land mine had been created by none other than the *Times*'s star investigative reporter, James Risen. For more than a year he had been at work on his own book about the war on terrorism, titled *State of War: A Secret History of the CIA and the Bush Administration*. The NSA surveillance program was framed as its most important revelation, the one guaranteed to generate headlines and possibly propel it onto the best-seller lists. Simon & Schuster had slated the book for release in mid-January 2006. By the late autumn of 2005, the clock was thus ticking away inside the offices of the newspaper. In a manner of speaking the *Times* was being blackmailed by its own reporter. Risen's threat was unmistakable, and he possessed the means to carry it out: Either put the story into print, or it will come out in my book and you will be forced either to fire me—the move, he recognized, was a potential "career-ender" at the paper—or be scooped by a member of your own staff.[30]

For the *Times*, as Lichtblau was later to recount, the book was "one trigger for reconsidering the story."[31] It was in no small part the quandary created by the book's impending release that prompted "another round of internal discussions over the NSA's program and what to do with it."[32] In short order the editors reversed course and called on Risen and Lichtblau to update the draft that had been moldering more than a year. It was only in this period of updating in late 2005 that the paper discovered, as Lichtblau later explained, that there "were deep concerns within the administration that the President had authorized what amounted to an illegal usurpation of power."[33]

But this characterization is verbal sleight of hand. Lichtblau artfully makes it appear as if the "deep concerns" within the administration were ongoing. He obscures the fact that by this juncture they had long been allayed. The Madrid bombings had put the controversy to rest in March 2004. In other words, by December 2005 the *Times* was poised to disclose a counterterrorism program no longer deeply controversial within the government; rather it was going to blow a program behind which, after fierce arguments, a consensus had been forged regarding both its legality and vital importance.

If the *Times* management was pushing forward for competitive reasons—a desire not to be scooped by its own reporter's book—there were additional motivations in the mix that have been little discussed but should not be ignored. One of them is politics.

The *Times* prides itself on being a nonpartisan purveyor of news. In the words of Adolph S. Ochs, the founding father of the modern *Times*, the newspaper's goal is "to give the news impartially, without fear or favor, regardless of party, sect, or interests involved." Political bias of any sort is strictly forbidden by the *Times*'s own published rules of the road. "No one may do anything that damages our news staffs' reputation for strict neutrality in reporting on politics and government," read the *Times*'s "Ethics in Journalism" guidelines.[34] Journalists working for the *Times*, the guidelines continue, "do not take part in politics [and] they must do nothing that might raise questions about their professional neutrality or that of our news operations." Over the years the *Times* has given such regulations force. Thus when its Supreme Court correspondent Linda Greenhouse marched in a pro-abortion parade in 1989 she was roundly reprimanded by her editors.

But the two reporters who drove the NSA story repeatedly made not even a minimal effort to disguise their deep contempt for George W. Bush and his policies. Risen's *State of War* opens with the observation that the president, under the influence of "a cadre of neoconservative ideologues," had embarked on a "radical departure from the centrist traditions of U.S. foreign policy" and "allowed radical decisions to take effect rapidly with minimal review."[35] In going to war in Iraq such laxity led him to take "an enormous gamble with American policy in the Arab world—and with the lives of American soldiers."[36] As part of a "broader and disquieting pattern," it approved surveillance programs that make "a mockery of long-standing privacy rule."[37] The administration also engaged in "outrageous operations"[38] and sanctioned "many questionable actions" that have "lower[ed] the bar on what is acceptable when it comes to the government's ability to intrude into the personal lives of average Americans."[39]

Eric Lichtblau was of a piece. In his book he editorializes without inhibition, calling the Bush administration's tactics in the war on terrorism so "over the top" as to pose an existential threat to our political order and basic rights.[40] Indeed, in his view, in what the Bush administration was either doing or proposing to do, nothing less than the fate of the Constitution itself was at stake. The terrible question raised by Bush's conduct was, "Which side of it were you on? Were you for upholding it, or tearing it down?"[41] Lichtblau's own answer was supplied by the title of his book: *Bush's Law: The Remaking of American Justice.*

Accompanying the ideological passions driving the story were pecuniary interests. Editors of the *Times* would firmly reject any suggestion that the newspaper's coverage is ever tailored to court favor with advertisers, the financial lifeblood of their industry. To ensure that the news is not contaminated by such courting, the powers that be have erected a firewall between the news and business sides of the institution. But what prevents the pecuniary interests of *reporters* from shaping the news?

Here, too, there are strict rules. "The good name of our company and of our business unit or publication does not belong to any of us," state the guidelines. "No one has a right to exploit it for private purposes."[42] In particular, "No newsroom or editorial page employee may exploit for personal gain any nonpublic information acquired at work, or use an association with our news organization to gain favor or advantage."[43] Even the "*appearance* of abusing nonpublic information for financial gain" is proscribed.[44]

The rules extend explicitly to the writing of books, and govern even those, like Risen, who take a leave of absence to write one: "Staff members who plan outside writing or other outside creative work must never permit an impression that they might benefit financially from the outcome of news events."[45]

It would be indecorous to contend that Risen's major objective in bringing forward the NSA story was to gain financial profit from the sale of his book. He is a serious investigative journalist with a long if controversial track record of digging into important stories. But it would be a serious omission, on the other hand, not to take note of the financial rewards that, as the *Times* was deliberating over his story, would accrue to him by having a wave of publicity about his revelations carried in the paper shortly before its publication.

Indeed, as it happened, only weeks after the *Times*'s NSA story appeared, Risen's *State of War* ascended onto the best-seller lists, bringing its author royalties estimated to be in the low six figures. Not only did this create the "appearance" that a reporter would "benefit financially from the outcome of news events," a reporter actually *did* benefit. And the news event in question was a leak that compromised American security.

THE TIMES DID NOT have to permit any of this. Its ethics guidelines warn that any intentional violation is "a serious offense that may lead to disciplinary action, potentially including dismissal."[46] But the newspaper chose another course entirely. Speaking at a ceremony at Harvard where Risen and Lichtblau were awarded the Goldsmith Prize (no relation to Jack Goldsmith) for breaking the NSA story, Keller hailed the two for "perform[ing] an extraordinary feat of reporting."[47]

What explains such readiness to break its own rules and then celebrate the outcome? Asking the question hardly seems necessary. The obvious answer, taken for granted by many critics of the paper, is that Keller and other executives at the paper share the same political premises of Risen and Lichtblau, including abiding hostility toward the Bush administration. This ideological congruence in turn would also explain the curious detail that, after holding the NSA story for more than a year, the *Times* chose to publish it the very day before the Senate was to take up an extension of the Patriot Act, legislation that the *Times* editorial page—and Risen and Lichtblau—stridently opposed.

But the crude intrusion of editorial views into news decision making is not the full story, if it is the story at all. The entire episode belongs instead inside a larger and more interesting frame than raw political bias. As their ethics guidelines make plain, the editors of the *Times* conceive of themselves as strictly nonpartisan gatherers and disseminators of information. Even if some of them dwell so far inside the mental universe of Left liberalism that they are unable to recognize when they stray from their ideal of objectivity, we do well to take them at their word that neutrality is the standard they are striving for.

Seen in this light, the decision to disclose a national security secret was not taken first and foremost to kneecap a White House toward which some inside the paper were plainly hostile. Rather, it flowed from an adversarial conception of journalism that, ever since Vietnam and Watergate, has come to dominate the profession.

For the first two-thirds of the twentieth century, objectivity was the watchword of journalism: Reporters and editors were to be the dispassionate purveyors of information that would lubricate the operations of democracy by providing the public with all it needed to know. This stance often thrust journalists into conflict with the government. Even before the pervasive suspicion of government engendered by the Vietnam War and the Nixon presidency, officials and the media were often fundamentally at odds over issues of secrecy merely by virtue of their differing institutional functions.

The two competing imperatives were captured neatly by the *Times* columnist Arthur Krock in the 1950s: A journalist's obligations in publishing a story, Krock wrote, were limited to answering some elementary questions: "Is it true? Has it been legitimately acquired? Is it fit to print—public property or a private matter? These satisfactorily settled, the facts are ready for their bath of printer's ink." But as the statesman considers disclosure, he has other considerations. For him the key questions are: "Is it premature? Will publication make the going more difficult? Will publication tend to confuse, rather than to clarify, the popular mind?"[48]

By the 1960s and 1970s, as time-honored verities were overturned by foreign war, domestic social upheaval, and real and imagined transgressions of law by the U.S. government, a novel dispensation took hold. The matter-of-fact assumptions about journalistic objectivity implicitly endorsed by Krock came to be regarded as their own peculiar form of bias, one that, in the words of the historian of the American press, Michael Schudson, "represent[s] collusion with institutions whose legitimacy was in dispute."[49] A new set of values came to inform the journalistic mind, and with it came a reflex to regard all centers of power—both private and public—with unrelenting suspicion, except journalism itself.

From this oppositional stance followed several corollaries. The press, for one thing, came to conceive of journalism not as a craft but as a calling with a salvific social and political mission of burning importance. For another, the press began by establishing itself as the most qualified and disinterested judge of what constitutes the public interest. It ended with the press regarding itself not merely as the Fourth Branch or the Fourth Estate—a checking and balancing force supplementing the three branches of the U.S. government— but as *the* sovereign power, *above* the three branches, and free to violate their democratically enacted laws in pursuit of its mission.[50] In entering the realm of national security, it has bestowed upon itself the role of final arbiter of what government secrets can and cannot be published, regardless of what is at stake.

The *Times* ethics guidelines speak of the paper's "solemn responsibilities under the First Amendment" to serve as an unfettered provider of information to the American people. "It's an unusual and powerful thing, this freedom that our founders gave to the press," wrote Bill Keller in an open letter to readers defending his paper's publication of yet another highly controversial national security leak in 2006. "The people who invented this country," he continued, "saw an aggressive, independent press as a protective measure against the abuse of power in a democracy and an essential ingredient for self-government. They rejected the idea that it is wise, or patriotic, to always take the President at his word or to surrender to the government important decisions about what to publish."[51]

But is Keller right about the "inventors" of this country and what they intended? Or is he engaging in what has been called "retrospective symmetry," in which a vision of the past is imposed upon the present, in this instance for the purpose of giving it a patriotic gloss?

CHAPTER 2

SECRETS OF THE FOUNDERS

ONE POINT OF ENTRY into the question raised by Keller's comments is the thinking of one of the more preeminent such inventors, Benjamin Franklin. Writing in the momentous year 1789, Franklin extolled liberty of the press, calling it something "which every Pennsylvanian would fight and die for." But he wondered at the same time about the limits of this liberty: "Few of us," he wrote, "have distinct Ideas of its Nature and Extent." Himself indisputably the most accomplished writer and printer of the era, Franklin had his own sharply articulated view of the appropriate limits. "My proposal," he wrote, is "to leave the liberty of the press untouched, to be exercised in its full extent, force, and vigor."[1] Bill Keller could presumably rest his case right there.

But Franklin continued with a qualification. Along with untouched liberty of the press, he also favored "the liberty of the cudgel." If an "impudent writer" attacked the reputation of a citizen, he wrote, "you may go to him as openly and break his head." In the public sphere Franklin counseled only a slightly gentler corrective to journalistic "licentiousness." If the government was libeled, he wrote, "I would not advise proceeding immediately to these extremities; but that we should in moderation content ourselves with tarring and feathering."[2]

However sardonic Franklin was waxing, his words shed considerable light on attitudes toward the press—and press freedom—in the year in which the Bill of Rights was ratified, in a land where tarring and feathering of writers and public figures, particularly those of royalist bent, was not unknown. Indeed, the framers of our Constitution were far from the consistent libertarians they are so often made out to be in our own libertarian era. As we shall see, the system they designed came complete with machinery to contain and control information, both as it flowed among the branches of government and as it was distributed to the public.

From the very outset the perils of secrecy, and the necessity of secrecy—and striking the proper balance between the two—was one of their central preoccupations. At moments when the new Republic was in imminent danger of being strangled in its cradle, the problem rose conspicuously to the fore. As the Republic grew more secure, concern for secrecy receded and the virtues of openness were more unrestrainedly trumpeted. Over the long haul of American history, this pattern—oscillation between a sense of vulnerability and a sense of self-confidence—mirrors precisely the fluctuations in our attitudes toward openness and secrecy right to the present day.

Then as now the effort to guard national security secrets ran directly against the principle of "freedom of the press." Yet as we shall also see, those four words meant very different things to eighteenth-century Americans than they do to us. Although the framers were bitterly divided among themselves on many issues, there was broad consensus, encompassing even the most radical proponents of openness, that safeguarding national security secrets was an imperative that could not be ignored. The publication of secret government information in pamphlets, books, and newspapers, though rare, was not unheard of in that era. How best to guard against such occurrences was the subject of heated discussion and, as a practical problem to be solved, a thicket of thorns.

Although in the founding era there were no specific statutes proscribing leaks to the public per se, the constitutions of the various states, and then later, the federal Constitution itself, contained a mechanism to punish those breaches that gravely compromised national security. If no satisfactory solution was ever settled upon to handle less egregious disclosures, this did not reflect indifference, let alone the view that the press was free to publish whatever it would without fear of sanction.

To be sure, it will not do to tread the same path as Bill Keller and hold up the handiwork of the Founding Fathers as a template for our contemporary circumstances. The presidency has grown hugely in scope and power since 1789. Successive technological revolutions have given the executive branch surveillance and information-storage powers of astounding reach. We enter this historical terrain not out of some originalist impulse to embrace the standards of the eighteenth century and impose them on our own institutions; as far as secrecy is concerned, the historical model erected by the Founding Fathers would not serve our needs. Our purpose rather is to dispel a mythology that in many quarters is uncritically embraced. The picture that emerges in its place is rich with suggestive implications for understanding the tension between transparency and secrecy over more than two centuries of American life.

THE MEN WHO declared independence in 1776, like those who gathered in Philadelphia in 1787, knew that they would have to build an entirely new political structure. What emerged from their deliberations was a system based on openness of a kind the world had not previously seen. As the historian Daniel N. Hoffman makes plain in his *Governmental Secrecy and the Founding Fathers*, at the very core of the democratic experiment was the question of transparency.[3] Secrecy was a cornerstone of monarchy, a fundament of an unaccountable political system built in no small part on what King James I had called the "mysteries of state." Secrecy was not merely functional, a requirement of effective governance, but intrinsic to the mental scaffolding of autocratic rule.[4]

Standing in diametrical opposition to authority based upon

inscrutability was an elementary proposition of democratic theory: Legitimate power could rest only on the *informed* consent of the governed. Along with individuals at liberty to give or to withhold approval, informed consent requires, above all else, information, freely available and freely exchanged. Official secrecy was anathema to this conception. What republican theory accomplished, in Hoffman's formulation, was "to reverse the old presumption in favor of secrecy, based on the divine right of kings and nobles, and replace it with a presumption in favor of publicity, based on the doctrine of popular sovereignty."[5] No one has put this proposition more forcefully than James Madison: "A popular government, without popular information, or the means of acquiring it, is but a Prologue to a Farce or a Tragedy, or, perhaps both. Knowledge will forever govern ignorance: And a people who mean to be their own Governors, must arm themselves with the power which knowledge gives."[6]

The roots of these revolutionary conceptions of transparency and publicity ran deep. As democratic ideas entered the consciousness of Anglo-Saxon elites, they had a subtle and slow but corrosive impact on the institutions of the old order. Parliamentary proceedings in England, long closed, began to be recorded in regularly published journals in 1722. But these appeared only in what Jeremy Bentham called a "meagre and dry" form, with a record of the formal proceedings and tallies of votes, but no account of the actual debates.[7] English practices were mirrored and to some considerable measure augmented in the American colonies, two of which, by law, conducted their legislative business in public, and eight of which invested their legislatures with the power to review the minutes of executive bodies.

But if antipathy toward governmental opacity was a powerful current, at no time in either the revolutionary or federal period was it in theory or practice an absolute. Even Bentham, an unvarnished advocate of maximum transparency, held open the need for exceptions. Openness, he maintained, "ought to be suspended" in those cases, among others, when it "favour[s] the projects of an enemy." Rules, he acknowledged, including very much his own "rule of publicity"—the proposition that government should be an open book—"are made for a state of calm and security," and "they cannot be formed for a state of trouble and peril."[8]

Trouble and peril were precisely what was gathering on the horizon as the First Continental Congress assembled in Philadelphia in 1774. It began by establishing rules of conduct for the deliberations that lay ahead. High on the register was the requirement that "the doors be shut during the time of business." Members were to consider themselves "under the strongest obligations of honour, to keep the proceedings secret, until the majority shall direct them to be made public."[9] With critical financial, diplomatic, and military decisions under debate, impending war made secrecy inescapable, a matter of life and death.

The Second Continental Congress, meeting in 1775 when the cannonballs were already flying, exhibited an even more intense preoccupation with security. The body imposed a compulsory oath of secrecy in which each member pledged "under the ties of virtue, honour and love of his country, not to divulge, directly or indirectly, any matter or thing agitated or debated in Congress" unless Congress gave its express permission.[10] Concern for secrecy was particularly acute, then as now, in the realm of intelligence, a sphere which George Washington deemed vital. "The necessity of procuring good Intelligence is apparent & need not be further urged," he wrote to a subordinate: "All that remains for me to add is, that you keep the whole matter as secret as possible. For upon Secrecy, Success depends in Most Enterprizes of the kind, and for want of it, they are generally defeated, however well planned & promising a favourable issue."[11]

In what amounts to an antique version of our present-day intelligence community, the Continental Congress set up several clandestine arms with different if overlapping functions. One was the Committee (later called the Commission) for Detecting and Defeating Conspiracies, our country's first counterintelligence body, with responsibility for apprehending British spies, couriers, and sympathizers. Operating in parallel with it was the Secret Committee, established in the autumn of 1775. This body was granted a handsome budget and near-free rein to obtain armaments for the Revolution. In addition to entering into secret contracts with manufacturers of arms and gunpowder, it also conducted covert operations, organizing raids on British facilities in the southern colonies. So intent was the Secret Committee upon fulfilling the mandate embedded in its name that it destroyed the records of its own transactions to minimize the possibilities of disclosure.

The Committee of Correspondence (soon thereafter renamed the Committee of Secret Correspondence and not long after renamed yet again the Committee of Foreign Affairs) was yet a third body. Though charged ostensibly with "the sole purpose of corresponding with our friends in Great Britain, and other parts of the world," that was by and large a cover. In actual fact the committee served as an intelligence directorate, carrying out both operational and analytical functions. Composed of only five members, precisely, as the historical record makes evident, to minimize the danger of leaks, its operational side organized clandestine operations, disseminated propaganda, devised codes and ciphers, employed a network of secret agents abroad, developed a maritime intelligence service parallel to that of the navy, intercepted and screened private mail, and established a secure courier system. Its analytical side acquired foreign publications for study of developments abroad.[12]

So sensitive did the Committee of Secret Correspondence deem some of its own activities that it could not in all cases entrust knowledge of its handiwork even to its parent body. When France agreed to supply munitions and funds to the American revolutionaries, Benjamin Franklin concurred with Robert Morris, his colleague on the committee, "that it is our indispensable duty to keep it a secret, even from Congress." A revealing reason was offered by way of explanation; damaging unauthorized disclosures had cropped up too often before. "We find, by fatal experience," wrote Franklin, that the Congress "consists of too many members to keep secrets."[13] Congress in that era consisted of approximately 50 members at any given time, not one of them with a staff. The echoes resound. Our often-porous Congress today is composed of 535 members, aided by thousands of personal and committee staff members.

The secrecy in which the Continental Congress wrapped itself in its sessions did not become entrenched or total, which would have been an irony in light of the democratic sentiments impelling the American revolutionaries forward in their fight. These sentiments pushed matters in a different direction, toward ever more publicity. As early as 1777, as conditions allowed, Congress took to the periodic publication of its proceedings, including tallies of votes. These congressional journals then began to appear on a regular schedule, either weekly or monthly. Only specific sensitive matters requiring secret handling were excluded from publication and entered into a separate journal, an early version of our modern system of classification.[14] From the outset, national security enjoyed a privileged status. Among those items marked for special handling outside public view were matters "relating to treaties, alliances or military operations."

But if congressional proceedings were, with the noted exceptions, recorded and made available, the doors of Congress remained shut; observers were barred from attending. By the 1780s this practice became a subject of fierce contention, caught up not only on the principle at issue, but in the sectional rivalries that were perpetually being hammered out in the chambers, with southern delegates fearing that openness would augment the power of northern merchants.[15] A series of proposals to open the doors for all of its sessions, "'unless otherwise ordered by a vote or by the rules of the house," was defeated.[16] Publicity continued to have its limits.

If this held true through the period of the Articles of Confederation, it held true as well for the Constitutional Convention that gathered in 1787 in the Pennsylvania State House, where the political machinery was built under which we now, more than two centuries later, continue to govern ourselves. The sessions in Philadelphia were conducted in a total information blackout, with sentries posted at the doors and the Convention's deliberations protected under the rule that "nothing spoken in the House be printed, or otherwise published or communicated without leave."

Of course by 1787 the war with the British was over; the Treaty of Paris had been signed and the conflict settled. National security could no longer be the rationale for shrouding in secrecy the deliberations that were to give birth to the basic document of American democracy. Why then the shuttered doors? The answer was spelled out by George Washington, the president of the convocation, as he chastised one member who had been "neglectful" of the Convention's secrets, leaving a copy of its records in public view in the state house. "I must entreat Gentlemen to be more careful," admonished Washington, "lest our transaction get into the News Papers, and disturb the public repose by premature speculations."[17]

This fear of disturbing the "public repose"—a most curious rationale for imposing secrecy in a democracy—itself caused disturbances. The information blackout spurred, as secrecy so often does, "wild speculation."[18] Among the proliferating rumors was the conviction that the Convention was poised to offer a foreigner, the bishop of Osnaburgh, the American crown.[19] But the framers offered reasons they found compelling for keeping their deliberations out of the newspapers. These had nothing to do with monarchical plots or threats from abroad and everything to do with forging consensus.

The records of the Convention are replete with passages lauding the manifold advantages of secrecy for this purpose:

> It was likewise best for the convention for forming the
> Constitution to sit with closed doors, because opinions
> were so various and at first so crude that it was necessary
> they should be long debated before any uniform system
> of opinion could be formed. Meantime the minds of the
> members were changing, and much was to be gained by a
> yielding and accommodating spirit. . . . Had the members

committed themselves publicly at first, they would have afterwards supposed consistency required them to maintain their ground, whereas by secret discussion no man felt himself obliged to retain his opinions any longer than he was satisfied of their propriety and truth, and was open to the force of argument.[20]

Our political system was thus born in secrecy: "No Constitution would ever have been adopted by the Convention," explained Madison, "if the debates had been public."[21]

The secrecy that was necessary to get through the Convention remained necessary to get through ratification of its handiwork by the states. "Had the deliberations been open while going on, the clamours of faction would have prevented any satisfactory result," wrote Alexander Hamilton, and "had they been *afterwards disclosed*, much food would have been afforded to inflammatory declamation. Propositions, made without due reflection, would have been handles for a profusion of ill-natured accusation."[22] Madison and Hamilton, two of the Revolution's most outstanding thinkers, thus adhered to the paradoxical idea that the midwifing of democracy had to be concealed from the demos itself. The public, they believed, was dangerously susceptible to demagoguery.

This dread of public reaction was not universally shared. Thomas Jefferson, writing from Paris as the American minister to France, was appalled, calling the "tying of the tongues" of the delegates an "abominable" precedent: "Nothing can justify this example but the innocence of their intentions, & ignorance of the value of public discussions."[23] Opinion was thus sharply split over the Convention's own secrecy. The divisions were mirrored in corresponding splits over the shape of the constitutional structure being drawn.

THE FRAMERS were far from being of one mind about the flow of information in the new order. On one side were the more radical libertarians, who would tilt toward Jefferson's view, placing a premium on openness; *informed* consent was the vital principal that should be elevated above all else. Where there was agreement, bringing aboard even those most inclined toward expanding the reach of popular sovereignty, was that national security was the single area where the new government needed the latitude to keep its operations hidden. Excessive openness in national security had been one of the more persistent weaknesses of the Articles of Confederation: "So often and so essentially have we heretofore suffered from the want of secrecy and dispatch," wrote John Jay in *Federalist* no. 64, "that the Constitution would have been inexcusably defective, if no attention had been paid to those objects."[24]

But where to draw the line? This question, as applied to both the newly envisioned bicameral legislature and to the executive, was to precipitate sharp disagreements. The Committee of Detail, charged with preparing a draft of the Constitution for the Convention's consideration, entertained a plan that would have left it to the two houses of Congress themselves to decide when to disclose their deliberations. But the advocates of openness prevailed: The committee ended by giving the House no discretion in the matter whatsoever. Its deliberations had to be open.

The Senate was a different matter. The Committee of Detail divided the Senate's functions into legislative and executive components, with the former to be open and the latter to be entirely secret. The full Convention took up the issue. By a vote of seven states to three, it adopted a proposal for the regular publication of a congressional journal that would report on *all* proceedings without exception for sensitive matters. A revision put forward by Madison and John Rutledge of South Carolina to give the Senate discretion to keep secret "non-legislative activity" was defeated by ten states to one.

These two tallies would seem to be an overwhelming rejection of secrecy. But in the final draft a more practicable compromise emerged. By a six-to-four vote (with one abstention) the Senate acquired the power to deliberate in secret when necessary. So, too, did the House of Representatives. In the finished Constitution, Article I, Section 5 makes plain that secrecy was to be at the discretion of both chambers: "Each House shall keep a journal of its proceedings, and from time to time publish the same, excepting such parts as may in their judgment require secrecy."

If Congress was ultimately invested with the discretion to keep its proceedings secret, the executive branch was granted even more leeway. To meet the weighty responsibilities of his office, the president was granted extensive powers, including that of commander in chief of the armed forces, and made the ultimate guarantor of national security. On one side the president's almost kinglike authority gave way to alarm in anti-Federalist quarters. With so much power concentrated in one individual, would he evolve into a tyrant? No, answered Alexander Hamilton in *Federalist* no. 69. Given the way his powers were clipped at every turn, there could be "no comparison between the intended power of the President and the actual power of the British sovereign."[25] But in protecting against the danger of tyranny, and in designing institutions to preserve the president's accountability to the people, the framers had also to guard against a countervailing danger: that the president would be too feeble an executive to carry out his job. "Decision, activity, secrecy, and dispatch," were the qualities required of the office, argued Hamilton famously in *Federalist* no. 70, countering proposals for designing an executive even weaker than the president already was to be.[26]

But how was secrecy to be reconciled with responsibility to the public? Here was a pivot point of the debate. "Secrecy, vigor & despatch are *not* the principal properties reqd. in the Executive," replied John Dickinson of Delaware to Hamilton. "Important as these are, that of responsibility is more so, which can only be preserved; by leaving it singly to discharge its functions."[27] The tension between publicity and secrecy thus lay at the heart of the great constitutional dilemma of constructing a democracy that would sail neither too close to the Scylla of autocracy nor to the Charybdis of anarchy.

The course on which the framers fixed was the separation of powers and the checks and balances they imposed on presidential authority. The energetic executive was to operate in conjunction with the courts and the legislature, requiring the latter's assent for expenditures, for appointments of ranking officials, and for decisions of great moment, like declarations of war.

For Congress to carry out its checking-and-balancing function, it necessarily required access to information about the activities of the executive branch. But the Constitution says markedly little about how and under what circumstances the requisite information was to flow. The Committee of Detail came up with the formulation that the president "shall from Time to Time give Information to the Legislature of the State of the Union," which made its way into the Constitution with only a cosmetic change. Yet the Constitution set in place no formal mechanism by which Congress could demand information from the executive. This lacuna in the document has been a perennial source of conflict among the branches from national inception to the present day, framed as battles over "executive privilege"—the presidential assertion that the executive branch has the right to keep aspects of its operation from disclosure.

Whatever the vagaries of the arrangements regulating the flow of information among the branches of government, when it came to scrutiny by the populace itself, the framers drafted the Constitution with the assumption that the president would be a remote figure, operating largely out of public view. And nowhere was this made more explicit than in the area of national security. "It seldom happens in the negotiation of treaties, of whatever nature, but that perfect *secrecy* and immediate dispatch are sometimes requisite," wrote Jay in *Federalist* no. 64.[28] At issue was not merely the narrowly construed secrecy required to protect the country against external threats to its security in and around wartime, but the more blanket-like secrecy required for the successful conduct of foreign relations even in peacetime.

Such limits on openness in the draft did not satisfy absolutist defenders of openness, and the issue emerged saliently in the broader discontent with the Constitution voiced by the anti-Federalists. Two of the most adamant anti-Federalists, Elbridge Gerry of Massachusetts and George Mason of Virginia, cited the deficit of transparency (among other things they found intolerable in the document) as reasons for declining to sign the Constitution. Even here, however, the principal objection revolved around the fact that Congress was held to such a vague timetable—"from time to time"—for offering a public accounting of government expenditures. The fact that secrecy would on some occasions be required for purposes of assuring national security was not something they contested.[29]

In a similar vein Patrick Henry, at that juncture an anti-Federalist nonpareil, was greatly exercised by the provisions limiting publicity. His complaint is revealing of the balance that even the most ardent advocate of greater transparency aimed to strike. On the one hand, wrote Henry, "The liberties of a people never were, nor ever will be, secure when the transactions of their rulers may be concealed from them." Indeed, "to cover with the veil of secrecy the common routine of business is an abomination in the eyes of every intelligent man, and every friend to his country."[30]

This was rousing language, but Henry was by no means an absolutist. Even as he called secrecy an abomination, he explained that "I am not an advocate for divulging indiscriminately all the operations of government."[31] In particular, "Such transactions as relate to military operations or affairs of great consequence, the immediate promulgation of which might defeat the interests of the community, I would not wish to be published, till the end which required their secrecy should have been effected."[32]

The qualifications like those entered here by Patrick Henry reveal that, in the final analysis, and despite the fierce quarreling, there was a remarkable degree of consensus about the limits of openness. In the constitutional plan, "Secrecy is only used when it would be fatal and pernicious to publish the schemes of government," was the answer of John Marshall, the future Chief Justice, to Henry.[33] Hoffman captures the balance aptly: "Without exception," the framers were agreed that "justification for secrecy was limited to the most highly sensitive military and diplomatic affairs; they only differed over whether the Constitution made this sufficiently clear."[34]

CHAPTER 3

"HIGHLY DANGEROUS TO THE PUBLICK SAFETY"

NOTWITHSTANDING the limitations on openness built into the foundation, the framers had crafted a political system with a high degree of transparency. And the most crucial counterpoint to whatever provisions limited that transparency in the Constitution came in the first Congress with the enactment of the Bill of Rights and, specifically, the First Amendment. Its words are seemingly unequivocal: "Congress shall make no law . . . abridging the freedom of speech, or of the press." This constitutional provision is today celebrated as one of the hallmarks of our political order, ensuring, in the words of the Supreme Court, that our "profound national commitment to the principle that debate on public issues should be uninhibited, robust, and wide-open."[1]

But what did the words "freedom of the press" mean to the framers, and how did the phrase fit together with official secrecy? Ben Franklin's cudgel aside, the framers were hardly the apostles of libertarianism that they are today made out to be by Bill Keller and many others. And the First Amendment was not designed to protect the press from punishment for anything and everything it might publish, including government secrets.

As we learn from the historian Leonard Levy's pathbreaking

Emergence of a Free Press, the dividing line drawn between the permissible and the impermissible by the revolutionary generation was drastically different from our own.[2] As they pressed upon the world in the Declaration of Independence, the Founding Fathers sought to sever the chain that connected the colonies to the king of England. But whatever radical ideas they held in opposition to the monarchical system, they were also, at the same time and to lesser and greater degrees, very much products of the mother country's intellectual milieu. They shared the outlook of its great legal minds—preeminently William Blackstone—whose four-volume treatise, *Commentaries on the Laws of England*, exerted a profound influence on the legal thinking of the era. They embraced the English system of common law that Blackstone so deeply explored and had been adopted by the American states in all cases where statutes were silent.

Outlawed in England, among other pertinent things, was "seditious libel," a crime that consists of assaulting the government with mere words. The same crime was on the books, by common law or by statute, of all of the American colonies. It encompassed not merely defamation or ridicule of government and/or government's officers and acts, but also—significantly for our purposes—words that had the effect, even indirectly, of breaching the peace.[3] Remarkably, to our modern minds, there was no contradiction perceived between such laws and freedom of expression. As Blackstone explained, "Where blasphemous, immoral, treasonable, schismatical, seditious, or scandalous libels are punished by English law . . . the liberty of the press, properly understood, is by no means infringed or violated."[4] Punishment was to come only *after* publication. It was only prior restraint, in the form of censorship or special taxes, that was incompatible with the Blackstonian tradition. The press, as in our era, was to have the freedom to print whatever it would, and government, unlike in our era, had the freedom to prosecute the press whenever it crossed the line into the forbidden.

The acquittal in 1735 of John Peter Zenger, editor of the *New York*

Weekly Journal, charged with libeling the governor of New York, has been heralded as the era's signal contribution to the development of freedom of expression on American soil. But despite Zenger's acquittal, the principal behind seditious libel laws remained universally accepted; the only innovation introduced by the case was that a jury was persuaded that the truth of the alleged libel could serve as a defense. The act of jury nullification in the Zenger case hardly nullified the statutes themselves.

After Zenger seditious libel laws remained on the books of all the colonies, a state of affairs that remained intact even after the colonies declared their independence. Indeed, as Levy has noted, not only were seditious libel laws retained, but "no state adopted truth as a defense during the period 1776–89."[5] If actual prosecutions for seditious libel were sporadic after Zenger, the threat of prosecution remained a dangling sword, deterring printers from publishing works that might skirt the line, crossing from what was deemed proper discussion into defamation. This hovering repression was not, to the thinkers behind the American experiment in freedom, an unhappy condition.

James Alexander was the legal powerhouse behind Zenger's defense and a man at the hub of the intellectual life of the era: a founder of the American Philosophical Society, attorney general of New Jersey, an editor at America's first politically independent newspaper, Zenger's *New York Weekly Journal*, and a celebrator of Zenger's acquittal as an epochal victory for freedom of speech. He was the first colonial figure, writes Levy, "to develop a philosophy of freedom of speech-and-press."[6] And from our modern vantage point, what a crimped and self-contradictory philosophy it was.

On the one hand Alexander held that "the Liberty of the Press is a liberty for every man to communicate his sentiments freely to the public, upon political or religious points." He stressed that true liberty hinges on the ability to communicate "without the Fear of Danger of being punished." Yet on the other hand, and without any awareness of the inconsistency, he maintained that "Abuses that dissolve society and sap the Foundation of Government are not to be sheltered under the Umbrage of the Liberty of the Press." He could not conceive, he wrote, "how any man can see a liberty, and an essential liberty of a constitution, abused with impunity."[7] And what was the nature of the "abuses" that so concerned Alexander? Ill-founded criticism of the government: Anyone who spoke "irreverently and disrespectfully of Magistrates," he wrote, "was and is, always will be, criminal."[8]

Alexander, the period's foremost exponent of liberty of the press, was of his time. Indeed, no libertarian theorist of the era extending from the early seventeenth century through to the American Revolution challenged the notion that seditious libel was a crime. Some scholars have since contested that assertion. Zechariah Chafee, Jr., writing in the *Harvard Law Review* in 1919 on "Freedom of Speech in War Time," holds up Thomas Jefferson as an apostle of an unrestricted free press.[9] He cites Jefferson's well-known preamble to the Virginia Act for Establishing Religious Freedom, which calls it a "dangerous fallacy" to "suffer the civil Magistrate to intrude his powers into the field of opinion, and to restrain the profession or propagation of principles on supposition of their ill tendency." Chafee argues that this line of reasoning "holds good of political and speculative freedom," and could be taken as repudiation by Jefferson of seditious libel laws. Dumas Malone, Jefferson's leading biographer, goes even further, asserting that "freedom of thought was an absolute for Jefferson"[10] and without full freedom of expression there can be no freedom of thought.

But Chafee's extrapolation is as dubious as Malone's brush is overbroad. Whatever contradictions this may have entailed, Jefferson's view of freedom of religion differed markedly from his view of freedom of the press. In the draft of the constitution of Virginia that he drew up in 1783, the press was to be "subject to no other restraint than *liableness to legal prosecution* for *false* facts printed and published."[11] Five years later Jefferson could be found arguing in favor of the First Amendment, but only by offering a qualification of its seemingly categorical meaning. "A declaration that the federal government will never restrain the presses from printing anything they please," explained Jefferson, "will not take away the liability of the printers for false facts printed."[12]

In other words Jefferson's departure from Blackstonian principles was only a partial one. Truth, once again as in Zenger, would be a defense to the charge of seditious libel, but in cases of falsehood, a criminal conviction for libeling the government or its officers could hold. Presented with the final text of Madison's amendments to the Constitution, Jefferson demurred, suggesting instead a far more explicit restriction on the press than the words on offer in the First Amendment. According to the substitute language Jefferson put forward, "The people shall not be deprived or abridged of their right to speak or otherwise to publish anything but false facts affecting injuriously the life, liberty, property, or reputation of others or *affecting the peace of the confederacy with foreign nations.*"[13]

JEFFERSON'S explicit concern for not protecting words "affecting the peace" of the new country returns us to the subject of leaks. If the publication of false facts injurious to the government was to be deemed a criminal act, what did that suggest for the publication of *true* facts that were secret, exposure of which could be even more injurious than almost any conceivable libel? On its face it would seem safe to infer that the framers would deem leaking to be beyond the pale of acceptability and outside the protection of the law and the Constitution, including the Bill of Rights. But unauthorized disclosure of classified information was not quite the common practice in the Revolutionary era that it has become today. Indeed, it was only rarely a subject of explicit discussion, let alone a matter that came before courts. Nonetheless a survey of historical episodes bearing on our account, might, surprisingly, be taken to offer a partial vindication—with heavy emphasis on the word "partial"—of Bill Keller's invocation of the past.

As we have noted, the Second Continental Congress had its members swear an oath of secrecy. For violations of the pledge, it set penalties, not all of them specific but draconian in nature: "If any member shall violate this agreement, he shall be expelled this Congress, and deemed an enemy to the liberties of America, and liable to be treated as such."[14] In other words leakers were to be deemed traitors. In actual practice, however, punishment did not rise to the threatened level.

One of the more notable leaks of the era came in the Beaumarchais imbroglio. Pierre-Augustin Caron de Beaumarchais, was a brilliant watchmaker, musician, pamphleteer, and an intimate member of the court of Louis XV, where he served as a music tutor to the king's daughters. With the ascension of Louis XVI to the throne, he also became a spy, working to assist the American patriots. A fervent believer in the American Revolutionary cause, in 1776 he organized a massive covert infusion of French financial and material assistance to the hard-pressed American forces.

At a time when the French were still publicly neutral but actively supporting the American insurrection behind the scenes, the financial connection had to be a closely held secret. But in 1778 it was divulged to the public in an essay by Thomas Paine, then the secretary of Congress's Foreign Relations Committee. The disclosure, which severely embarrassed France, provoked outrage all around. A leak investigation ensued, with John Jay the chief inquisitor. Paine was summoned to appear before him. "I am directed by Congress to ask you if you are the author." Replied Paine, "Yes, sir, I am the author of that piece."[15]

In his Crisis pamphlets Paine had pleaded for openness in government as a necessary adjunct of democracy. "A government or an administration who means and acts honestly, has nothing to fear, and consequently has nothing to conceal."[16] In the wake of his leak, he was unrepentant, using words that precisely echo the justifications put forward by contemporary leakers: "My wish and my intentions in all my late publications were to preserve the public from error and imposition. . . . I have betrayed no trust because I have constantly employed that trust to the public good. I have revealed no secrets because I have told nothing that was, or I conceive ought to be, a secret."[17]

For his transgression Paine was subject to scorching attacks— "treason" was a charge bandied about—forfeited his post as secretary of the Foreign Relations Committee, and was expelled from Congress. Yet he was scarcely treated as an "enemy to the liberties of America." Indeed, he suffered no further penalty beyond the expulsion. Whatever damage his reputation suffered did not last. Years later, on Washington's recommendation and after his own incessant pleading, he was rewarded for his services to the Revolution with an estate in New Rochelle. His part in the Beaumarchais affair had become but a dim memory.

Even more striking in some respects is the outcome of leak cases that occurred in the early years of the new Republic. In one episode in the midst of the 1796 presidential campaign, a private communication from the French minister to the American secretary of state was leaked to the press. It lambasted Washington's administration and suggested the election of Thomas Jefferson. Federalists were outraged. Samuel Chase, then an associate justice of the Supreme Court, called for prosecution: "I think the Printer ought to be indicted for a false and base libel on our Government." A free press, he continued, "is the support of Liberty and a Republican Government, but a licentious press is the bane of freedom, and the peril of society, and will do more to destroy real liberty than any other Instrument in the Hands of knaves and fools."[18]

But despite the clamor, no prosecution resulted or was contemplated; indeed, the leak was government inspired, an attempt to embarrass the opposition, and once the document was in the public domain, the administration saw to it that it was given wide circulation. Here, in other words, was an early example of a practice now widespread: the elected government itself leaking secret information for partisan ends.

Revealing in a different way was the "Vindication" of Edmund Randolph, the nation's second secretary of state, written by him in 1795 after he was forced out of office by Washington for allegedly engaging, as he describes it, in a conspiracy "to destroy the popularity of the President, and thrust Mr. Jefferson into his chair."[19] As he defended his own conduct, Randolph jettisoned every consideration of secrecy. Along with the record of his conversations and the letters he exchanged with Washington, and intimate accounts of presidential decision making, he published diplomatic correspondence with France in full.

Once again no prosecution for leaking resulted. From the outset a criminal indictment would have been unfeasible. One obstacle was that Washington, in acrimonious correspondence with Randolph, had given him blanket permission to divulge whatever he would. "You are at full liberty," wrote the president, "to publish, without reserve, any and every private and confidential letter I ever wrote you; nay, more, every word I ever uttered to, or in your presence, from whence you can derive any advantage in your vindication."[20]

This generosity from the chief executive left Randolph free from liability, but it was intrinsic to Washington's rebuke. Randolph had made his case in the newspapers, and the president sought to place his side of the saga before readers as well. "I have no wish," Washington wrote to Randolph, "to conceal any part of my conduct from the public. That public will judge, when it comes to see your vindication, how far, and how proper it has been for you to publish private and confidential communications. . . . And it will, I hope, appreciate my motives, even if it should condemn my prudence, in allowing you the unlimited license herein contained."[21]

James Monroe, for his part, not long after Randolph was pushed out of office, was recalled by Washington from his position as minister to France. Evidence had emerged that he was leaking diplomatic secrets to the opposition press. Defending himself from the charge, Monroe published his own self-justification, accompanied by "authentic documents," including diplomatic correspondence. In other words, in defending himself from the charge of leaking, Monroe leaked even more prolifically, writing a pamphlet that laid bare the entire record of Franco-American relations, almost all of it rich with the potential to complicate relations with both Paris and London. Although the revelations badly rattled the administration, yet again the leaking elicited no prosecution, and no record has come to light suggesting that handing up an indictment was even contemplated.[22]

In another even more consequential case involving relations with France, in 1798 Benjamin Franklin Bache, editor of the *Philadelphia Aurora*, obtained and put into print diplomatic correspondence from Talleyrand to Elbridge Gerry. Once again the Federalists were infuriated. They demanded to know, writes Hoffman, "how Bache had obtained a copy and by what authority he had published it." In short order Bache stood "accused of carrying on a 'treasonable correspondence' with Talleyrand. Abigail Adams demanded that the hapless editor be 'seazed.' "[23] Bache insisted that his source for the leaked material was "domestic, not foreign." The explicit logic of this defense claim was that publication of a leak based on a foreign source might indeed be treasonable, but one drawn from a domestic source fell within legitimate and lawful parameters. Bache was indeed "seazed" and indicted for seditious libel. But the charges revolved around his attacks on the president and Congress, not his publication of secrets. Bache died of yellow fever before he could be put on trial.

The leaking and the stream of vituperation in the *Aurora* directed against the government were key factors leading to the passage in 1798 of the Sedition Act. Though the act constitutes one of the most extensive infringements on freedom of the press—and freedom generally—in American history, it did not itself make leaking per se a crime. The reticence in punishing leaking was a deliberate policy choice and part of a common outlook that even the Federalists shared. Protecting government secrets certainly was a concern in the era. Before the Sedition Act was enacted, a congressman had urged passage of a law against leaks by former officials, noting that his constituents "viewed with concern a defect in the laws of the United States, which suffered persons employed by the United States, after they were discharged from office, to print with impunity the secrets of Government, and praying that measures may be adopted to prevent this evil in the future."[24] Yet this proposal went nowhere in the House, and the "evil" was left unaddressed.

The failure to enact an antileak law is a puzzle. The most compelling explanation is that such a law would have been superfluous. For one thing some of the leakers who retailed U.S. diplomatic correspondence were foreign officials who could not be sanctioned. For another thing, when it came to leaking, the Federalists were themselves not shy about engaging in the practice, and came to see that an antileak statute might be used to turn the tables against them. There was also a de facto recognition that in a democracy some secret information would inevitably make its way into the public domain, and that the passage of a specific statute enjoining unauthorized disclosure would not be the appropriate way to stanch the flow. Hoffman suggests that in the final analysis the free-speech principles of the day, which allowed for the punishment of the dissemination of "false facts," would have frowned upon a law touching "true facts," which, after all, is the essence of leaked information. An antileak law would therefore have been regarded as "unconstitutional."[25]

YET AT A JUNCTURE in which the right of free speech was being trampled on left and right, it seems far fetched to think that the Federalists were inhibited by constitutional considerations, and there is scant evidence for such a conclusion in the documentary record. Perhaps the lacuna might best be explained by the fact that there already existed laws on the books, first of every colony, then of every state, and finally in the new U.S. Constitution itself, that would have made truly egregious disclosures punishable as a crime. The name of the crime is treason.

Typical is the Massachusetts Bay Act of August 31, 1706. It

defined treason not merely as the levying of war against the king. The offense also encompassed "holding a traiterous [*sic*] correspondence with any of her majesty's enemies, by letters or otherwise, whereby they shall give them intelligence tending to the damage of her majesty's subjects or interests, or to the benefit or advantage of the enemy."[26] A leak of vital military plans or covert intelligence operations, published for all to read, including enemies of the king, would arguably fall within the perimeter of this language. "The striking characteristic of all of the pre-Revolutionary [treason] legislation in the colonies," writes James Willard Hurst in his classic study of the law of treason, "is the evident emphasis on the safety of the state or government, and the subordinate role of any concern for the liberties of the individual."[27]

In the Revolutionary period the states redrew the colonial-era treason statutes to fit the exigencies of the wartime situation. Now included in the crime were such offenses as "traffic with the enemy," giving "aid and comfort" to the enemies of the Revolution, and "disloyal utterances." In New Jersey, for example, legislation enacted in 1778 noted that "many disaffected Subjects of this State do keep up an Intercourse and Communication with the Subjects or Troops of the King of Great-Britain, highly dangerous to the Publick Safety."[28] Such communication, when conducted without official permission, was deemed treasonous, even when undertaken without specific intent to aid the enemy. In New York, treason also could consist of certain kinds of speech, including endeavoring to "maliciously and advisedly seduce or persuade, or attempt to persuade or seduce any Inhabitant of this State, to renounce his or her Allegiance to this State."[29]

In Virginia the treason statute reached anyone who "by any word, open deed, or act, advisedly and willingly maintain[ed] and defend[ed] the authority, jurisdiction, or power, of the king or parliament of Great Britain."[30] Though the actual record of prosecutions in the revolutionary era is scant, one might see how, with the charge defined in terms so favorable to the preservation of security, it could be readily applied to the egregious disclosure of government secrets. Hurst's conclusion about the treason laws of the states is apposite: "Apart from their prima facie meaning, the terms of such statutes are obviously capable of being applied to sweep in all manner of incautious political talk in a time of stress."[31]

Treason is more narrowly defined in the U.S. Constitution itself. Even as they sought to preserve the security of the new federal government, after much debate the framers settled on the language that we know as Article III, Section 3:

> Treason against the United States, shall consist only
> in levying War against them, or in adhering to their
> Enemies, giving them Aid and Comfort. No Person shall
> be convicted of Treason unless on the Testimony of two
> Witnesses to the same overt Act, or on Confession in open
> Court.

In drawing the treason provision in this way, the framers were intent upon skirting a danger cited by Montesquieu that "if the crime of treason be indeterminate, this alone is sufficient to make any government degenerate into arbitrary power."[32] Treason was thus defined in a manner that would preclude prosecution for purely political crimes like voicing unpopular opinions. Stringent requirements of proof—the testimony of two witnesses to an "overt act" or a confession in "open" court—were a direct answer to the abuses of the notorious English Star Chamber proceedings of an earlier day.

But the illicit disclosure or publication of military secrets—a form of speech uniquely destructive of security—might nonetheless constitute an "overt act," lending "aid and comfort" to the enemy under the Constitution's terms. It is significant that under English law, while mere words could never amount to treason, there was also the crime of "constructive treason," under which words or acts, such as advocating the deposition of the king, could indeed lead to prosecution.

Likewise, in the American context, it remained more than a

theoretical possibility that words might also be deemed treasonous. One only need recall that after publishing the correspondence of Talleyrand, Bache was accused of precisely that (even as he was formally charged with seditious libel). It is also noteworthy that even in the modern era, with our far more capacious view of freedom of speech, certain kinds of utterances have been deemed treasonous by the courts. Most famously Ezra Pound was indicted for treason for his broadcasts on behalf of Fascist Italy during World War II. Pound was found not guilty by reason of insanity (and confined in Saint Elizabeth's Hospital in Washington, DC, for twelve years), but other American citizens were convicted of the crime on similar grounds. Iva Toguri d'Aquino, better known as "Tokyo Rose," was sentenced to ten years in prison for her wartime broadcasts on behalf of imperial Japan.

One might also call attention to the extraordinary World War II–era prosecution of the isolationist fanatic William Dudley Pelley, not for treason but for the arcane crime of seditious libel. In April 1942 he was charged with making "false statements with intent to interfere with the operation or success of the military or naval forces of the United States or to promote the success of its enemies."[33] Among other utterances deemed indictable was his declaration that President Roosevelt "chose to surround himself with Zionists and a fearful war resulted from their counsels."[34] For that and similar statements a jury convicted Pelley on eleven counts. The U.S. Court of Appeals for the Seventh Circuit upheld his conviction. The Supreme Court declined to hear a further appeal. Pelley served ten years of a fifteen-year sentence.*

---

*Geoffrey Stone is sharply critical of Pelley's conviction, arguing that "In the fervor of the moment, angry, ill-tempered criticism [of the government] was transformed into criminal falsehood," and that it is "very dangerous to allow the government to pick and choose which false statements in public debate it will prosecute and which it will tolerate." Stone's judgment is unassailable. But as I have pointed out, leaking and the publication of government secrets raises an entirely different set of issues, involving not the dissemination of false facts but of true ones. See Stone, *Perilous Times*, 260–72.

———

OUR HISTORY, old and not so old, demonstrates that speech in the realm of foreign affairs is by no means treated by our constitutional system as a right without boundaries. In his *Commentaries*, Joseph Story, the preeminent nineteenth-century interpreter of the U.S. Constitution, bluntly stated that the idea that the First Amendment "was intended to secure to every citizen an absolute right to speak, or write, or print, whatever he might please, without any responsibility, public or private . . . is a supposition too wild to be indulged by any rational man."[35] Still, the fact also remains that the publication of leaked secrets—unlike the theft of secrets in classic espionage—has never led to an actual criminal prosecution for treason or sedition in the founding era or since. Indeed, even if Bill Keller is blithely mistaken about what the inventors of this country intended, he can still take comfort from the fact that, in our early history, warnings of severe sanctions for such conduct came together with rather benign punishment in virtually every case.

Indeed, prosecutions for publication of leaks, as best as I can ascertain, do not appear in the historical record. Leakers themselves were not treated with particular harshness; the usual penalty, if there was a penalty at all, was forfeiting one's official position and suffering some measure of disgrace in the public eye. The same laxity with regard to publication arguably prevails today, with government officials issuing dire warnings not to publish sensitive material but then doing nothing more than throwing up their hands when the press ignores their pleas. Then as now, there was perhaps recognition that a cure would be worse than the disease.

But there is another side to this coin. For when one assesses the content of the major leaks of the founding era, one cannot but be struck by the innocuous nature of the disclosed material, at least in relative terms. Almost every leak that received public attention involved either diplomatic communications or White House decision making. The revelations were often acutely embarrassing and had repercussions in both domestic politics and for the conduct of foreign affairs.

But in an age in which open warfare was either under way or threatening to break out, and the survival of the Republic was often at risk, truly sensitive military or intelligence information involving, say, the disposition of American forces or the characteristics of American codes and ciphers, was never the subject of a public breach. In this respect the contrast with our own era is stark. In the twentieth century, which began with a world war and ended with the proliferation of weapons of mass destruction and global terrorism, leaks of classified information can have—and have had—very different consequences than in an age of musket fire and wind-borne ships.

CHAPTER 4

CLEAR AND PRESENT DANGER

S EPTEMBER 11, 2001, is for all of us indelible. But the night of July 30, 1916, is not one that New Yorkers of a different era would easily forget. Shortly after 2 a.m. a massive explosion detonated on a pier on Black Tom Island across the Hudson just off Jersey City. Windows shattered in an area with a radius of twenty-five miles from the epicenter. In Times Square shards of glass littered the streets. Shrapnel from the blast lodged in the Statue of Liberty, causing the closure of her arm and torch to visitors to this very day.[1] The earth shook as if a quake measuring more than 5.0 on the Richter scale had struck; people as far away as Maryland were roused from their slumbers. Property damage was estimated to be $20 million ($377 million in today's dollars). There was only one saving grace: For all the explosion's power, casualties were remarkably low. Reports vary, but as few as seven people may have perished.

Black Tom Island was the site of a munitions depot. On the night of the blast some two million pounds of ammunition, and one hundred thousand pounds of TNT, were stored at the facility in railcars and on barges, matériel heading to Britain and France for use in the war raging in Europe. German agents had infiltrated the facility and placed the bombs that effectively removed the munitions from the fray. The Black Tom blast was not the most dramatic act of sabotage of the era. Four months later German operatives succeeded in setting fire to a munitions factory in Kingsland (now Lyndhurst), New Jersey. Over the course of four hours approximately five hundred thousand high-explosive shells detonated, destroying the entire plant in a pyrotechnic display visible in Manhattan and more spectacular than the Black Tom explosion.

Arthur Zimmermann, Germany's foreign secretary—later immortalized in history as the author of the intercepted Zimmermann telegram—had boasted to the American ambassador in Germany that in the event of war "there are half a million trained Germans in America who will join the Irish and start a revolution," eliciting the ambassador's famous retort: "In that case there are half a million lamp-posts to hang them on." However exaggerated Zimmermann's threat, there was significant reason for concern.

When World War I erupted in August 1914 Germany's ambassador arrived in the United States bearing $150,000,000 in German treasury notes, all earmarked to underwrite a propaganda campaign.[2] For this initiative there was fertile ground to till. The U.S Census of 1910 put the number of persons born in Germany at more than 1.3 million, and it estimated that more than 10 million Americans were of German descent. Yet by April 1917, when America was finally provoked into joining the fight, Germany sympathizers and German intelligence agents were hardly the only internal problem with which the Wilson administration had to contend. The greater challenge was mobilization, for the European war was without precedent in the scale of the economic and social transformation that waging it required.

Hundreds of thousands of men had to be conscripted, fed, trained, armed, and transported across the ocean in the teeth of submarine attacks, which in turn demanded the production of an enormous quantity of weapons and other goods. This effort would have been challenging under any circumstances, but along with it the government had to counter fierce left-wing opposition to American entrance into the war, and opposition in particular to conscription, both of which took the form of agitation, demonstrations, and labor strikes.

The Russian Revolutions of February and October 1917 further energized domestic radicals and prompted alarms of another sort; a "red scare" was soon to ensue with widespread arrests of Communists and anarchists, real and suspected. When terrorism again reared its head after the war—eight bombs were set off in 1919 outside the homes of prominent Americans, including that of the new attorney general, A. Mitchell Palmer—the hysteria only intensified. The so-called Palmer raids began.

Woodrow Wilson, presiding over this cascade of calamities, began as an apostle of transparency, exceeding even Jefferson in the absolutism of his insistence on openness. Campaigning for the presidency, he had staked out an uncompromising position: "There is not any legitimate privacy about matters of government. Government must, if it is to be pure and correct in its processes, be absolutely public in everything that affects it."[3]

But as president, in the face of what he believed to be massive covert enemy infiltration, his sentiments about the purity of government went by the boards. Germany, Wilson warned, as he asked Congress for a declaration of war, had "filled our unsuspecting communities and even our offices of government with spies and set criminal intrigues everywhere afoot against our national unity of counsel, our peace within and without, our industries and our commerce."[4]

Inevitably, with the menace framed in this way, American entrance into the grand struggle served as a trigger for restrictions on liberty. Two days after declaring war Wilson presented Congress with a set of proposals to deal with the enemy within. Three months later, following a prolonged debate, Congress acted on Wilson's recommendations and passed the Espionage Act of 1917, which, among other provisions, provided steep fines and imprisonment for sabotage, spying, obstructing recruitment, and inciting insubordination.

The Espionage Act was itself a watered-down version of Wilson's much tougher initial demands. Both the original House and Senate versions of the bill had included a section that would have instituted a system of prior restraints on the press through government censorship. Wilson was adamantly in favor of such a measure, writing to Edwin Yates Webb of North Carolina, the Democratic chairman of the House conferees, that "authority to exercise censorship over the Press . . . is absolutely necessary to the public safety."[5] Yet he did not prevail.

Under fierce pressure from the press and a nascent civil liberties movement, Congress declined to enact the censorship provision. But the tide was not pulling in the direction of freedom. Not long after signing the Espionage Act into law, Wilson also put his signature on the Trading with the Enemy Act, which compelled all foreign-language newspapers and periodicals to submit to the post office English translations, prior to publication, of all content pertaining to the war or the operations of government. Then came the Alien Act of 1918, which provided for the deportation, without trial, of foreign residents suspected of disloyalty or who advocated the violent overthrow of the government. This was followed by the Sedition Act of May 1918—actually a set of amendments to the Espionage Act of 1917—adding nine more offenses to its coverage, including the punishment of any citizen who uttered anything "disloyal, profane, scurrilous, or abusive" about the U.S. government, the Constitution, the flag, and the uniform of the army or navy.

These statutes are highly significant to our story. For one thing, in provisions of the Espionage Act that were hotly controverted at the time, Congress devoted significant attention to the disclosure of closely held government information, the first occasion it had done so in our history. Its handiwork in this area remains the legal backbone of our secrecy regime to the current day. For another thing some three thousand Americans were prosecuted under the Espionage Act and associated statutes. Though leaks of sensitive information were not involved in any of these cases, the litigation left a body of precedents that defined the limits of free expression for that era and for our own. These precedents were to form a standard by which the disclosure and/or publication of classified information might be punished without treading on constitutional norms.

REMARKABLY, in the century and a half that had nearly elapsed since the founding of the United States, the Supreme Court had never before frontally considered the reach and limits of the First Amendment. Now, amid the domestic turmoil provoked by war, landmark rulings came in a flurry. *Schenck* was the first of a trilogy of free-speech cases—*Frohwerk* and *Debs* were the two others—that reached the Court in early 1919, just months after the war had come to its end with the spectacular collapse of the Central Powers.

Charles Schenck was the general secretary of the Socialist Party. A jury in a lower court had found him guilty of "causing and attempting to cause insubordination in the military and naval forces of the United States," and seeking "to obstruct the recruiting and enlistment service . . . when the United States was at war with the German Empire," all in violation of the Espionage Act.[6] The evidence against him consisted of minutes from a session of the executive committee of the party. A resolution approved there had called for printing fifteen thousand leaflets and mailing them to draftees. According to the summary offered by the Court, in impassioned language the leaflet "intimated that conscription was despotism in its worst form and a monstrous wrong against humanity in the interest of Wall Street's chosen few."[7]

In his defense Schenck asserted that the Espionage Act was an unconstitutional abridgement of free speech and a free press. In distributing the pamphlets he and members of his party were doing nothing more than exercising their fundamental rights. The Supreme Court unanimously disagreed. Oliver Wendell Holmes, the author of the Court's holding in this and the other two cases, forthrightly recognized that the First Amendment offered protection of speech extending beyond the mere prohibition of prior restraints. He also acknowledged that "in many places and in ordinary times the defendants in saying all that was said in the circular would have been within their constitutional rights." The problem posed by the leaflet, however, was one of "proximity and degree," for "the character of every act depends upon the circumstances in which it is done."

In words now famous, continued Holmes:

> The most stringent protection of free speech would not
> protect a man in falsely shouting fire in a theatre and
> causing a panic. It does not even protect a man from an
> injunction against uttering words that may have all the
> effect of force. The question in every case is whether the
> words used are used in such circumstances and are of such
> a nature as to create a clear and present danger that they
> will bring about the substantive evils that Congress has a
> right to prevent. . . . When a nation is at war many things
> that might be said in time of peace are such a hindrance to
> its effort that their utterance will not be endured so long as
> men fight and that no Court could regard them as protected
> by any constitutional right.[8]

Schenck's pamphlet, in its effects on the operation of the system of conscription, was judged equivalent to falsely shouting fire in a crowded theater. Accordingly, governmental suppression of it did not, the Court ruled, violate the First Amendment.

In *Frohwerk*, a second unanimous decision, the Court extended and clarified its reasoning. Jacob Frohwerk, a onetime copyeditor at the *Staats Zeitung*, a Missouri-based German-language newspaper, had been convicted and sentenced to ten years' imprisonment for "attempts to cause disloyalty, mutiny and refusal of duty in the military and naval forces of the United States," by means of "being engaged in the preparation and publication of a newspaper."[9] Articles published by his paper, in the Court's summary of the evidence, had extolled the "unconquerable spirit and undiminished strength of the

German nation." The *Staats Zeitung* had declared it "a monumental and inexcusable mistake to send our soldiers to France," a decision amounting to "outright murder" taken at the behest of the trusts of Wall Street. The newspaper had painted a picture, wrote Holmes, "made as moving as the writer was able to make it, of the sufferings of a drafted man, of his then recognizing that his country is not in danger and that he is being sent to a foreign land to fight in a cause that neither he nor any one else knows anything of, and reaching the conviction that this is but a war to protect some rich men's money."[10]

The issues in *Frohwerk*—speech directed against conscription—were nearly identical to those in *Schenk*, to which Holmes adverted in upholding Frohwerk's conviction. "We have decided in *Schenck*," wrote Holmes, "that a person may be convicted of a conspiracy to obstruct recruiting by words of persuasion." He then added a more explicit discussion of how these convictions fit together with the free-speech and free-press clauses of the Constitution. The First Amendment, Holmes continued, while prohibiting legislation against free speech in general, "obviously was not intended to give immunity for every possible use of language. We venture to believe that neither Hamilton nor Madison, nor any other competent person then or later, ever supposed that to make criminal the counseling of a murder within the jurisdiction of Congress would be an unconstitutional interference with free speech."[11]

IN CONSIDERING these decisions upholding the Espionage Act and the broader legal picture of the World War I era, what leaps out at first, of course, is the appalling fashion in which civil liberties were jettisoned wholesale. "No government which is for the profiteers can also be for the people, and I am for the people," wrote the socialist Rose Pastor Stokes in a letter to the *Kansas City Star* in 1918.[12] For this simple utterance she was convicted of attempting to cause insubordination under the Espionage Act and drew a sentence of ten years in the penitentiary. For attending a radical meeting and contributing all of twenty-five cents to the cause, an Iowa man drew a sentence of twenty-five years. Today we recoil viscerally from the way in which our country so readily embraced practices that seem to us entirely un-American, including especially prosecutions for political speech.

Yet to many in the World War I generation, as so often happens in wartime, the rationale for the repression, if not for its application in every instance, was dismally compelling. It is striking to recall that not long before Congress passed the Sedition Act of 1918, the *Washington Post* editorialized in its favor, noting that "it will give the government full power to deal effectively with persons who are not in sympathy with the United States, and it is to be hoped that [when] it is written on the statute books the Department of Justice will proceed with its enforcement."[13] For Americans seeing bombs detonating on our territory, strikes directed against the war effort, rioting in the streets, and a sizable German immigrant population whose loyalty was suspect at a moment when our ships were being struck by German submarines, the threat seemed overwhelming. And in facing it, recent history was full of lessons. The American Civil War had concluded six decades earlier, within living memory of the World War I generation. The extraordinary steps taken to preserve the Union were fresh in the public mind, just as today the lessons of wars reaching back seven decades, like World War II, remain fresh in ours.

AMONG the episodes of the Civil War that particularly resonated was the imprisonment (commuted to expulsion to the Confederacy) in 1863 of Clement Vallandigham, the national leader of the Copperheads, for having publicly condemned the president, the Emancipation Proclamation, the war, and conscription. Like those of Schenck, Frohwerk, Debs, and many others sentenced during World War I to long prison terms, Vallandigham's crime involved no action beyond words; it was a pure specimen of seditious speech. But during the Civil War there were no statutes on the books that would allow for prosecution on such a charge. Yet the extrajudicial prosecution that ensued, carried out by military tribunal, bore the imprimatur of none other than one of our greatest presidents.

Abraham Lincoln's words defending the trial and conviction of Vallandigham spoke directly to the men and women of Wilson's era:

> Mr. Vallandigham avows his hostility to the war on the part of the Union; and his arrest was made because he was laboring, with some effect, to prevent the raising of troops, to encourage desertions from the army, and to leave the rebellion without an adequate military force to suppress it. . . .
>
> Long experience has shown that armies can not be maintained unless desertion shall be punished by the severe penalty of death. The case requires, and the law and the constitution, sanction this punishment. Must I shoot a simple-minded soldier boy who deserts, while I must not touch a hair of a wiley agitator who induces him to desert? This is none the less injurious when effected by getting a father, or brother, or friend, into a public meeting, and there working upon his feelings, till he is persuaded to write the soldier boy, that he is fighting in a bad cause, for a wicked administration of a comtemptable [sic] government, too weak to arrest and punish him if he shall desert. I think that in such a case, to silence the agitator, and save the boy, is not only constitutional, but withal, a great mercy.[14]

Lincoln's logic was as captivating as his rhetoric. In the extraordinary circumstances of the Civil War, with brother fighting brother on our own soil and the fate of the republic at stake, the silencing of Vallandigham is difficult to condemn. (Indeed, it is ironic in light of how the *New York Times* has since evolved that it took the lead among Northern newspapers in its unwavering enthusiasm for prosecuting Vallandigham and anyone else expressing similar ideas.)

Yet if Lincoln approved the trial and conviction of Vallandigham, he drew the line there. Urged early in the war to suppress the Copperhead newspaper the *Chicago Times*, he declined, declaring, "I fear you do not fully comprehend the danger of abridging the liberties of the people. A government had better go the very extreme of toleration than do aught that could be construed into an interference with or jeopardize in any degree the rights of the people."[15] When Gen. Ambrose Burnside nonetheless shuttered the *Chicago Times* in 1863 for repeated expressions of incendiary and disloyal sentiments, Lincoln compelled him to rescind his orders.

WOODROW WILSON deviated sharply from the path trod by his illustrious predecessor. The machinery of repression he set in motion during World War I crossed a line. By its all-encompassing sweep, by the zeal with which it was employed, and by the exaggerations of the danger that was its justification, the administration's response was anathema to a liberal democratic order. Yet the egregious overreaction, it must be emphasized, was not located in the Espionage Act of 1917 itself, at least as that statute was initially drawn before the sedition amendments were added in 1918.

Congress, as I have previously noted, had vociferously opposed Wilson's initial proposal for government censorship and rejected it in full. The resulting legislation was hardly a liberal's dream, but neither did it trample on the basic premise of the First Amendment. Today even an orthodox civil libertarian like Geoffrey Stone regards the statute in a respectful light. The Espionage Act, Stone writes in *Perilous Times*, "was not a broadside attack on all criticism of the war. It was, rather, a carefully considered enactment designed to deal with specific military concerns."[16] Congress's rejection of the president's more radical proposals, Stone continues, "reflected a genuine concern for the potential impact of the legislation on 'the freedom of speech, or of the press.' "[17]

The trouble thus lay less with the statute itself than with the Wilson administration's aggressively tendentious construal of it. In an atmosphere of panic in the face of a threat far less grave than the one Lincoln confronted in the Civil War, Wilson's Justice Department leapt far beyond the law's intent. Under the overzealous enforcement of Attorney General Thomas Watt Gregory, it became a crime to write a word in print or to speak a word in public against the war on the grounds that it *might* be read or heard by a soldier or draftee and cause insubordination.

In reacting to this perversion of our constitutional order—Stone aptly calls it "the death of free speech"—the task the Supreme Court took upon itself as cases like *Schenck* came before it was nothing less than determining the limits of permissible expression under the First Amendment at a moment of grave national danger. In other words it was attempting to reconcile the root tension, present in all democratic societies, between order and freedom.

The logic of Wilson's drastic approach was to punish all words that had some tendency, however remote, to incite violations of the law—in effect, as one legal scholar of the era put it, killing the serpent of sedition in the egg and not letting words hatch into lethal action.[18] But as the Supreme Court came to recognize, this "bad tendency" approach, whether rooted in the thoughts of the Constitution's framers or not, hardly corresponded to the requirements of our democracy at the dawn of the twentieth century.

The Sedition Acts of 1798 had driven home the unsuitability—and indeed the danger—of a seditious libel law for democratic governance. The fierce opposition it generated over the two years it was in force signaled the waning of the pure Blackstonian tradition in which the First Amendment was regarded as nothing more than a prohibition on governmental imposition of prior restraints. Then, in the mid-nineteenth century, in *On Liberty* and other writings, John Stuart Mill made the case for freedom and openness with unsurpassed clarity and persuasiveness. In *Schenck* and *Frohwerk*, the Supreme Court was taking cognizance of the century-long shift in the intellectual and legal landscape. Thus, the standard it set forward in both drew a binding nexus between speech and action. For speech to be lawfully proscribed it had to pose a "clear and present danger" and the banned words had to be employed "in such circumstances and are of such a nature as to . . . bring about the substantive evils that Congress has a right to prevent."

Whether Holmes and the Court rightly applied that test in upholding the convictions of Schenck, Frohwerk, and Debs is debatable. But the standard itself is unexceptionable. As Chafee put it at the time, if by "substantive evils" the Court meant "overt acts of interference with the war, then Justice Holmes draws the boundary line very close to the test of incitement . . . and clearly makes the punishment of words for their bad tendency impossible."[19] Indeed, in *Abrams*, which came along seven months after the Court decided *Schenck*, Holmes had an occasion to make explicit this limitation on government's suppressive power.

Along with four other defendants, all of them Russian émigrés, Jacob Abrams had distributed multiple copies of English- and Yiddish-language leaflets. One of them was an ardent plea to shun participation in the war. For this and similar utterances the five were charged with conspiring "to unlawfully utter, print, write and publish . . . disloyal, scurrilous and abusive language about the form of government of the United States . . . intended to bring the form of government of the United States into contempt, scorn, contumely, and disrepute. . . [and] intended to incite, provoke and encourage resistance to the United States in said war."[20]

In considering these charges Holmes stood by his prior rulings, declaring that he had "never . . . seen any reason to doubt that the questions of law that alone were before this Court in the cases of *Schenck*, *Frohwerk* and *Debs*, were rightly decided." But he also made a subtle shift, no longer speaking of a "clear and present danger" but of a "clear and imminent danger." To be criminal, words had to be tied to harm by a tight knot. This knot was absent in *Abrams*. Wrote Holmes, "Nobody can suppose that the surreptitious publishing of a silly leaflet by an unknown man . . . would present any immediate danger that its opinions would hinder the success of the government arms or have any appreciable tendency to do so." But this rejection of the "bad tendency" standard did not yet command broad assent. The conviction of Abrams was upheld by a vote of seven to two, with only Louis Brandeis joining Holmes in his dissent. Nonetheless, given the direction in which the Court was to travel over the following decades, *Abrams* was the moment at which our modern and capacious view of free speech and a free press was born.

IT IS NOT DIFFICULT to see how laws proscribing the publication of secret information might fit into this evolving understanding of the First Amendment. That the disclosure of a national security secret might in many circumstances, particularly in wartime, constitute a "clear and imminent danger," bringing about the "substantive evils that Congress has a right to prevent," would seem obvious on its face. Yet matters are not so simple. For the World War I generation, drawing up a statute that would protect secrets yet not unduly limit discussion of matters of vital public concern proved not to be a simple task. Subsequent generations have not found it any simpler.

As the United States entered the European war, the need for secrecy was almost immediately brought to the fore by the challenges of mounting military operations while defending both the homeland and the vital shipping lanes to Europe against attack by submarines. A 1911 statute, enacted in the aftermath of espionage scares and amid mounting tension in Europe, had proscribed various unauthorized information-gathering activities on military installations, and it had also criminalized the communication of defense information to persons "not entitled to receive it." But the statute was inartfully drafted, and among the many questions it left unanswered was whether defense information disclosed by "publication"—a word that did not appear in the 1911 law—was proscribed. Facing war in 1917, the president who was recently waxing poetically that "government ought to be all outside and no inside" had a sudden epiphany about the critical importance of secrecy.[21] Now Wilson veered to the other extreme.

Once again the experience of America's most recent major conflagration—the Civil War, in which the press had retailed military secrets wholesale—loomed large in Wilson's mind, and not his alone. "What we suffered from during the Civil War," declared Senator Knute Nelson of Minnesota, a Republican proponent of Wilson's censorship plan, "was the fact that our newspapers contained full information as the number of troops, their location, the movement of the troops, and everything." Like-minded senators and congressmen who pointed in this direction were hardly exaggerating. Numerous breaches of vital secrets could easily be recounted.

In one well-known case, reporters traveling with Gen. Burnside in 1862 as he sailed on an expedition to seize Roanoke Island had agreed to maintain an information blackout up to the moment when the first blow was struck. Nonetheless they conveyed detailed information on the size of the fleet and its accompanying land force to their editors, which was then almost immediately published in the *New York World* and the *Chicago Tribune*, endangering the mission and infuriating the War Department.

In that same year the forces of Gen. John Pope in Virginia were in jeopardy of being overrun by Confederate forces under the command of Robert E. Lee, who had mustered a force of some 24,000 men for the assault. Gen. George B. McClellan's army was urgently ordered to provide reinforcements to Pope. To the great consternation of the War Department, three newspapers, including the *New York Times*, published stories reporting that McClellan's army had pulled up camp, which it had not yet done but was preparing to do. Ulysses S. Grant telegraphed the secretary of war that the story in the *Times* was "the most contraband news I have seen published during the war."[22] The Confederate triumph that ensued only served to augment bitterness at the newspapers' cavalier conduct.

As became known after the war, Lee and other Confederate generals paid careful attention to Northern newspapers. Of special interest were the casualty rosters, which, as the historian J. Cutler Andrews has pointed out, "often gave full information about the position of brigades and regiments, the arrival of reinforcements, and the location and strength of battery units."[23] Although the fault for such laxity rested primarily with editors not reporters, the leaks, particularly the premature announcements of troop movements, "caused unnecessary battles and the needless expenditure of human lives."[24] With these Civil War episodes in the common memory of America's political elites, and at precisely the moment the debate over the antileak provisions of the Espionage Act was at its height, a sensational contemporary leak involving antisubmarine warfare roiled the debate.

The *New York Times* and the *New York Tribune* revealed that to protect New York Harbor from invasion, the navy was in the process of erecting a steel net a mile in length across the channel connecting Staten Island (then Richmond) to Fort Hamilton, the current site of the Verrazano Bridge. The *Tribune* tossed in the fact that "if the plan works, similar gates will be provided at every Atlantic port whose configuration lends itself to the scheme."[25] This was a most inopportune breach.

In 1915 the sinking of the *Lusitania* with 1,198 souls aboard, including more than one hundred Americans, had aroused the nation to the horrors of German submarine warfare. Although Germany subsequently held its submarines in check against neutral U.S. shipping, on February 1, 1917, the Germans announced the resumption of unrestricted submarine warfare. This was the instrument by which the kaiser hoped, within a matter of months, to strangle Great Britain. It was also, of course, the principal casus belli for American entrance into the war. The German navy then immediately began racking up successes, sinking eighty-six vessels in February. Overnight, American techniques to defend against submarine attack became one of the most sensitive military matters. The report in the *Times* two weeks after the United States entered World War I thus ignited a ferocious debate, with the episode becoming a touchstone of the discussion over how best to prevent future such disclosures.

Among other effects, the leak offered powerful ammunition to the backers of Wilson's proposal for government control of all information related to the war. But even so, despite the uproar, Wilson's proposal was defeated in the face of intense lobbying by a news media appalled at the comprehensive nature of the proposed censorship. The media's position was reflected in the debate by senators like Albert Cummins of Iowa, a Republican who called Wilson's proposals "an absolute suppression of free speech" and "an absolute overthrow of a free press."[26] Hiram Johnson of California, also a Republican, declared it would be "infinitely better" to have a publication that disclosed military secrets like the net across the narrows of the New York Harbor "than that the mouths of the citizens of the United States be gagged or the press be muzzled."[27] This liberal view prevailed. Wilson's censorship proposals were defeated.

Nonetheless, as a compromise—and in some respects a muddled one—the black-letter law enacted by Congress left open the possibility that the press could be punished for publishing secrets. The antileak provisions of the Espionage Act—codified as sections 793 and 794 of the U.S. Criminal Code—remain in force to the present day.[28]

A number of the prohibitions enumerated in Section 794 apply only in wartime. Given the gravity of the potential danger at times when American soldiers are in harm's way, Congress imposed the death penalty or life imprisonment for conveying "information relating to the public defense, which might be useful to the enemy" when done with the "intent that the same shall be communicated to the enemy." An explicit mention of "publishing" in the statute brings newspapers under its purview. But whether prosecutors could successfully convict a newspaper under its provisions—the statute has never yet been employed against one—is uncertain. It would seem, at least from our current vantage point, that editors could plausibly maintain that they were publishing the national defense information to enlighten the public; the fact that the enemy learned of it along the way would be incidental rather than the intent of their action.

But in the era in which the Espionage Act was enacted, that benign assumption about the motives of newspaper editors and reporters did not always obtain. Dozens of German-language newspapers, like the Detroit *Abend Post*, the Cincinnati *Volksblatt* and *Freie Presse*, and the St. Louis *Amerika* were then in circulation. Almost all fiercely opposed conscription and U.S. involvement in the war. Some of them were suspected, with good reason, of being under German control.

German intelligence and propaganda authorities certainly did not shrink from such methods. Among other things, not long before America entered the war, Germany had covertly purchased the *New York Evening Mail* for $1.5 million, a useful organ for reaching urban readers.[29] And as law-enforcement authorities discovered after the war from decrypted German cable traffic, some correspondents writing for mainstream publications, like William Bayard Hale of Hearst (formerly the Paris correspondent of the *New York Times*), were active German agents. In Hale's case the German Ministry of Propaganda was supplementing his Hearst salary to the tune of fifteen thousand dollars a year.[30] At the time the Espionage Act was enacted, in short, disloyal newspapers and disloyal newspapermen represented a genuine problem, which is what the drafters of Section 794 aimed to cover.

Section 793 of the Espionage Act applies when the country is *not* officially at war. It imposes less severe penalties: a maximum of ten years imprisonment and/or a ten thousand dollar fine. Falling under its reach are those who have either lawful or unlawful possession of information "relating to the national defense" who then "willfully communicate" that information to "any person not entitled to receive it." Unlike in Section 794, the crime in Section 793, as Congress defined it, does not require intent to abet the enemy. To run afoul of it all that is required is that the discloser has "reason to believe" that the information in question "could be used to the injury of the United States or to the advantage of any foreign nation."

This section raises numerous questions. Among other things it shares a problem of definitions with Section 794: What exactly constitutes "information relating to the national defense"? As numerous commentators have pointed out, this accordion-like construction is highly problematic in a world in which social and economic factors underpin national security. Would the statute forbid only discussion of sensitive details, like, say, the vulnerability of a particular design of tank armor, or would it extend more expansively to cover the amount of steel available for tank-armor production and from there outward to the amount of coke and iron ore for the production of steel? On this vital point the statute is not self-explanatory.

Vagueness as to what kinds of secrets it protects is not the statute's only deficiency. An obvious additional trouble spot is that gathering and communicating information about national defense is one of the primary activities of journalism. In the ordinary course of business there is continuous and voluminous exchange of information between the executive branch of government and the press. Yet the statute would seem to prohibit much of this activity, making it criminal. In an exhaustive 1973 study of the Espionage Act in the *Columbia Law Review*, Harold Edgar and Benno Schmidt, Jr., conclude that the law is "a loaded gun pointed at newspapers and reporters who publish foreign policy and defense secrets."[31] About this they are certainly right. But as we shall see, the gun is so ill-designed that even in the rare instances in which it has been fired, it has never successfully hit a journalistic target, even those journalists and writers who have put us all in danger.

The domestic scene during World War I is rightly remembered today as a dark and deplorable episode in the history of American freedom. But in the narrow area of protecting secrets, the often reviled Espionage Act was not repressive enough or, to be more precise, not specific enough. For its manifest deficiencies our country was to pay a high price. As we were to learn at Pearl Harbor on December 7, 1941, loose lips can indeed sink ships.

CHAPTER 5

THE BLACK CHAMBER

ON DECEMBER 5, 1941, two days before Pearl Harbor, Nagao Kita, a Japanese consular official based in Hawaii, acting as an intelligence operative in the service of the Japanese military, sent a telegram to Tokyo reporting his most recent observations:

1) During Friday morning, the 5th, the three battleships mentioned in my message #239 arrived here. They had been at sea for eight days.
2) The Lexington and five heavy cruisers left port on the same day.
3) The following ships were in port on the afternoon of the 5th:

   8 battleships
   3 light cruisers
   16 destroyers
   Four ships of the Honolulu class and [unreadable] were in dock.

On the following day, December 6, a cable from Tokyo came in reply, requesting an urgent update:

Please wire immediately re the latter part of my #123 the movements of the fleet subsequent to the 4th.[1]

Kita responded as instructed and added some vital details to his previous report:

On the American continent in October the Army began training barrage balloon troops at Camp Davis, North Carolina. Not only have they ordered four or five hundred balloons, but it is understood that they are considering the use of the balloons in the defense of Hawaii and Panama. In so far as Hawaii is concerned, though investigations have been made in the neighborhood of Pearl Harbor, they have not set up mooring equipment, nor have they selected the troops to man them. Furthermore, there is no indication that any training for the maintenance of balloons is being undertaken. *At the present time there are no signs of barrage balloon equipment.* In addition, it is difficult to imagine that they have actually any. However, even though they have actually made preparations, because they must control the air over the water and land runways of the airports in the vicinity of Pearl Harbor, Hickam, Ford, and Ewa, there are limits to the balloon defense of Pearl Harbor. *I imagine that in all probability there is considerable opportunity left to take advantage for a surprise attack against these places.*

2) *In my opinion the battleships do not have torpedo nets.* The details are not known [emphasis added].

For reasons having to do directly with secrecy—and, indirectly, a stunning breach of secrecy—none of these three telegrams was deciphered and read by U.S. intelligence in time for anyone in authority to ponder their significance.

Of course, even without having read these ominous communications, U.S. forces based in Hawaii were already on alert in response to an intensifying drumbeat of danger signals. On November 1 the United States had learned that the Japanese had taken a major step to tighten communications security, altering the twenty thousand or so call signs used to identify their ships. Over the following weeks the United States received numerous reports of Japanese naval vessels steaming southward toward an undetermined destination. On November 16 U.S. intelligence lost sight of Japanese aircraft carriers. On December 1 the United States observed Japanese naval vessels once again changing their call signals en masse, an extraordinarily unusual step following so soon upon the previous change, and regarded in Washington as a nearly certain indicator of imminent hostilities. On December 3 messages intercepted by U.S. intelligence revealed that Tokyo had issued orders that were an unambiguous signal of impending war.

A cable summarizing their contents was transmitted to American theater commanders. "Highly reliable information," it stated, "has been received that categoric and urgent instructions were sent yesterday to Japanese diplomatic and consular posts at Hongkong, Singapore, Batavia, Manila, Washington, and London to destroy most of their codes and ciphers at once and to burn all other important confidential and secret documents." On December 6 the FBI reported that local Japanese authorities on Pearl Harbor were burning papers. Smoke was also observed coming from the Japanese Embassy in Washington.

The U.S. military had not ignored these warning signs. On November 27, even before the December 1 change of call signs and the December 3 order to destroy codes and ciphers, naval intelligence had issued a war warning. Army intelligence followed suit the next day. In response to the alert, American forces at Pearl Harbor adopted various precautionary measures, including increasing the hours in which aircraft-warning radar stations were manned. But these steps were far from sufficient; despite the indicators there was a distinct lack of urgency in implementing defensive measures. When the bombs came raining down on December 7, the Japanese achieved total surprise, sinking five of eight battleships, destroying most of the island's combat aircraft, and sending more than 2,400 Americans to their graves.

The reasons for this intelligence failure—the worst in American history up until September 11, 2001—have been exhaustively explored, most compellingly by Roberta Wohlstetter in her brilliant *Pearl Harbor: Warning and Decision.*[2] One prime factor was the boy-who-cried-wolf effect. American officials had grown inured to warning signals that had led to three previous alerts, one in 1940 and two in 1941, that had been followed by no particularly noteworthy Japanese action. There had also been earlier intercepts of highly detailed Japanese telegrams laying out the state of fortifications and the disposition of ships at Pearl Harbor. But such specific reporting was not taken as a sign that Pearl Harbor was a likely target for a Japanese opening offensive. Rather, it was chalked up to the methodical nature of the Japanese intelligence services, which were observed gathering similar data at numerous other military installations as well. The latest intercepts therefore did not set off special alarms.

If by the first week of December 1941, U.S. intelligence was confident that a Japanese strike was imminent, the consensus held that the most likely target would be somewhere in Southeast Asia, with diversionary attacks also possible, perhaps on the Philippines or in Thailand. Pearl Harbor, so distant from the Japanese theater of operations and the site of such a powerful naval force, was not judged a likely place for the Japanese to attack.

In any event the various pieces of data suggesting Pearl Harbor was the target were drowned out in a cacophony of signals—"noise" is the intelligence term of art—either not comprehensible or pointing in other directions. Underpinning the supine American posture was the conviction, sharply expressed by Adm. Husband E. Kimmel, commander in chief of the U.S. Pacific Fleet, that it would be "national suicide" for the Japanese to strike Pearl Harbor and therefore unthinkable. No one dreamed that, as Wohlstetter has best put it, a mighty deterrent would itself make an inviting target.

But what if U.S. intelligence on December 5 and 6 had decoded Kita's last telegrams and read their contents in time? The December 6 telegram was startlingly different from all previous communications obtained by the United States. Along with the urgency of the request from Tokyo for details about military preparations, including in particular a focus on such defensive instruments as barrage balloons and antitorpedo netting, there was that most pregnant sentence: "I imagine that in all probability there is considerable opportunity left to take advantage for a surprise attack against these places." At the very least such words would have been a powerful stimulus for a reexamination of basic assumptions at that moment of high alert, leading to what might have been a last-minute upgrade of military readiness at Pearl Harbor, denying the Japanese the total surprise they achieved.

But the United States did not process Kita's last telegrams. On December 2 Kita, like other Japanese diplomats in vulnerable locations around the world, followed orders from Tokyo to destroy all the codes that had been their primary means of secure communication. Only a code known as PA-K2 was to be retained in operation, and it was used to send and receive the dispatches of December 5 and 6. PA-K2 was one of the simplest of the various Japanese codes then in use. Until the beginning of December all Japanese communications then being intercepted by American listening stations, including those transmitted in PA-K2, were sent to Washington for decryption and analysis. But PA-K2 was so easily broken that the U.S. radio-traffic-analysis staff had begun to process these messages locally. Their procedures, however, were not yet regularized or refined, and there was a time lag in both decryption and dissemination. The typical PA-K2 message required somewhere between six hours and six days to decipher, with three days the average.[3] The December 5 and 6 telegrams were not processed until December 7. Too late.

———

A DELAY in handling these time-sensitive Japanese communications was not the only problem afflicting U.S. intelligence. We are fond of recounting our triumphs—and they were considerable—but we do not always dwell on our limitations and failures. Among the triumphs, in August 1940 in a great feat of cryptanalysis, William F. Friedman, the head of the U.S. code-breaking effort, had cracked Purple, the top-priority Japanese diplomatic code, after more than a year of mind-numbing labor that led him to nervous collapse. A number of other lesser codes had also been solved, the collective output of which was given the designation MAGIC. One of the most closely guarded Allied secrets of World War II, MAGIC offered an intelligence bonanza that contributed significantly to our understanding of Japanese capabilities and long-range plans, and, most crucially, to preserving the lives of American soldiers and sailors as they carried out their daily operations.

But Friedman's feats notwithstanding, a huge volume of Japanese communication still remained inaccessible. The achievements of American code breakers may have been glorious, but by December 7, 1941, they had not finished their job. Up until and past American entrance into the war, the most modern Japanese military codes remained completely secure. Only some of the lower-level naval codes had been partially cracked by army and navy intelligence. On the eve of Pearl Harbor the United States was only able to understand about 10 percent of these communications.

Given the enormous emphasis on secrecy in the Japanese planning of the Pearl Harbor strike, we cannot say for a certainty that timely access to the interactions encoded in the higher-level Japanese naval codes would have averted Pearl Harbor. But we do know that the Japanese, having high (and misplaced) confidence in the unbreakability of *all* their codes and ciphers, communicated freely in these presumably secure channels. If we had been listening in, it is more than likely that December 7, 1941, would today not be remembered as a day of infamy.

What explains the weakness of U.S. code breaking at this momentous turning point? Part of the answer—whether or not it is the critical part, by the nature of things historical, cannot be proved decisively—is traceable to one of the most sensational leaks in all of American history. The breach occurred in 1931, a decade before Pearl Harbor, and it is now largely forgotten, but its consequences for American security were long lasting and profound.

THE STORY of the 1931 leak—the Black Chamber affair, as it has come to be called—actually has its origins more than a decade earlier in the aspirations, ultimately dashed, of an extraordinarily ambitious code clerk by the name of Herbert O. Yardley. Yardley's career, recounted in close detail in *The Reader of Gentlemen's Mail* by the cryptological historian David Kahn, began as a telegraph agent for the railroad at a junction in his home town of Worthington, Indiana, where he had been taught telegraphy by his father.[4] By 1912, already highly proficient at sending signals in Morse code to trains, he entered the civil service as a government telegrapher. In short order he landed a slot in Washington, DC, as a code clerk in the Department of State. By the time World War I erupted, he was earning one thousand dollars a year sending and receiving diplomatic cables, many of them encrypted.

Handling these sensitive documents on a daily (and nightly) basis, Yardley could not erase a question from his mind. The pursuit of an answer filled his life with a single-minded purpose that it had hitherto lacked: Could American diplomatic codes be broken by foreign powers or anyone else? "I would devote my life to cryptography," he was later to write. "I now began a methodical plan to prepare myself."[5] Immersing himself in the scant collection of materials available in the Library of Congress, and trying his hand at encrypted telegrams from foreign embassies provided to him by well-connected friends, Yardley found himself making rapid headway in his newly chosen craft.

A breakthrough—not in the mysteries of cryptography but in his career as a code breaker—came one evening when an encoded message came in to President Wilson from his intimate friend and adviser Colonel House, then engaged in a delicate mission in Germany. "As the telegram flashed over the wire I made a copy," wrote Yardley. "This would be good material to work on, for surely the President and his trusted agent would be using a difficult code." To his amazement Yardley found himself able to read the message in plaintext within two hours.[6]

The White House was using what Yardley called a "schoolboy" cipher, its putatively clandestine communications bare for all foreign powers to read. This cryptographic feat, such as it was, was followed not long after by a genuinely taxing achievement: Yardley's demonstration to his superiors that he had penetrated the State Department's more formidable system of secret communications, which he presented to their shock in a hundred-page typescript labeled "Exposition on the 'Solution of American Diplomatic Codes.'"

With the U.S. entry into the war in 1917, Yardley's cryptographic prowess, now well known in American military and diplomatic circles, was suddenly in demand, and he found himself named chief of Military Intelligence, Section Number 8, the official designation for the code-and-cipher unit in the War Department. Yardley proved himself to be not merely a gifted code breaker but also a superb administrator. Starting from a near-zero baseline, he built up a smooth-running operation, and MI-8 rapidly tallied a series of significant successes, solving the codes and ciphers of eight foreign governments.

The end of World War I did not end official interest in cryptanalysis. After some squabbling over budgetary matters both the State and War Departments agreed to contribute funds for a new operation. Because there were legal restrictions on additional State Department personnel working within the confines of the capital, New York City was chosen as the site for a new agency. Yardley—now all of thirty-one years old—was appointed its chief.

He called the outfit the American Black Chamber, borrowing the name from the sixteenth-century *cabinet noir*, the secret letter-opening and resealing facility of King Henry IV of France. It was not long before a small staff of twenty-five top linguists and cryptographers from across the U.S. government were toiling away in a nondescript three-story building at 3 E. 38th Street.

Almost immediately Japanese communications, hitherto virgin territory for American cryptanalysts, became a target. Tensions with Tokyo had been on the rise. Flush with energy from its newly obtained footholds in China and Siberia, Japan was taking the first steps on the expansionist path that would bring it utter devastation. His superiors, wrote Yardley, "begged me to turn all my efforts to the unraveling of Japanese secrets, and I, in a moment of enthusiasm, had promised them either a solution or my resignation within a year."[7]

But breaking the Japanese codes was a maddeningly complex project; parsing and reparsing the encoded cables searching for recognizable patterns became literally an obsession to Yardley. After prolonged and arduous labor, the solution, fittingly, came to him in a dream: "One night I wakened at midnight, for I had retired early, and out of the darkness came the conviction that a certain series of two-letter codewords absolutely *must* equal *Airurando* (Ireland). Then other words danced before me in rapid succession: *dokuritsu* (independence), *Doitsu* (Germany), *owari* (stop). At last the great discovery! My heart stood still, and I dared not move. Was I dreaming? Was I awake? Was I losing my mind? A solution? At last—after all these months!"[8]

By February 1920, having pieced together the broader picture from these initial pieces of the puzzle, Yardley was able to report to Washington that he had broken the Japanese code known as Ja, a feat his superior in Washington, Gen. Marlborough Churchill, head of Military Intelligence, called "the most remarkable accomplishment in the history of code and cipher work in the United States."[9] But the Japanese were not standing still. They had hired a Polish cipher expert to help them construct more complicated and secure codes, some of which entailed dividing up a single message and encoding each portion in one of ten different codes.

By May, Yardley had cracked these, too, and also finally Jp, a code of an entirely new type. This was to prove a breakthrough of staggering consequence. Jp was the code, it turned out, that the Japanese intended to use to secure their communications at the Washington Naval Conference set to open in November 1921, a conference of consummate importance to Tokyo's realization of its aspirations in Asia.

President Harding's purpose in convening the gathering was to curtail the naval rivalry in the Pacific that had already begun to gather steam. He sought to put in place fixed limits on the fleets of the major powers. The American opening gambit in the parley was a ratio in overall tonnage for the United States, Britain, and Japan of, respectively, 10:10:6. Japan, which was counting on adding new capital ships to its navy, was adamant that its proportion be a minimum of 70 percent. On November 28, just one week into the conference, the Black Chamber deciphered a most interesting cable:

> From Tokyo
> To Washington.
> Conference No. 13. November 28, 1921.
> SECRET.
> Referring to your conference cablegram No. 74, we are of
> your opinion that it is necessary to avoid any clash with
> Great Britain and America, particularly America, in regard
> to the armament limitation question. You will to the utmost
> maintain a middle attitude and redouble your efforts to
> carry out our policy. In case of inevitable necessity, you will
> work to establish your second proposal of 10 to 6.5. If in
> spite of your utmost efforts, it becomes necessary in view
> of the situation and in the interests of general policy to fall
> back on your proposal No. 3, you will endeavor to limit the

power of concentration and maneuver of the Pacific by a guarantee to reduce or at least to maintain the status quo of Pacific defenses and to make an adequate reservation which will make clear that [this is] our intention in agreeing to a 10 to 6 ratio.

No. 4 is to be avoided as far as possible.[10]

Yardley appraised this as "the most important and far-reaching telegram ever to pass through the Black Chamber's doors."[11] Indeed it was. From nearly the opening day of the negotiations, the United States knew the Japanese bottom line, and the American negotiators had only to hold fast until the Japanese retreated to it. After weeks of fruitless negotiating that is what they finally did.

For this and other accomplishments Yardley was awarded the Distinguished Service Medal (DSM). But given the nature of his work, there could be no public recognition. Indeed, his very identity was treated as a deep secret. "My name was not permitted in the telephone book, mail addressed to me was through a cover address, etc.," Yardley was both to complain and boast. The DSM citation, too, was carefully drafted so as not to reveal his profession. "If foreign governments learned that we were successful," wrote Yardley later, "they would immediately change their codes, and we would be obliged after years of struggle to begin all over again."[12]

The Black Chamber was to continue its work throughout most of the decade. But the DSM (and a second awarded in 1926) was to prove the high-water mark of Yardley's government career. The first hint of trouble came, comically, later in the 1920s with the appointment of a new director in the State Department in charge of supervising the Black Chamber's work. Yardley, in Washington to sketch out the activities of his unit, broached to his new superior the fact that the Vatican codes seemed vulnerable and might be usefully tackled next. This elicited an unexpected reaction: "I noticed with amazement that the Director's face went very white. At the same moment the executive officer gave me a vicious kick under the table.

It scarcely needed the injury to my shins to make me realize that the Director was a Catholic."[13] Instantaneously Yardley reversed course: He found himself explaining to his new superior that "I personally feel that it is unethical for us to inquire into the Vatican secrets."[14]

By 1929, after Herbert Hoover's election, scruples about code breaking had assumed a more ecumenical dimension. A new secretary of state, Henry A. Stimson, assumed office. As was his custom, Yardley furnished his new superior with decrypts, hoping to impress him with the skill of the Black Chamber and the importance of its work. The reception was once again not what Yardley anticipated. When informed of the clandestine doings in New York, Stimson "totally disapproved of our activities and ordered that all State Department funds be withdrawn from our support, and that the State Department have absolutely nothing to do with our organization."[15] Stimson, steeped in a uniquely American puritanism, was shortly to utter his most famous—and given his responsibilities, fatuous—pronouncement: "Gentlemen do not read each other's mail."

Cut off from funds, the Black Chamber was doomed, and so was Yardley's career as a cryptographer. At age forty-one he found himself in hard times. One day he was earning the handsome salary of $7,500 a year; the next, he was out of a job in the midst of the Great Depression. And here, in Yardley's financial difficulties and his bitterness over the Black Chamber's dissolution, was the proximate cause of the unprecedented leak.

With a wife and young child to support and without savings, for he both loved money and was careless with it—poker was not his only mistress; there were evidently some flesh-and-blood ones, too—Yardley began to cast about for income. Earlier in the twenties he had approached the War Department for permission to write about intelligence matters for *Collier's*, one of the large-circulation popular magazines of the era. Even with the War Department offered the right of prepublication review, it denied permission. Security policies "covering use of confidential files," wrote an official, "make it impossible to grant your request."[16] But Yardley now resurrected his journalistic plan, and this time without worrying about official consent.

Yardley first approached Viking Press. But Viking consulted Military Intelligence on its own and demurred after being warned of harm to the national interest. Yardley persisted. He found a literary agent, George T. Bye, to represent him. Bye was soon peddling a proposal to major New York publishing houses. It was not long before Bobbs-Merrill agreed to go where Viking dared not tread. One of its editors, George Shively, fired off an ecstatic note to a colleague that "Bye may have dug up [a] best-seller. This morning he sent in a chap named Yardley, who was chief of a secret bureau of the Intelligence Dept. during and for some time after the war. . . . It's an amazing story, and if true ought to make the front page of every paper in the world."[17] After Yardley sent in a formal outline the editors at Bobbs-Merrill were even more enthused, but they also began to express qualms. "It is likely that some careful maneuvering will be necessary," wrote Shively. "Maybe we'd all be charged with treason and shot at sunrise."[18] Flippant or not, Bobbs-Merrill was entering into a relationship with Yardley with some awareness of what was at stake.

Yardley for his part lost no time in writing the book. Working feverishly, within seven weeks he was done and had also had completed a series of accompanying articles for publication as teasers. On January 31, 1931, in the same week he completed his manuscript, he attempted to resign from Military Intelligence, where he remained under commission as a reserve officer. He claimed in his resignation letter that he had come to disapprove of the division's policies. But the true reason, Kahn explains, "was fear of a court-martial."[19]

The fear was not unjustified. Military Intelligence was alarmed by what they were learning about Yardley's intentions. They warned him that he had continuing obligations to protect official secrets. Inquiries followed up and down the chain of command about whether Yardley could be enjoined from publishing. As quickly became apparent, nothing in American law would allow for a prior restraint. In the end the War Department accepted Yardley's resignation and concluded it could do little to halt publication except to threaten him with prosecution under the Espionage Act if he went ahead.

Both Bye and Bobbs-Merrill retained counsel to consider their next steps. The two legal teams came to starkly differing conclusions. Bye's attorneys believed that the contents of Yardley's book were potentially so damaging that even a prior restraint might be allowed by the courts: "It is a reasonable assumption," they wrote, "that the publication of this book would be opposed with the utmost possible vigor by a number of very powerful interests, and as indicated above we believe that such efforts would be likely to meet with success."[20] Such fears proved overdrawn.

Bobbs-Merrill's lawyers moved in the opposite direction. Their line of reasoning strikingly anticipates the defensive volley let loose by the *New York Times* seven decades later in the NSA affair. The secrets contained in Yardley's manuscript, they pointed out, were in the main "obtained by the government by improper methods," and by a unit of government that was not regularly constituted. Under such circumstances "I do not believe that there would be any liability on the part of the house in publishing the manuscript."[21] Yardley may have betrayed the government's trust, but Bobbs-Merrill did not think it would be on the hook for this.

YARDLEY himself was far from free of worries about his own legal liability. As an official employee engaged in clandestine activity, he had taken a security oath (although he was later to deny that he had). He had also always been intensely security conscious. "I have consistently fought against disclosing anything about codes and ciphers," he wrote to a colleague in 1924. "My reason is obvious; it warns other governments of our skill and makes our work more difficult."[22] He had his office walls in the Black Chamber plastered with warning posters with messages like: "SECRET! If enemies learn that we

can decipher their present codes, they will try to devise more difficult forms. Let's keep them ignorant of our success," or "SECRET!
Remember that making public a single code message deciphered by
MI-8 may lead to a discontinuance of the code and thereby nullify
the labor of months."[23]

But now he assumed a new pose, and was renouncing the work of
the Black Chamber and defending the publication of his manuscript
as an act of virtue. Indeed he enumerated the benefits that would
accrue to the U.S. government from his disclosure. Since the current administration was no longer interested in breaking codes, his
book would at the very least serve, he said, "as an exposé of America's defenseless position in the field of cryptography" and spur the
United States to employ more secure codes and ciphers than it was
currently using for its own communications.[24]

In the late spring of 1931, after some deletions in the manuscript,
and some alterations of names so as not to reveal the identity of various players, Yardley's book went to press. Before being distributed
to bookstores, portions of it were serialized in the *Saturday Evening
Post*, which boasted a massive circulation of 2.8 million readers. The
book itself, published as *The American Black Chamber*, caused a sensation. It was a front-page story in leading newspapers, and rapidly
ascended the best-seller lists.

The huge public reaction is not hard to explain. Yardley let spill
an astounding array of government secrets. As an internal National
Security Agency reappraisal was to note many years later, it was "as
if an NSA employee had publicly revealed the complete communications intelligence operations of the Agency for the past twelve
years—all of its techniques and major successes, its organizational
structure and budget—and had, for good measure, included actual
intercepts, decrypts, and translations of the communications not
only of our adversaries but of our allies as well."[25]

As both a literary exercise and an exploration of the hidden workings of government, *The American Black Chamber* gained some lauda-
tory reviews. "Simply as entertainment," wrote the *Saturday Review*

of Literature in a typical vein, "this exposé . . . . is well worth the price. . . . To a person with curiosity to know something of what goes on behind official draperies, it provides more than entertainment, and this even though it is quite impossible to check up on many of its statements and incidents."[26] But there were other voices, scathing attacks on Yardley for his breach of trust. The *New York Evening Post*—one of the leading dailies of the era—lambasted Yardley for "betray[ing] government secrets with a detail and a clarity of writing that makes one gasp."[27]

Within the fraternity of code breakers there was shock at Yardley's disloyalty and dismay at the quantity and quality of secrets laid bare. Friedman, who went on to break the Japanese Purple code, and at that point still a friend of Yardley, called the publication "a terrible blow." Writing to Yardley he expressed distress at "the amount of valuable information disclosed."[28]

Friedman did not know the full extent of the betrayal, and neither did any other of Yardley's contemporaries. That was only to become apparent decades later. In 1967 Ladislas Farago, a Hungarian immigrant and the author of many books on espionage, published *The Broken Seal: "Operation Magic" and the Secret Road to Pearl Harbor.*[29] Although littered with mistakes and full of doubtful opinions, it leveled a disquieting accusation. In 1928, three years before publishing *The American Black Chamber*, Yardley had sold the secrets that were later to appear in the book—and other secrets, too—directly to the Japanese. The great cryptographer, according to Farago, had not only leaked American secrets, he had engaged in espionage.

Kahn, who has delved more deeply into Yardley's life than anyone else, has harsh judgments of his subject but does not go quite as far. "Yardley's fault," Kahn writes, "was his greed for money and the inattention to duty it entailed." Yardley was "an opportunist, and he breached the trust his country had placed in him when he published his book." That action, writes Kahn, was "despicable," and "was rightly castigated by many people." But Kahn rejects the charge of treason: "He never sold information to Japan or to anybody else, and he never worked against the United States." Yardley, he concludes, "was a rotter, not a traitor."[30]

But Kahn's assessment of the treason allegation is not the last word. When Farago's book appeared, the National Security Agency was appropriately skeptical. Given the manifold deficiencies it found in the book, it sought to verify independently the startling accusation. Copies of the relevant Japanese Foreign Ministry documents, acquired by the United States after the Japanese surrender, were on deposit in the Library of Congress. The agency had its Japanese translators review the material, which was done "not once, but several times."[31] The NSA's findings: Some elements of Farago's account "could not be confirmed" or were "found to be wrong." But the "key document" underpinning the allegation of treason did in fact exist. It was an "internal Foreign Ministry memorandum saying that the Japanese paid Yardley $7,000 for copies of deciphered Japanese messages and cryptanalytic techniques."

The NSA bruited the possibility that the memo was a fabrication, but concluded that this was highly improbable: "the ruse was not only superintricate in concept, but it failed in its purpose since the material remained undiscovered for thirty-five years, long after it had any practical value." The overall finding of the inquest: "NSA's investigations tend strongly to substantiate Farago's basic claim."[32] One way or the other—in fact, probably in two ways—Yardley had conveyed American secrets to the Japanese.

WHAT, PRECISELY, was the harm? Looking back at it from our vantage point in the twenty-first century, it can be seen to have come in several forms. There was, to begin with, plain vanilla diplomatic damage. Yardley gloats in his book that "We solved over forty-five thousand cryptograms from 1917 to 1929, and at one time or another, we broke the codes of Argentine, Brazil, Chile, China, Costa Rica, Cuba, England, France, Germany, Japan, Liberia, Mexico, Nicaragua, Panama, Peru, Russia, San Salvador, Santo Domingo, Soviet

Union, and Spain."[33] Not one of these countries, we can say with high confidence, was pleased to learn that its secret communications were being read by Washington. Whatever else the book was, it was not balm for smooth relations with a far-flung set of countries.

Indeed, some countries were particularly incensed, Japan foremost among them. Yardley had boasted of the Black Chamber's success at the 1921 Washington Naval Conference, noting that American cryptanalysts had read *all* Japanese code messages received or sent by the Japanese representatives. "Stud poker," he noted sardonically, "is not a very difficult game after you see your opponent's hole card."[34]

Unsurprisingly this was a bombshell in Japan, where *The American Black Chamber* enjoyed a frenzied reception. First it was excerpted at length in a leading publication. It then appeared in translation in full, practically flying out of bookstores; sales in the first year were quadruple those in the United States. Driving the intense interest was outrage. "Betrayal of International Trust," was the headline of one leading Japanese paper. "Treachery at the Washington Conference" and "Disgrace to the Convener of the Conference," were the headlines of others. In the face of a national humiliation, a new wave of anti-Americanism swept Japan. Several Japanese politicians associated with the concessions made at the Washington Conference were assassinated by militarists;[35] Japanese militarism itself was energized by the revelation of American treachery.

All this was bad enough, but more narrowly, and more tangibly significant for American security—and the factor that returns us to the subject of Pearl Harbor—was the jolt forward that the disclosure delivered to Japanese cryptographic efforts. Stimson may have halted the State Department's funding of the Black Chamber, but code breaking continued apace at the War Department. Yet after 1931 the cryptographers there found themselves increasingly hobbled; Yardley's disclosures had prompted Tokyo to engage in a whole series of short- and long-term upgrades of code security.

To demonstrate to its staff the consequences of cryptographic laxity, the communications department of the Japanese Foreign Ministry sent 138 copies of Yardley's book to its legations around the world. Japan, a U.S. military report later noted, almost immediately changed its diplomatic codes. The U.S. Navy reported in 1931 that its ability to read the communications of a certain "foreign power"— that is, Japan—had suddenly lapsed because "the systems of convey this information have undergone a complete change."[36] The Japanese military infused new funds into research on cryptographic security, which led within three years to the development of a machine-generated cipher, a precursor to the famously complex Purple code machine. Some sensitive communications were no longer transmitted over the airwaves even in encrypted form. Instead a worldwide courier system was introduced to ensure their secure delivery.

Kahn maintains that the injury caused by Yardley was not as great as commonly assumed. In particular he discounts the short-term damage, noting that reports of immediate changes by some American analysts were based upon ignorance of cryptographic realities. "Nations rarely stock backup cryptosystems because of expense and the dangers of theft and obsolescence, and when they want a new one, they must devise it, test it, produce it, distribute it, and teach it before they can use it."[37]

But there are contradictory accounts from reliable sources. Lawrence F. Safford, a captain in the U.S. Navy, and himself one of the giants of American cryptanalysis in the 1920s, notes in his own history of U.S. communications intelligence that in December 1930 the old Japanese Naval Code was replaced by a new code that remained in effect until October 31, 1938, "giving the U.S. Navy Comint organization a severe, although temporary, setback." The new code, writes Safford, "was never used without a cipher; the cipher had to be stripped off before the code could be reconstructed."* Breaking this layered system "was the most difficult cryptanalytic task ever performed up to that date and possibly the most brilliant."[38] The year

---

*A cipher is a cryptographic system in which units of plain text, usually letters, are transposed by some regular system into other symbols. A code works at the level of words and requires senders and recipients to both have a code book to encode and decode messages.

1930, it should be noted, was before the publication of *The American Black Chamber*, but two years after Yardley had consummated his private "sale" to the Japanese, just enough time for the Japanese to have devised, tested, produced, and distributed a new system.

Of course Kahn is right in noting that even without Yardley, Japan would have been tightening its code security over the 1930s; enhancing security is what nations do even without revelations like Yardley's. But Kahn's attempt at partially exculpating Yardley misses the point. The net effect of Yardley's revelations was to increase greatly Japanese consciousness of their own vulnerabilities. If their response was not immediate and/or uniform, it still was a response, and it was one with a cumulative effect. It may have taken a few years, but by 1935, as a joint U.S. Army-Navy study recognized, the Japanese began to tighten up in the weak areas, and "a definite trend toward complete communications security became evident."[39]

Among other things, over the period 1935–39, the Japanese navy began to display "improvements in circuit discipline, more frequent changes of calls, encipherment of ship-movement reports, a decrease in plain language messages, interception of U.S. Naval messages, and a raising of the standards of the Japanese Naval codes."[40] Kahn himself acknowledges that Yardley's book "lastingly impressed Japan—ten years later the foreign minister mentioned it in connection with a communications matter."[41]

To be sure, U.S. cryptographers in this era repeatedly demonstrated that they could crack any code the Japanese could devise. But it took tremendous resources, and it took something even more valuable: namely time. To penetrate a new code or cipher system sometimes required as much as two years. If by December 7, 1941, the United States was not able to read crucial Japanese communications in a timely fashion, or read them at all, Yardley's indiscretions (not to mention his acts of treachery) carried a share of the blame.

In public Yardley had turned on the activities of the Black Chamber and suggested that its work—and the best work of his own life—was criminal in nature. In private he himself was the criminal. Although he was never charged by prosecutors fearful of spurring even more revelations, Yardley understood the damage he was inflicting on his country. For the thirty pieces of silver he was thrown by Bobbs-Merrill (and an additional thirty pieces, it would seem, by the Japanese government), he shuttered his eyes. They had not always been closed. In May 1920 Yardley had warned: "If the Japanese should learn that we can read their messages they may make such a violent change in their codes that we could never read them."[42] This was an overstatement. Even after Yardley's own betrayal prompted the Japanese to make a "violent change" in their codes, American cryptographers did manage to continue reading their communications. But precious time was lost. So were American lives.

Yardley is today scarcely remembered. Though he was almost certainly a traitor, he lies undisturbed in Arlington National Cemetery in a grave next to those of our greatest heroes. If nothing else, our country is liberal to a fault, and sometimes extraordinarily generous toward those who would do it harm.

CHAPTER 6

THE PRICE OF IMPUNITY

MPUNITY BREEDS IMPUNITY. As the 1930s wore into the 1940s, the consequences of the laxity displayed toward Yardley became more visible. Venality was seldom the motivating force. More typical was wanton disregard for the damage that could follow unauthorized disclosures. The 1930s thus saw a rash of cases that instilled fear in the War Department that the huge labors of its code-breaking unit would be nullified.

In one instance, in 1939, an article in the *Washington Times-Herald* reported (accurately) that the Federal Communication Commission (FCC) had created its own Black Chamber to decode international transmissions.[1] The *Los Angeles Times* committed a far more egregious transgression in 1941 when it regaled readers with a detailed account of the FCC's intelligence capabilities and facilities, describing eleven counterespionage radio stations, roving mobile units, and the technology used for recording intercepted messages.[2] To the acute dismay of the military, press discussions of America's cryptographic capabilities continued even after Pearl Harbor brought the United States into the war.

Indeed, on the very day after the Japanese attack, the *New York Daily News*, citing well-placed sources, reported that the War Department was reading encrypted Japanese communications, and that Tokyo was probably aware that we were reading them, which may explain why Tokyo declined to inform its diplomats in Washington of the impending strike. Days later the *Daily News* amplified its report, explaining that the United States had cracked Japanese codes as far back as 1932.[3]

Perhaps the most horrifying episode of all—known as the "May Incident"—came not from the pages of a publication but from the mouth of an elected official whose gratuitous disregard for security was then transmitted to the Japanese by the American press. Andrew Jackson May, a congressman from Kentucky, was the chairman and ranking Democratic member of the powerful House Military Affairs Committee throughout the war. In June 1943 he toured American facilities in the Pacific theater and was briefed extensively on the shortcomings and strengths of our submarine campaign to cripple Japanese shipping. Among other things May learned that much of our success against Japanese convoys in the undersea struggle was due to the fact that Japanese antisubmarine depth charges were fused to detonate too far above our hunter-killer submarines, enabling them to launch their torpedoes at close range and then survive the ensuing counterattack.

At the close of his tour May staged a press conference at which he boasted of the high survival rate of American submarines, attributing it directly to the Japanese miscalibration of their depth charges. May's disclosure was picked up by wire services and ran in a number of newspapers. According to some accounts it did not take long to make its way to the attention of Japanese intelligence, and soon thereafter led the Japanese to adjust their depth charges to a less shallow setting. "I hear . . . Congressman May . . . said the Jap depth charges . . . are not set deep enough," wrote Vice Adm. Charles A. Lockwood, commander of the U.S. submarine fleet in the Pacific, to a subordinate. "He would be pleased to know the Japs set 'em deeper now." Lockwood was later to estimate that May's irresponsibility resulted in the loss of ten submarines and the death of eight hundred crewmen.[4]

That may well have been an exaggeration or even flat wrong; documents from the Japanese military archives confirming that they took any notice of May's indiscretion have yet to appear. But the Roosevelt administration had no alternative but to assume the worst. Yet Congressman May was regarded as too powerful a politician to confront, and the White House did nothing more than throw up its hands. Ultimately however, justice was done, if on an entirely different count. Two years after the war May was convicted and sentenced to prison for accepting bribes to help steer wartime contracts to a munitions firm.

If appalling stupidity like May's was one facet of the security problem, its even more significant side came as a nasty brew of one part recklessness and nine parts politics. Enter Col. Robert R. McCormick, the publisher-editor of the *Chicago Tribune* from the mid-1920s through the 1950s. Aristocratic in demeanor, Anglophobic to the core, ardent Republican and determined isolationist, he seemed to hate Roosevelt more than he hated Hitler or Hirohito. One charge of his indictment: his conviction that FDR, as revealed by his New Deal program, was an aspiring tyrant who aimed to impose nothing less than "a proletarian dictatorship" on the United States.[5] A major subtheme, and evidence of FDR's power grab, was McCormick's conviction that the president intended to eviscerate freedom of the press.

Intrinsic to his eclectic conservatism was a passionate devotion to the First Amendment, which, much like the *New York Times* today, he regarded as an unlimited license to print whatever he would. As chairman of the Committee on the Freedom of the Press of the American Society of Newspaper Editors, he occasionally joined forces in court cases with the ACLU, an otherwise improbable ideological bedfellow. (One such case, *Near v. Minnesota*, the Supreme Court's most significant pronouncement on prior restraints of the press until the Pentagon Papers case, will figure later in our story.) He regarded Roosevelt's proposal to license businesses, including news organizations, as the first building block of an emerging tyranny. "Power to license," he wrote, "gives the power to control, and such power potentially completely abridges the freedom of the press."[6]

For this and many other of FDR's transgressions, the pages of McCormick's broadsheet and his own lips directed a steady stream of vitriol at the president, assailing his patriotism above all else. "The trouble is that Mr. Roosevelt *is* a Communist," he wrote to a reader of his paper on one occasion.[7] When Democrats held their convention to renominate Roosevelt in 1936, "The Soviets Gather At Philadelphia" was the headline in the *Tribune*. McCormick's belief that New Deal America had been thoroughly penetrated by Communists was not just a public show, staged to hawk newspapers. "I am constantly receiving rumors that Trotsky is in this country directing a revolution," he told a subordinate before asking him to follow up: "What can you get from the Immigration and State Department?"[8]

If Roosevelt as a Red was one strand of his thinking, another was his conviction that the president was determined to drag America into a second European conflagration. He lauded the isolationist Charles Lindbergh and lavished praise on his America First movement in the pages of the *Tribune*, generously lined its coffers, and had Lindbergh as a frequent house guest. Lindbergh's notorious September 11, 1941, speech in Des Moines, in which he accused "the British, the Jewish, and the Roosevelt administration" of trying to entangle the country in a foreign war, did not fray McCormick's ties to the aviator in the least. Though the *Tribune* feebly scolded him for his remarks, it simultaneously featured a display of his medals.

With the outbreak of the European war in 1939, McCormick only redoubled his efforts to keep America out. The *Tribune* denounced the provision of arms to England under Lend-Lease as "the Dictator Bill." After Hitler invaded the Soviet Union, the prospect that Lend-Lease aid would reach not only England but the USSR filled him with disgust: "Are we to send an army to reestablish atheism in Russia and the slaughter of the priests?"[9]

———

THIS INTELLECTUAL-IDEOLOGICAL stew is essential to understanding McCormick's handling of military secrets in World War II. But before we examine the role played by the *Tribune* in dispensing secrets in wartime, we should take note of some biographical details that make his personal responsibility clear. First, McCormick was no stranger to the world of secret intelligence. During World War I, while retaining his post at the *Tribune* he engaged in derring-do on behalf of the Allied cause. Among other relevant things, he was entrusted with communications intelligence secrets of a high order. In 1915, on the very day of his wedding, he received a sealed box from the Russian Embassy in London containing the top-secret naval signal flags essential for coordinating movements of the British and Russian fleets in the Black Sea. He then set out with his bride on a circuitous mission to deliver the container to agents of the czar in Petrograd, traversing the Mediterranean, the Balkans, and Bulgaria, and guarding—revolver on his person—his sensitive goods against a succession of menacing German agents.

A year later, now serving in the army in Paris (earning his colonelship along the way), he was assigned as liaison to French intelligence. There he worked with the most sensitive of all intelligence materials: intercepted German radio communications. Such active service was not all. Before and after World War I, McCormick maintained a lifelong fascination with matters military and was steeped in the literature and history of war. That he grasped the critical importance of secrecy in statecraft cannot be doubted.

Second, McCormick was never a hands-off editor-publisher, content to let his staff write about the world as they saw fit. On the contrary, he was intimately engaged in editorial decisions large and small, from the assignment of reporters to stories he deemed important (one persistent passion was demonstrating that recipients of public relief had high rates of syphilis) to firing those who failed to toe his isolationist line in their news coverage. His principal biographer, Richard Norton Smith, has observed that as the 1930s progressed and "events overseas spun out of control, McCormick exercised an even tighter rein on those he employed to report and interpret foreign developments."[10]

It is only with all this in mind that one can fully understand a sensational story, the first of a series based upon leaked military documents, that appeared in the *Tribune* during World War II. On December 4, 1941, three days before Pearl Harbor, a banner front-page headline ran in the paper:

FDR'S WAR PLANS!
GOAL IS 10 MILLION ARMED MEN
HALF TO FIGHT IN AEF

The story beneath it, by the reporter Chesly Manly, detailed Rainbow Five, the army and navy's joint "confidential" plan for total air and ground war against Germany in theaters in Asia, North Africa, and on the European continent. A thousand ships would carry the five million men as the body of the Allied Expeditionary Force (AEF) that would begin to liberate Europe not later than July 1, 1943.

In Washington the story appeared to be an unmitigated political disaster for a president who, having assiduously courted a wary public in the 1940 election campaign, pledged that he would not send American boys to fight and die in a conflict across the ocean. Keeping out of the fray was hardly Roosevelt's true inclination, however. But now, thanks to the *Tribune*, at the very moment when Great Britain's survival was at stake, the antiwar forces of both parties were greatly keyed up by the disclosure.

The nation has been "betrayed," declared one congressman as a firestorm of protest carried isolationist sentiment forward. Senator Burton K. Wheeler of Montana, the leading isolationist in Congress, who had only recently forecast that Roosevelt would "plow under every fourth American boy,"[11] declared that the revelation proved his point. The Roosevelt administration, for its part, attempted to present Rainbow Five as a contingency, not an actual war plan. But the *Tribune* bent every effort to show otherwise. It adduced a letter from Roosevelt himself requesting the plan from the military. McCormick called Manly's story "the greatest scoop in the history of journalism."[12]

Gen. Albert C. Wedemeyer, the author of the Rainbow Five plan, was in the War Department's headquarters on the day the story appeared. Years later, interviewed by the historian Thomas Fleming, he recounted how "officers were standing in clumps, talking in low tones. Silence fell, and they dispersed the moment they saw me. My secretary, her eyes red from weeping, handed me a copy of the *Times Herald* [a Washington affiliate of the *Tribune*] with Manly's story on the front page. I could not have been more appalled and astounded if a bomb had been dropped on Washington."[13] Unsurprisingly within the War Department a hunt commenced for the leaker.

Wedemeyer, who was acquainted with Lindbergh and was known to have sympathies for the America First movement—he had attended some of its meetings—himself became a prime suspect. He was summoned to the office of John McCloy, assistant secretary of war, and, though not formally accused, was given a dressing-down. "There's blood on the fingers of the man who leaked this information," said McCloy as he kept the general standing at attention.[14]

Henry Stimson, secretary of war at this juncture (and now older, wiser, and an avid reader of the "other gentlemen's mail" that he had formerly shunned) averred that the leaker was "wanting in loyalty and patriotism" and the newspapermen who published the story had exactly the same deficits. At a cabinet meeting on December 6, Harold Ickes, secretary of the interior and Roosevelt's close confidant, pressed for prosecution of the *Times* and the *Tribune*. Just as matters were coming to a head, events intervened—great events: On the following day the Japanese struck Pearl Harbor. The United States was now in the war, but it was a Pacific war, not the European one envisaged in Rainbow Five. The controversy instantly disappeared from public view.

Behind the scenes the FBI nonetheless continued its investigation of the leak under the personal supervision of J. Edgar Hoover. Wedemeyer, who steadfastly maintained his innocence, was interrogated for months. Manly was also grilled by the FBI and military intelligence investigators, but to no avail; he declined to reveal his confidential sources.

In the end Hoover amassed an investigative file of some twelve hundred pages. It showed that thirty-five copies of the Rainbow Five plan had been distributed to the army, navy, and army air corps, with "several hundred Army and Navy officers and civilian employees in both the War and Navy Departments having legitimate access" to the document.[15] As is typical of leak investigations to the present day, with so many individuals having handled the document, the culprit was never uncovered, at least while the investigation was active. Today we do know that Wedemeyer was innocent. Senator Wheeler, who had received a copy from a contact within the army, had leaked it to the *Tribune* for the express purpose of using it to denounce Roosevelt. In his memoirs written years later, Wheeler openly claimed "credit" for the deed.[16]

IF THE RAINBOW FIVE leak was overshadowed by Pearl Harbor, its chain of consequences continued. Here indeed was an instance in which an adversary took full cognizance of the secret information that had been dropped in its lap for inspection.

As one would expect, the *Tribune* story had been immediately cabled to Berlin by the German Embassy in Washington. Within hours it was on Hitler's desk. Hitler had long intended to fight the United States, but without a proper navy this was not yet feasible; an intensive shipbuilding program was an unfulfilled prerequisite. The "Roosevelt war plan," as the Germans called Rainbow Five, did not alter his fundamental reckoning that war with the United States would have to wait. But Pearl Harbor did alter it. With Japan now locked in battle with the United States, the American navy would be engaged in the Pacific, and Germany had what it regarded as a naval superpower—Japan—fighting on its side. In the fuhrer's fevered calculation the moment for war with the United States had become ripe.

On December 11 Hitler went before the Reichstag and delivered a long harangue, focusing characteristically on the way in which the Jews surrounding Roosevelt, filled with an "Old Testament thirst for revenge" and "diabolical meanness," were intent on plunging the United States into a European war. Adverting explicitly to the *Tribune* leak, he explained that "with no attempt at an official denial there has now been revealed in America President Roosevelt's plan by which, at the latest in 1943, Germany and Italy were to be attacked in Europe by military means." Hitler finished his speech by declaring war on the United States.[17]

It would be a stretch to assert that Hitler acted in response to the leak alone. As one student of the decision has noted, the evidence "supports the notion that psychological considerations, not rational factors . . . were paramount in determining the timing of Hitler's decision."[18] But the leak clearly colored his thinking and may have been a spur to his impulsive action.

Whatever Hitler's motives, as seen in retrospect—and as seen in the White House at the time—the result was not a calamity but a godsend. Roosevelt's politically induced hesitations about joining the British in resisting Hitler were finally by the boards. On December 11, the United States declared war on Germany and Italy. By declaring war on the United States, Hitler had sealed his own fate; in the grand strategy adumbrated by Roosevelt, victory in Europe was now the first priority.* Wheeler had leaked Rainbow Five with

---

*The convenient way in which the *Tribune* leak ultimately played into Roosevelt's hands has given rise to speculation that the president had actually engineered the disclosure, aiming to goad Hitler into declaring war. This view was given its fullest elaboration by William Stevenson in his 1976 *A Man Called Intrepid*, about the British spy William Stephenson. The evidence behind the theory is shaky, and the theory itself is highly speculative. Like many conspiracy theories it posits an ability on the part of the alleged conspirators to foresee the course of inherently unforeseeable events.

the intention of keeping the United States out of the war. The gods of history played a trick on him.

THE COLONEL, for his part, unpunished and undeterred, was soon to strike again. The Battle of Midway concluded on June 7, 1942, exactly six months to the day after Pearl Harbor. Although it could not be perceived at the time, from the historian's vantage point, it was the most significant American victory of the entire Pacific war, a watershed. The Imperial Japanese Navy had determined to attack the Midway atoll with its carriers, destroying the American fleet, seizing the island, gaining a vital foothold in the Pacific, opening the way for offensives across its southern expanse and into the Indian Ocean, and dealing the United States a demoralizing blow that would compel Washington to negotiate an end to hostilities on terms that would leave Japan predominant in Asia.

But things did not go as planned for the Japanese. There were many flaws in the campaign worked out by Admiral Yamamoto. Chief among them was the fact that by now the United States had broken the Japanese naval code and was able to discern the sequence of the planned attack. The Japanese had blindly gambled that in seizing the Midway atoll, they would first confront the forces on the American base there and only afterward a defensive action by the American navy. Thanks to MAGIC, however, they faced both simultaneously. An American task force was marshaled from Pearl Harbor and dispatched to defend the atoll. In the ensuing battle the Japanese lost all four of the aircraft carriers deployed in the attack, and along with them hundreds of planes and pilots and thousands of experienced naval personnel.

The cryptographic effort involved in breaking those communications and discerning the Japanese plans had been epic. Following the Battle of the Coral Sea in early May, U.S. intelligence knew that the Japanese had formed a second strike force of unprecedented size. But they did not know its destination or precise time of attack, although they were able to narrow it to between May 20 and June 20.

Decrypted traffic flowed in indicating that the target would be a location that the Japanese had given the two-letter designation AF. But what was AF? U.S. intelligence was in the dark. There were grounds to believe it was Midway, but it might also have been the Hawaiian island of Oahu. A ruse—now famous in the history of cryptography—was set in motion to see if the Japanese could be tricked into disclosing the identity of the target. The navy sent a message in plaintext from Midway reporting that the island's distillation plant had broken down and a severe shortage of potable water was setting in. A reply cable was then sent, also in plaintext, replying that water barges were being sent. As hoped, both communications were picked up by Japanese intelligence. Shortly thereafter U.S. intelligence intercepted a cable disseminated by Tokyo stating: "AF is short of water." The scheme had worked; the target was indeed Midway.

Identifying the target was hardly the only achievement of MAGIC in the Battle of Midway. It revealed almost all the critical details that enabled the United States to have its own powerful naval force lying in wait to ambush and destroy the Japanese armada. Indeed, it was thanks to communications intelligence, as one American historian of naval intelligence has pointed out, that the commander in chief of the U.S. Pacific Fleet, Adm. Chester W. Nimitz, "knew more about the Midway Operation than many of the Japanese officers involved in it. He knew the targets; the dates; the debarkation points of the Japanese forces and their rendezvous points at sea; he had a good idea of the composition of the Japanese forces; he knew of the plan to station a submarine cordon between Hawaii and Midway; and he knew about the planned seaplane reconnaissance of Oahu, which never took place because he prevented their refueling at French Frigate Shoals. He even knew when and where many of the forces involved would anchor on their return to Saipan."[19] Clearly Comint had come into its own as an instrument of destruction. Given its contribution over the entire course of the war, one might even say that it was the second most powerful weapon next to the atomic bomb.

WAS THE *CHICAGO TRIBUNE* oblivious to the vital and sensitive nature of Comint? Or was it something else that led it, on June 7, the last day of the Midway battle, to run a front-page story titled "Navy Had Word of Jap Plan to Strike at Sea, Knew Dutch Harbor Was Feint"? Attributing its information to "reliable sources in . . . naval intelligence," the paper reported that the "strength of the Japanese forces which the American Navy is battling somewhere west of Midway Island . . . was well known in American naval circles several days before the battle began." The story then proceeded to list the names, tonnages, and armaments of all the Japanese vessels that had taken part in the battle. The implication of the dispatch was inescapable: U.S. intelligence was reading Japanese naval communications.

Both the Justice Department and the War Department commenced a criminal investigation. A navy board of inquiry began closed hearings into the matter. Summoned before it, the *Tribune's* managing editor, J. Loy Maloney, explained that the *Tribune's* reporter, Stanley Johnston, had been on board the USS *Barnett* and seen the battle firsthand. In piecing together a picture of the Japanese order of battle, Johnston, he said, had relied exclusively on *Jane's Fighting Ships*, the authoritative naval publication. He could not have knowingly revealed secret cryptographic information, asserted Maloney, because the *Barnett*, a mere marine transport, would not be carrying such intelligence.

In the public arena McCormick echoed Maloney's explanation. Denouncing the investigation as a sham, the latest step in Roosevelt's "Get the *Tribune* Offensive," McCormick insisted that the government's allegations were preposterous: "I know and every military man knows that secret documents are not sent to sea aboard fighting ships. The commander is given only the information that is necessary to the carrying out of his mission."[20]

Naval investigators had a very different story to tell, and they began to tell it before a federal grand jury convened in early August by Attorney General Francis Biddle at the navy's request. A key witness was the captain of the *Barnett*, who testified that his vessel did indeed have intelligence materials aboard and one of his subordinates had been careless with a secret document of great significance—a decrypted summary of the Yamamoto plan to seize Midway. The officer in question had befriended Johnston and given him access to classified operational documents on the condition that he not write about them, a promise that was violated.

There can be no dispute about the veracity of the captain's testimony. That Johnston cribbed from a classified document—and not, as he claimed, from *Jane's Fighting Ships*—has been definitively demonstrated by the historian Dina Goren, who has compared the Johnston's story in the *Tribune* to the actual secret cable sent by Admiral Nimitz on May 31, 1942, to all the commanders of the Pacific Fleet. The cable read:

> CINC PACIFIC FLEET ESTIMATE MIDWAY FORCE
> ORGANIZATION X STRIKING FORCE 4 CARRIERS (AKAGI KAGA
> HIRYU SORYU) 2 KIRISHIMAS 2 TONE CLASS CRUISERS 12
> DESTROYERS SCREEN AND PLANE GUARD X SUPPORT FORCE
> IDV OR XCV 2 KIRISHIMAS 4 MOGAMIS 1 ATAGO 1 ? BD SCREEN
> XX OCCUPATION FORCE 1 TAKAO 1-2 MYOKOS (QUESTION) 1
> CHITOSE 1 CHITOYODA 2-4 KAMIKAWA MARU 4-6 AK 8-12 AP
> 12 DESTROYERS X APPROXIMATELY 16 SS RECONNAISANCE
> AND SCOUTING MISSION MID PACIFIC HAWAIIAN ISLANDS
> AREA.

As Goren's historical detective work reveals, both Nimitz's ultrasecret message and Johnston's story "include identical versions in the spelling of Japanese ship names."[21] Johnston had referred to the Kirishima just as it was spelled in the Nimitz cable. *Jane's*, on the other hand, called the ship the Kirisima. Johnston had clearly relied upon *Jane's* to add in the tonnages of the ships and calibers of the guns aboard them that he discussed in his story. But he had not bothered to correct the orthography and make it conform to his ostensible source.

In short, Johnston had committed a crime under the Espionage Act, copying, conveying, and arranging for the publication of the contents of closely held national-defense information in wartime. Then, with the connivance of his editors, he had engaged in a cover-up.* It would not have been difficult for the grand jury sitting in Chicago to hand up an indictment. Indeed, an intelligence officer was scheduled to testify before it to explain the significance of this document Johnston had seen and the harm that flowed from his story. But then, at the last minute, the officer's invitation to testify was quashed, and on August 19, 1942, the grand jury was disbanded.

William D. Mitchell, formerly Herbert Hoover's attorney general, who was managing the government's case, put out a carefully crafted statement:

> The Grand Jury, considering the matter of the publication
> of June 7, 1942, in the *Chicago Tribune* and in other
> newspapers of an article relating to the Japanese Fleet
> in the Midway Battle, have decided that no indictment
> should be returned. I was asked by the Attorney General to
> come here and conduct the inquiry and in so doing to see
> that the Grand Jury had before them all the facts. I have
> conducted the inquiry as fully and as fairly as I know how.
> Those under investigation were given the unusual privilege
> of appearing before the Grand Jury and explained their
> connection with the incident. The Jury has considered the
> case fully and its conclusion that no violation of the law was
> disclosed settles the matter.[22]

---

*Among other steps taken to mask the origin of Johnston's revelations, *Tribune* editors gave his story a false Washington, DC, dateline.

But this was only an explanation for the public, duly celebrated by the *Tribune* on its front page the following day. Behind the scenes in the government there was turmoil as prosecutors reversed course. One factor behind the turnabout was that grand jurors, ordinary citizens lacking security clearances, would have had to be read into the crown jewel of American secrets. There would also be continuing press attention to the proceedings, which posed a different kind of problem. For as the navy scrambled to understand the actual damage that had been incurred by the *Tribune* story, considerable uncertainty remained about whether the Japanese had in fact taken cognizance of the disclosure.

A flurry of newspaper articles had already compounded the danger by speculating that the Japanese had indeed reacted by altering their codes. Congressman Elmer Holland of Pennsylvania put a semiofficial gloss on this reporting, taking to the floor of the House, where he declared that "it is public knowledge that the *Tribune* story . . . tipped off the Japanese high command that somehow our Navy had secured and broken the secret code of the Japanese Navy. That is a priceless advantage in war—to know your enemy's plans through your knowledge of his code. Three days after the *Tribune* story was published the Japs changed their code."[23]

In fact, Holland was himself drawing attention to a breach that the Japanese had thus far—inexplicably—ignored. There was initial confusion surrounding this because the Japanese had never stood utterly still in their cryptographic efforts. While they had continuously employed the J-25 code since June 1, 1939, they would periodically—approximately every six to twelve months—change the additives, and the Americans would then need to crack the freshly indecipherable communications.

One such change—presumably for operational security—had been introduced over the course of May, just on the eve of their planned assault on Midway. American cryptographers, who had already harvested such a rich trove of information about the war plan, were temporarily left in the dark. But then in August, just as the grand jury was considering the evidence, navy code breakers caught up with the latest Japanese changes. This was almost proof positive that the Japanese had *not* reacted to the *Tribune* story by introducing some fundamentally new system.

Secretary of the Navy Frank Knox therefore opted to call off the grand jury proceedings lest it prove yet another point of leakage and finally alert the Japanese to the breach. Knox's decision caused intense bitterness in the Justice Department, which had embarked on the controversial path of indicting a powerful newspaper, only to be asked to turn around and drop the matter. Mitchell, dumbfounded by the abrupt reversal, denounced the decision in a private letter to the War Department for having "sold me down the river and the Department of Justice as well."[24] *Newsweek*, reporting on the contretemps, was equally acerbic: "Knox pushed Biddle out on a limb, followed him there, then sawed them both off."[25]

But there were sound reasons for the shift. Aiming to mollify Mitchell, Secretary Knox replied to him in a letter that he insisted be destroyed immediately upon reading: "I think that you are entitled to know, confidentially and personally," he wrote,

> why this change of attitude occurred on the part of the Department. . . . The truth was that we had just again successfully broken the Japanese code and this fact was of immense value to us in operations then in progress. Naturally, this made the military end of the Navy extremely apprehensive lest any talk of code breaking in the newspapers in the United States lead the enemy to take action to cut off this highly valuable source of information. . . . It was an extremely difficult choice to make but in the light of the very great value access to Japanese information had, even I was compelled to admit that the decision must be negative, even though it cost us a chance of bringing the offenders in the *Tribune* to the book.[26]

A major mystery left by the entire episode is why the Japanese did not react to the *Tribune* leak and change their codes. A legend has taken root that the Japanese simply failed to notice the story. But this is unlikely. The initial Johnston dispatch appeared in four newspapers and itself became a subject of controversy in many others. Indeed, the commentary and radio personality Walter Winchell had taken to the airwaves in early July to celebrate the fact that "advance knowledge" of enemy plans had saved American forces from defeat on at least two occasions.[27] The fact that proceedings were initiated against the *Tribune* was also widely commented on in the country's newspapers. It beggars the imagination to suggest that Japanese intelligence agents in the United States did not keep abreast of a story so central to Japanese security.

An explanation for the astonishing Japanese laxity in code security has never emerged from the Japanese archives. The best we can do is informed conjecture. This is the direction traveled by Kahn, who ascribes it to Tokyo's monumental hubris:

> the Japanese trusted too much in the reconditeness of their language for communications security, clinging to the myth that no foreigner could learn its multiple meanings well enough to understand it properly. In part they would not envision the possibility that their codes might be read. . . . Perhaps their own failures with American ciphers convinced them that cryptanalysis was a practical impossibility. In any event they hypnotized themselves into the delusion that their codes were never seriously compromised.[28]

Thus the great irony is that the two most significant leaks of World War II, both in the pages of the *Chicago Tribune*, wound up by strange chains of events doing no harm. The first of them quite arguably—and certainly inadvertently—did more than a modicum of good.

Yet that outcome was merely the great good fortune of the United States: Things could have easily gone the other way. If the United States, thanks to the *Chicago Tribune*, had lost its window into Japanese military communications, the war in the Pacific would still have ended in certain Japanese defeat; that outcome was all but assured by the atomic bomb. But three years were to elapse before that terrible weapon was ready for use. In the interim, without the priceless advantage of knowing Tokyo's every next move in advance, thousands—tens of thousands—of American soldiers and sailors would have died needlessly. Colonel McCormick's place in our history would be even lower than the low place in which it already resides. Or is it a low place at all? In some quarters, as we shall see, his spirit is very much alive.

CHAPTER 7

THE "PATRIOTIC PRESS"

"Now I AM become Death, the destroyer of worlds," were the words from Hindu scripture that the principal inventor of the atomic bomb, the physicist J. Robert Oppenheimer, uttered to himself as he stood in the New Mexico desert north of Alamogordo on July 16, 1945, and watched the fireball and the mushroom cloud of the world's first atomic explosion unfold before his eyes. Three weeks later on August 6, 1945, "Little Boy" was dropped on Hiroshima, killing more than 100,000 people in a millisecond and incinerating a living city. Literally in a flash the world had changed, and so had the place of secrecy in American life.

The terrible peril posed by atomic weapons was perceived well before the bomb was actually birthed. The initiation of a self-sustaining nuclear chain reaction by Enrico Fermi in 1939 confirmed to our country's leading physicists, almost all of them refugees from Hitler's Europe, that the devastating power bound up in the atom could be unleashed for military purposes. Everything must be done, they concluded, both to obtain the technology and to deny it to Nazi Germany and imperial Japan. In a famous letter Albert Einstein explained the reason to FDR: "This new phenomenon would . . . lead to the construction of bombs, and it is conceivable—though much less certain—that extremely powerful bombs of a new type may thus be constructed. A single bomb of this type, carried by boat and exploded in a port, might very well destroy the whole port together with some of the surrounding territory."[1] The creation of the atomic weapon thus transformed the effective control of secret information from potential advantage to survival imperative. After Hiroshima and Nagasaki the public learned what a select group of scientists and political leaders already knew—namely that a Pearl Harbor in the nuclear age could spell the end of our civilization.

An obvious first step in response to the danger was to contain any information even suggesting that such destructive technology was in the offing. Legislation passed on the eve of the war had strength-ened the Espionage Act and given Roosevelt authority to protect military information at his discretion. By executive order, the first of its kind in the security realm, Roosevelt extended the definition of "military installation" in sweeping fashion to include within its pur-view "*any* commercial establishment" engaged in the development or manufacture of military arms. By creating, for the first time, three levels of classification—"Secret," "Confidential," and "Restricted"— he also laid the basis for a hierarchy of secrets that, with modifica-tions, has survived to the present day.[2] In a subsequent executive order, Roosevelt broadened controls to cover information "relating to the national defense," a phrase that by virtue of its vagueness gave him virtually unlimited power to place subjects behind the curtain of security.[3]

Befitting its extreme sensitivity, nuclear research was treated in a special fashion. As the crash bomb-building program known as the Manhattan Project got under way, a regime of censorship was erected, supervised by a succession of improvised organizations. The National Defense Research Committee (NDRC) initially emerged as the primary guardian of militarily significant scientific infor-mation. Its purview rapidly expanded as it assumed control over screening the personnel engaged in nuclear research, classifying information pertaining to atomic weaponry, and providing physical security to the installations engaged in the endeavor.[4] Yet as research and production facilities sprang up across the country from Hanford in Washington state to Oak Ridge, Tennessee, tens of thousands of scientists, engineers, and ordinary laborers were drawn into the program. The security requirements multiplied apace. It shortly became necessary to put the U.S. Army in charge as the only arm of government that had sufficient resources for the task. The civilians working on the bomb thus came to be guarded by thousands of military personnel whose function it was to patrol the perimeter of manufacturing sites, monitor the shipping of sensitive goods and documents, and account for confidentially appropriated funds whose purpose, initially at least, was concealed even from Congress.

Within the heart of the project, at the research laboratory at Los Alamos, New Mexico, where Oppenheimer and other physicists labored, truly extraordinary procedures were put in place. As far as the rest of the world was concerned, the Los Alamos site did not exist. Outgoing mail bore the nondescript return address: "PO Box 1663, Sandoval County Rural, New Mexico." Incoming and outgoing mail was censored. Relatives (other than spouses and children) were not permitted to visit the site, civilian employees had their travel restricted to a one-hundred-mile radius of the site. Army counterintelligence placed undercover officers in Santa Fe bars and hotels to eavesdrop and make sure that classified information was not being casually discussed or surreptitiously funneled to enemy agents. Leading physicists were assigned pseudonyms. Oppenheimer assumed the code name James Oberhelm. Fermi became Henry Farmer. Hans Bethe was Howard Battle. The information in their heads was deemed so valuable that specially selected and trained army counterintelligence officers—disguised as drivers—trailed their every step.

This secrecy regime was by no means free of cost. Indeed, the Manhattan Project was repeatedly hamstrung by the very measures designed to protect it. Compartmentalization, as is so often the case in intelligence matters, was the major culprit. Manhattan Project regulations restricted information to each individual employee to "the minimum necessary for the proper performance of his duties." The same principal applied to organizations affiliated with the enterprise on the outside, with the regulations specifying that employees "shall be organized into small working groups or teams so far as possible, each working on its own phase of the job and not being permitted to inspect or discuss the work being done by others." As a means of safeguarding information, this was basic fare. As a means of running a vast scientific and engineering endeavor it was a formula for dysfunction.

Such compartmentalization collided directly with the nature of scientific endeavor, which hinges on the rapid diffusion of knowledge. It was especially burdensome in that the army often applied the principle in extreme fashion, insisting that, as an official postwar account recorded, "production plant blueprints be broken down and distributed in such a way as to reveal as little as possible to any one individual about the overall character of the project" and that "equipment orders to commercial firms specify that an item not be manufactured and assembled at the same location."[5] When production facilities actually reached the point of operations, plant managers were instructed "to split up orders for raw materials among a number of suppliers so that the purpose for which they were being used could not be readily ascertained."[6] Many workers did not even know the nature of the end product they were constructing. At some installations project officials invented "plausible but inaccurate"[7] explanations of what was actually being produced in the facilities at hand.

Under these circumstances conflicts frequently arose between the civilian researchers and their military overseers over access to information. But Gen. Leslie Groves, the military master of the sprawling secret enterprise, regarded compartmentalization as "the very heart of security," and was seldom flexible in its application. To him the principal that "each man should know everything he needed to know to do his job and nothing else" was not a drag on scientific inquiry at all but quite the opposite: something that "greatly improved overall efficiency by making our people stick to their knitting." Its overriding virtue was that "it made quite clear to all concerned that the project existed to produce a specific end product—not to enable individuals to satisfy their curiosity and to increase their scientific knowledge."[8]

After the war Groves's compartmentalization policies were to draw harsh criticism from many of the scientists who had taken part in the effort. A major complaint was that the Los Alamos researchers were kept in the dark about complementary work on reactors being conducted in Chicago. Edward Condon, one of the great pioneers of quantum mechanics, declared that the policy put the bomb-building scientists "in the position of trying to do an extremely difficult job with three hands tied behind your back."[9] Leo Szilard, another distinguished physicist, testified before Congress that information-security policies were a gross hindrance to rapid progress in the fundamental objectives of the program, one that possibly prolonged the war in the Pacific for more than a year. Compartmentalization of information, he complained, "was the cause for failure to realize that light uranium U-235 might be produced in quantities sufficient to make atomic bombs. . . . We could have had it eighteen months earlier. We did not put two and two together because the two two's were in a different compartment."[10]

DID THE AMERICAN press go along with the extraordinary secrecy regime and permit its arguably dysfunctional aspects to escape public scrutiny? The question scarcely needs to be asked. The "good war" took place in an era very different from our own, with a very different kind of press. It was, in FDR's words, a "patriotic press,"[11] a phrase that could not be uttered today by an American president, or anyone else, without a tinge of irony.

The First War Powers Act passed by Congress two weeks after Pearl Harbor included a provision for press censorship. On the day following its enactment, Roosevelt rolled out, again by executive order, an Office of Censorship to organize the system. "It is necessary to the national security that military information which might be of aid to the enemy be scrupulously withheld at the source," declared the president. Our government, he continued, had therefore called upon our "patriotic press and radio to abstain voluntarily from the dissemination of detailed information of certain kinds."[12]

Domestically circulated news was thus subjected to controls. However, as Roosevelt indicated, compliance was to be "voluntary." What this meant in practice was that instead of government agents being assigned to monitor individual publications and radio stations, blocking certain kinds of reports in advance, newspaper editors and broadcasters were issued a "Voluntary Censorship Code" that they were asked to follow. The Office of Censorship lacked the power to punish violators, but it could shame them—and impair their business—by disclosing their names; in egregious cases it could also refer them, as occurred in the *Chicago Tribune* case, to the Justice Department for prosecution under the Espionage Act.

Significantly, the man Roosevelt selected to run the censorship operation was not a military or nuclear expert but a journalist: Byron Price, executive news editor of the Associated Press. His deputy was another newspaperman: Nathaniel Howard, editor of the *Cleveland News*. Virtually from the outset of Price's tenure, strenuous efforts were made to keep the American press in the dark about the immense nuclear undertaking. Or, it might be more accurate to say, strenuous efforts were made to keep the American public in the dark, for key members of the press, by one of the paradoxes of voluntary censorship, were partially entrusted with the secret.

Price's approach thus relied upon two complementary prongs. On the one hand a battalion of censors, many of them from the Women's Army Auxiliary Corps (WAAC), scanned the leading dailies and magazines looking for references to anything that might disclose secret information or draw attention to the nuclear project. This effort gradually expanded until some 370 newspapers and periodicals were under its scrutiny. Yet to make such a system workable—and here was the second prong—the editors and radio broadcasters under scrutiny had themselves to be informed in considerable detail about what they could *not* publish or discuss. The Office of Censorship thus issued periodically updated bulletins containing specified subjects and terms to which the press was not to advert.

In June 1943, for example, editors and broadcasters were asked to refrain from public discussion of "new or secret military weapons or experiments." The censorship mandate then itself proceeded to lay out extremely sensitive information, proscribing references to such subjects as:

- [The production] or utilization of atom smashing, atomic energy, atomic fission, atomic splitting, or any of their equivalents.
- The use for military purposes of radium or radioactive materials, heavy water, high voltage discharge equipment, cyclotrons.
- The following elements or any of their compounds: plutonium, uranium, ytterbium, hafnium, protactinium, radium, thorium, deuterium.[13]

By and large the system of censorship was highly successful. Journalists, conceiving of themselves in that distant era not as neutral observers but as an integral part of the war effort, were eager to comply. Don Anderson, the publisher of the *Wisconsin State Journal*, to take but one example from the hinterland, was too old to enlist or cover the war in person. He chose instead to monitor, as a volunteer "missionary," compliance by the 340 publications of his home state, and educate violators when they went wrong.[14]

Similarly Russell B. Porter of the *New York Times*, when he was not reporting the news for his paper, was keeping tabs on his colleagues. After attending a talk by the muckraking columnist Drew Pearson, he wrote a memo to his editors noting, "At the beginning of his speech, Pearson said he was going to tell things he could not write in his column or say on the radio, and that the newspapers could not print." Porter found it highly objectionable that Pearson had unilaterally "set himself up as the authority" as to what military information can be disclosed. "It would seem to me," he continued, "that no one should be allowed to go around the country lecturing to large groups of people at public dinners, or even at one such event, and reveal as 'inside stuff' information so secret and so useful to the enemy that the newspapers and radio are not allowed to publish it. . . . [N]o one can be sure that there was not an Axis agent or sympathizer in the room."[15]

Upon receiving Porter's memorandum, editors at the *Times* did not dismiss it as the work of a snitch or rat and contrary to the ethos of journalism. Rather they eagerly passed it along to Arthur Hays Sulzberger, the paper's publisher-owner, who duly conveyed it to the Office of Censorship, whence it traveled to the White House. An FBI inquiry into Pearson commenced and lasted eight months. It ended inconclusively, with Pearson insisting he had not violated the code during his speech despite his representation to the contrary. He had merely, he said, been engaging in showmanship.

Even with such avid compliance by local and national publications, there were more than a few breaches of the censorship regime over the course of the war. Indeed the violations totaled in the thousands, but those that occurred in the atomic-weapons sphere (as in other spheres as well) were overwhelmingly not of the Colonel McCormick variety, born of political ideology and personal hatred. Rather they stemmed from the sheer impracticality of walling off all information about an enterprise of such scope. Thus, when the government requisitioned large tracts of land for facilities like Hanford, displacing longtime residents by the hundreds, it was unavoidable that there would be discussion of the turmoil in the local newspapers and awkward questions asked.

The Office of Censorship wisely tolerated some release of information, recognizing, as an official postwar study of security arrangements noted, "that complete suppression of information about activities at these locations would actually draw more attention than a policy of judicious release of news of local interest, carefully controlled so as not to reveal any vital secrets."[16] Rather than crack down, the censors themselves visited the editorial offices of newspapers and radio stations to caution them in person about the boundaries of acceptable discussion.

Inevitably, alarming leaks occurred despite such counseling. A *Washington Post* columnist let slip the suggestive report that the Truman Committee—the Senate's watchdog on wasteful military expenditures (named for its chairman)—was investigating a half-billion-dollar War Department project, reportedly "one of the largest single projects that's to be built from scratch in the nation's history."[17] The story was picked up by wire services and ran across the country. Within days another story appeared in newspapers in Tennessee citing a brigadier general who had spoken of "secret war production of a weapon that possibly might be the one to end the war."

In Minneapolis the *Morning Tribune* ran a story in August 1944 that said "all known explosives are popgun affairs compared to the dreadful power sub-atomic energy might loose," and then continued to explain that uranium sales were being restricted by the U.S. government. That same month Arthur Hale, the host of the *Confidentially Yours* program on the Mutual Broadcasting network, a show that reached two million listeners, regaled his audience with news that the army would soon create a new weapon based upon the splitting of the atom. None of these transgressors was punished. Rather, agents of the Office of Censorship swooped in to trace the source of the leaks, to try to contain the story, and to warn the editors and broadcasters away from a repetition of the violation.

As the Manhattan Project came closer to fruition, Gen. Groves sought to hire an "official journalist" to handle the dissemination of the information that it would unavoidably have to disclose to the public after the bomb was used in anger against Japan. Groves had his eye on William L. Laurence, a science reporter for the *New York Times* who had followed nuclear developments before the war and published an important article about their military implications in 1940 in the *Saturday Evening Post*. Before approaching Laurence directly, Groves arranged a meeting with Edwin L. James, the managing editor of the *Times*, asking him to have Laurence standing by in case his presence was necessary.

At the meeting, while offering no details about the project itself, Groves simply told James that for reasons of "extreme importance" the government "needed a newspaper writer for a number of months."[18] After some discussion of Laurence's fitness for a sensitive assignment, the reporter was brought into the meeting. "We want you to come work for us," said Groves. Laurence's reply did not evince even a tinge of ambivalence: "I have been waiting for a long time for an opportunity to serve. When do I start?"[19] His demeanor, Groves was later to write, "only made us more certain than ever that this was the man we wanted." A conversation about practical matters ensued. "It seemed desirable for security reasons, as well as easier for the employer," noted Groves in his memoirs, "to have Laurence continue on the payroll of the *New York Times*, but with his expense to be covered by the [Manhattan Project]."[20]

Also for security reasons Groves asked James to keep Laurence's assignment "as secret as possible," a commitment to which the *Times* editor readily assented. Indeed, the *Times* participated in generating a diversionary cover story for their reporter as he disappeared into the government's black world. The newspaper published an article bearing Laurence's byline with a false London dateline. "This was helpful," writes Groves, "in throwing off suspicion." It was also helpful in calming the anxiety of Laurence's wife, "who was wondering where he was and why he would not tell her what he was doing."[21]

Taking up the newly created reporter-in-residence slot inside the Manhattan Project, Laurence was made privy to the most intimate details of the program, receiving extensive briefings at Oak Ridge, Hanford, and Los Alamos. After having been brought up to speed, he was permitted to witness the Trinity test at Alamogordo, for which he prepared alternative statements for public release, thereby hedging against the possibility of a disaster that killed the scientists and engineers involved in the blast. Traveling to Tinian, the base from which the nuclear attack on Japan was to be launched, he arrived too late to join the observation plane for the Hiroshima bombing. He did make it on board a flight to watch as Nagasaki was reduced to cinders by the detonation of "Fat Man." Hours after the bombing of Hiroshima, President Truman, returning from the Potsdam Conference aboard the USS *Augusta*, informed the public that the explosion was "an atomic bomb, harnessing . . . the basic powers of the universe. The force from which the sun draws its power has been loosed against those who brought war to the Far East."[22] The words were written by Laurence.

After the war Laurence returned to the *Times* and resumed his journalistic career; no conflict was perceived at the newspaper between his role as a reporter and his role as what would be derided today in the newsroom as a government flack. Quite the opposite: "Mine has been the honor, unique in the history of journalism, of preparing the War Department's official press release for worldwide distribution," boasted Laurence in his own memoir. "No greater honor could have come to any newspaperman, or anyone else for that matter."[23] The journalistic world concurred, awarding him a Pulitzer Prize in 1946 for his story about the bombing of Nagasaki and ten subsequent articles tracing the development of the A-bomb, all reported while he was on the government payroll. As for Byron Price, in 1944 the Pulitzer committee bestowed upon him a "special award" for "the creation and administration of the newspaper and radio [censorship] codes."[24]

ALL THIS contains irony wrapped inside irony. On one side there could be no more powerful indication than these unthinkable Pulitzers of how profoundly American journalism has changed in attitudes toward government secrecy in the decades since World War II. Today, indeed, voices in the journalistic world are calling for Laurence to be stripped of his prize. He stands accused of betraying his professional responsibility by collaborating with the government in carrying out the nuclear attack on Japan.[25] On the other side is the inescapable fact that, even as journalists enthusiastically aided government in guarding its greatest secret, the entire system proved ineffective in its most crucial objective: keeping the nuclear secret out of the hands of foreign powers.

From the outset the security establishment assumed that some leakage was inevitable. With a huge number of individuals from widely divergent backgrounds and at so many disparate locations involved in the research and manufacturing program, even stringent background checks and clearance procedures would prove insufficient to keep out spies. In this they were correct. But the scope of the hemorrhaging far exceeded the imagination of the responsible officials. As is well known today but was a terrible shock back then, the Manhattan Project had been infiltrated by Soviet intelligence, which had succeeded in recruiting a number of Communists and Communist sympathizers inside the project.

Just as the bomb was nearing completion in late 1944 and early 1945, David Greenglass, an Army sergeant at Los Alamos, conveyed classified data from the laboratory to his brother-in-law, Julius Rosenberg, and to Morton Sobell, who in turn passed it on to the USSR. All three (along with Rosenberg's less complicit wife, Ethel) were apprehended five years later, put on trial, and convicted of espionage. The theoretical physicist Klaus Fuchs, a German refugee and member of the British delegation assisting at Los Alamos, was also apprehended as the spy ring crumbled. The Rosenbergs were both executed while the others were imprisoned for lengthy terms.

Thanks to such treachery, and the security shortcomings that allowed it, the USSR was able to develop an atomic bomb much earlier than forecast. But Joseph Stalin's prowess in espionage can hardly be taken to mean that the secrecy surrounding the Manhattan Project was for naught. However gravely damaging to American security was the Soviet spying, the USSR was a wartime ally. The key fact is that our mortal wartime enemies, Germany and Japan, did not manage to peer through the shroud we had draped over the bomb effort. Germany's leading nuclear physicists, captured by the British after VE-Day and detained in a facility in England where their every word was surreptitiously recorded, evinced astonishment when informed of the Hiroshima detonation.[26] The Japanese, for their part, were as mystified as they were terrified by the hellfire that descended upon them in August 1945 and impelled them to surrender.

Without doubt, in key respects our nuclear secrecy was dysfunctional and inadequate, as secrecy almost always is. Like all instruments of national power its use involves trade-offs among competing objectives. And like all instruments of national power it can be fouled up by shortsightedness and incompetence or simply fall victim to happenstance amid the fog of war. It can also be foiled, as we learned, by an ingenious foe determined to pierce the veil. But in reaching a supreme objective in World War II—building the bomb while keeping the Axis powers in the dark—secrecy decisively proved its worth.

CHAPTER 8

TO THE "RAMPARTS"

T HE END OF World War II and the shortcomings of our secrecy
regime during the conflict did not lead to a fundamental change
of direction in the postwar era, or at least not initially. But looking
back on that moment, we can see that a great pendulum was poised
to swing and carry the country, with accelerating speed, from one
extreme to the other.

At the beginning of the postwar era, as it dawned on Americans that the hot war with Germany and Japan was giving way to
a cold war with the USSR, secrecy efforts were redoubled. Soviet
possession of the A-bomb after 1949 and, increasingly over the next
two decades, the means to drop the A-bomb on American cities
via bombers and missiles, meant that the two-ocean buffer we had
enjoyed throughout our history was a thing of the past: Suddenly we
were vulnerable and growing more so with the passage of each day.

The American-Soviet balance of terror thus brought about the
heyday of American secrecy, made manifest in new laws and new
institutions. Of the latter the most visible was the Central Intelligence Agency, established by the National Security Act of 1947 to
coordinate the clandestine intelligence functions of a gaggle of other
organizations scattered throughout the United States government.
Some of these, like the National Security Agency, which President

Truman created in 1952, were simply brought into being by presidential edicts that were themselves secret. As far as the public was concerned, as noted earlier, the NSA did not exist.

To be sure there was a significant relaxation of restrictions on information in the aftermath of the American victory over Germany and Japan. Wartime censorship was abolished at war's end, when Byron Price ceremoniously hung an Out of Business sign on the door of the Office of Censorship. Such measures were never thought appropriate for peacetime no matter how precarious the peace. But other restrictions were multiplied. When the Cold War erupted into a hot war on the Korean Peninsula in 1950, President Truman acted decisively to ramp up the secrecy system. For the first time elaborate procedures were set up specifying precisely what kinds of information were to be classified and, once classified, properly handled. Truman issued an executive order specifying in close detail the management of even the most mundane aspects of secrecy, covering things like how properly to dispose of "carbon-paper" material that had been employed to make duplicates of classified documents and even how to staple classified documents.[1]

The order also created a new category of Top-Secret information, the secure handling of which was likewise elaborated with great particularity. Such information, dictated the Truman order, "shall be stored in the most secure facilities available. Normally it will be stored in a safe, a steel file cabinet, or other steel container having a three position dial-type combination lock and being of such weight, size, construction, or installation as to minimize possibility of physical theft or damage by fire or tampering." Top-secret documents were only to be "destroyed by burning," although "the head of an agency may authorize destruction of documents other than by burning, provided the resulting destruction is equally complete." This stood in contrast to merely "restricted" information that could be destroyed not only by burning but also by "shredding or reduction to pulp."

It is easy to make such regulations seem absurd, a gross overreaction, as no doubt some of them were. But on the whole the new security mechanisms were reasonable given the danger and the frightening uncertainty, with war raging in Asia, about what the morrow would bring. Senator Joseph McCarthy may have been demagogically fingering innocent civil servants as Communists in this period, but that did not mean that there was no threat from Communist infiltration. The successful Soviet espionage at Los Alamos, and the sensational conviction of former State Department official Alger Hiss in 1950 on perjury charges (the statute of limitations of the Espionage Act had expired), made it plain that adopting stringent measures to protect secrets from the MGB, the KGB's predecessor organization, required concentrated attention.

Congress was of the same view. The Joint Congressional Committee for the Investigation of Pearl Harbor, a body enjoying high prestige much like the 9/11 Commission of our own era, included among its urgent recommendations the tightening of laws governing the dissemination of government secrets. Adverting to both the Yardley and McCormick cases, it saw the existing statutory framework as operating potentially "to the benefit of an enemy or other forces inimical to the Nation's security and to the handicap of our own intelligence agencies." It urged Congress to give serious study to "legislation *fully* protecting the security of *classified* matter."[2] This sounds unexceptionable, but it was a radical change of conception. Hitherto classification by itself was not relevant to the Espionage Act. This statute only protected "National Defense Information" (NDI)—that is, secrets the disclosure of which the government would have to prove in court could injure the United States.

The sweeping approach favored by the Joint Committee coincided with the preferences of both the army and the navy, which even before Germany and Japan had surrendered were pushing hard for legislation that would have strengthened various provisions of the Espionage Act, eliminating its culpability requirement of an "intent to injure" the United States and dramatically extending its scope to include *all* classified "military and naval intelligence" information.[3]

Though intensely concerned about security, Congress was reluctant to move in a direction that had the potential to place vast tracts of information off limits from public discussion. It sought instead legislative pathways to safeguard only the most sensitive secrets while leaving everything else to be covered by the looser provisions of the Espionage Act. This alone puts the lie to some of the more exaggerated depictions of the secrecy regime that was erected in the Cold War, including the morally noxious notion put forward by one scholar that we had erected our own "iron curtain" just as the Russians had done: Theirs had been built in 1946 "with tanks and barbed wire," while "ours is a curtain of our own design, woven with executive orders, legislation, and most of all, the system of classifying sensitive information."[4]

Indeed, Congress acted to preserve the American tradition of openness in one of the most trying times in our history. But there were realms that did require special protection, nuclear technology being the most obvious. Thus, not long after Tokyo capitulated, legislators turned their attention to containing the secrets of the atom. As originally drafted in the flush of Allied victory and before friction with the Kremlin had become so palpable, the Atomic Energy Act called for the establishment of a "program for the free dissemination of basic scientific information and for maximum liberality in dissemination of related technical information." This flirtation with transparency did not last. With relations with the USSR teetering on the brink of open conflict, by the time the bill arrived on Harry Truman's desk in August 1946, "free dissemination" and "maximum liberality" were out and the phrase "control of information" assumed their place.[5]

In particular the Atomic Energy Act provided especially stringent protection for "all data concerning the manufacture or utilization of atomic weapons, the production of fissionable material, or the use of fissionable material in the production of power." Communicating, transmitting, or disclosing such "restricted data" with "reason to believe it would be utilized to injure the United States or to secure an advantage to any foreign nation" was made a criminal offense punishable by death. A unique—and uniquely controversial—feature of this provision was that no affirmative action by the government was necessary to classify information about atomic weapons and fission. Anything that fell within the definition of restricted data, whether developed by the government or by scientists operating in private, was automatically walled off and protected at the moment it came into being. Hence such restricted data was said to be "born secret."

In successive sessions after the war, Congress also considered legislation that sought to do precisely what the Joint Committee on Pearl Harbor had recommended: proscribe the publication of *all* classified material. Once again, despite the extreme anxieties of the era, the American tradition of openness won out. By 1950, when proponents in Congress and the military finally recognized that an all-encompassing approach could not pass, they acted to safeguard another narrowly defined set of secrets nearly as sensitive as atomic energy, namely, communications intelligence.

The statute that emerged from Congress was Section 798 of Title 18, as it is codified, or the Comint Act, as it is sometimes called. Unlike the vague phrases of the Espionage Act protecting the nebulous category of National Defense Information, the new law was unambiguous and highly specific. It punishes "whoever knowingly and willfully communicates, furnishes, transmits, or otherwise makes available to an unauthorized person, *or publishes*" any classified material "concerning the communications intelligence activities of the United States [emphasis added]."

The Comint Act, still on the books today unchanged, was extraordinary in several respects. In line with the long-standing preference of the army and navy, it did not require the government to jump over the hurdle of proving "intent to injure" the United States. The knowing act of publishing secret Comint material was sufficient to secure a conviction. In other words, under the statute, and quite unusual in American law, the act itself is the crime while intent is irrelevant. Even more noteworthy is that here, for the first time, was a statute that, in punishing "*whoever* . . . publishes [emphasis added]," aimed not only at former government employees like Yardley, but also journalists, book publishers, and anyone else who chose to put such secret material into print.

The Comint Act enjoyed widespread support. It passed the Senate with barely a word of debate and sailed through the House without objection. Most remarkably it was endorsed by the American Society of Newspaper Editors, an organization in which leading editors of the *New York Times* were active members.[6] Such broad acceptance reflected, on the one hand, piercing recognition of how pernicious Yardley and McCormick's behavior had been and the urgency of preventing a recurrence in the nuclear age. At the same time, to those concerned about freedom of the press, precisely because the legislation was a compromise that averted tighter controls on far broader categories of intelligence information, it was welcomed with some relief. Still, when all is said and done, a law that criminalized and punished the *publication* of government secrets—potentially imposing on a journalist a sentence of up to ten years—enjoyed the backing of the nation's newspaper editors. The Cold War consensus had reached its height, and there it was to remain for a decade.

WHEN THE Korean War erupted in June 1950, a significant number of Americans were convinced it would lead to a nuclear exchange. Nonetheless, regarding Korea as a square on the global chessboard that the United States could ill afford to cede, the overwhelming majority—some 81 percent of voters polled in a Gallup survey—were willing to make the sacrifices and run the risks of providing military assistance to the beleaguered south.[7] The experience of appeasing tyrants in the years before World War II had taught lessons that had been deeply engraved in public consciousness. In this, the press differed little from the broader populace; Outliers aside, like the Soviet apologist I. F. Stone, the basic premise of containment, the need to resist the expansionist proclivities of the USSR, was hardly a subject of controversy within journalistic circles. And as in World War II, in the global struggle of the Cold War, American journalists did not regard themselves as neutral observers; rather they were on a side, the American side, and that shone through. They were fully part of the "vital center" of Cold War liberalism.

Thus when the North Koreans poured southward across the thirty-eighth parallel, journalists flocked to the front and conveyed the horrors of what they saw. But not every story from the front lines that today would have been rushed onto the front page actually got there. A good many, especially those reporting civilian casualties caused inadvertently by American actions, were spiked by a self-censoring press cautious about boosting enemy morale and/or losing the accreditation granted by the U.S. military. The shared premises of the Cold War thus kept the press from exposing every mishap of battle and every last drop of misery that Korean civilians suffered as American, North Korean, and Chinese troops laid waste the Korean Peninsula in their battle to control it.

But by the early 1960s the pendulum of change was fully in motion, and the vital center began to spin apart, including especially inside the journalistic elite. One of many illustrative cases in point can be found in the career of David Halberstam, who was assigned to Saigon by the *New York Times* in 1960. Halberstam is today best remembered for documenting the intellectual hubris of an anti-Communist worldview that led us into the morass of Vietnam. But what is today forgotten is that Halberstam was solidly in the center of the anti-Communist consensus, or at least he was solidly in its center until he wasn't anymore. Though he was loath to acknowledge it—making not a reference to his own political conversion in his celebrated 1972 book about the Vietnam War, *The Best and the Brightest*—in fact before he became a fervent dove he had been an even more fervent hawk.

As late as 1965, Halberstam was brooding over the dire consequences of American withdrawal, which would mean not only "a drab, lifeless, and controlled society for a people who deserve better" but also "that the United States' prestige will be lowered throughout the world, and . . . that the pressure of Communism on the rest of Southeast Asia will intensify. Lastly, withdrawal means that throughout the world the enemies of the West will be encouraged to try insurgencies like the one in Vietnam."[8] Such hawkish views were fully in accord with the editorial page of the *New York Times*, which that same year declared that America "went into Vietnam to contain the advance of Communism in that part of Southeast Asia. . . . The motives are exemplary and every American can be proud of them."[9]

It is only in the context of the widely shared anti-Communist outlook that we can understand one of the more striking facts—indeed for a time a highly secret fact—about the journalism of the 1950s and early 1960s. Top reporters and columnists, and approximately twenty-five news-gathering organizations, including the *New York Times*, Time Inc., and CBS, had been secretly cooperating with the CIA in all sorts of ways, some of which, by their own current lights, would undercut their standing as impartial purveyors of information.

This collaboration was first brought into the public view by the Church Committee hearings of 1976, and more details were shortly thereafter supplied by the investigative reporter Carl Bernstein, who found that reporters from major papers were in more than a few cases employed "to help recruit and handle foreigners as agents; to acquire and evaluate information, and to plant false information with officials of foreign governments. Many signed secrecy agreements, pledging never to divulge anything about their dealings with the Agency."[10]

At the height of the Cold War, in other words, the secrecy ran both ways. It is another lens through which to see how profoundly the relationship between the press and the government has shifted over the past five decades. The days are past when a leading columnist would say of his cooperation with the CIA, as Joseph Alsop did when interviewed by Bernstein, that "I'm proud they asked me and proud to have done it" and that "the notion that a newspaperman doesn't have a duty to his country is perfect balls."[11] From what was arguably an excess of deference in the Cold War, the press has moved to an excess of defiance. Governmental secrecy lay at the heart of the transformation.

A FIRST STATION on the journey came in the aftermath of the CIA-organized Bay of Pigs invasion of Cuba in 1961. As John F. Kennedy was pondering whether to move forward with the CIA plan he had inherited from the Eisenhower administration, stories appeared in some minor left-leaning publications reporting that something was afoot. Digging into the reports, the *New York Times* and the Associated Press learned of the impending operation and planned stories along similar lines.

At Kennedy's personal urging both news outlets reduced the prominence of the coverage to avoid giving the game away and forcing cancellation of the invasion. The operation went forward and ended as a bloody disaster on a Cuban beach. In the wake of a fiasco that made him appear vacillating and inexperienced, Kennedy had a change of mind. In a conversation with Orvil Dryfoos, then the publisher of the *Times*, he expressed regret that the news outlets had heeded his earlier admonition. If they had published what they knew, they would have saved him from his own foreign policy blunder. "I wish you had run everything on Cuba . . . I am just sorry you didn't tell it at the time."[12]

That was a breathtaking evasion of responsibility by a president who, campaigning against Richard Nixon in October 1960, had on the eve of the presidential election complained that the "fighters for freedom" who offer "eventual hope of overthrowing Castro" had gained "virtually no support from our government."[13] It was also a dip into hypocrisy by a president who reveled in secrecy, and who would have been appalled if the press had actually gone forward and divulged even a small fraction of the secret initiatives in which the United States came to be engaged—the American-instigated assassination of South Vietnamese premier Ngo Dinh Diem, for instance—during the remainder of his tragically abbreviated administration.

Unsurprisingly Kennedy's ex post facto judgment that the press was wrong to withhold its foreknowledge of the Bay of Pigs invasion is often deployed today by journalistic defenders of leaks as justification for putting anything and everything into print. Also unsurprisingly what those same defenders always seem to omit is that in his more considered moments the president was by no means offering the press a license to publish leaks at their own discretion.

In a speech to the American Newspaper Publishers Association (the source of one of the epigraphs of this book) not long after the collapse of his Cuban adventure, Kennedy proposed that the industry adopt a voluntary system to protect national security secrets, declaring it was time to "ask every publisher, every editor, and every newsman in the nation to reexamine his own standards, and to recognize the nature of our country's peril." Citing the precedent set in *Schenck* in the aftermath of World War I, Kennedy pointed out that "in time of 'clear and present danger,' the courts have held that even the privileged rights of the First Amendment must yield to the public's need for national security." And indeed, according to Kennedy, this was such a time:

> For the facts of the matter are that this nation's foes have
> openly boasted of acquiring through our newspapers
> information they would otherwise hire agents to acquire
> through theft, bribery or espionage; that details of this
> nation's covert preparations to counter the enemy's covert
> operations have been available to every newspaper reader,
> friend and foe alike; that the size, the strength, the location
> and the nature of our forces and weapons, and our plans and
> strategy for their use, have all been pinpointed in the press
> and other news media to a degree sufficient to satisfy any
> foreign power.
>
> . . . I am asking the members of the newspaper
> profession and the industry in this country to reexamine
> their own responsibilities, to consider the degree and the

nature of the present danger, and to heed the duty of self-restraint which that danger imposes upon us all. Every newspaper now asks itself, with respect to every story: "Is it news?" All I suggest is that you add the question: "Is it in the interest of the national security?"[14]

This was a ringing speech. But as far as secrecy and the press are concerned, it was one of the last gasps of the old regime. Change came and it came fast. The war to which Kennedy committed us in Vietnam was the strongest catalytic force. But other currents were flowing, too. The shock to the nation delivered by the assassination of the young president in 1963, the flowering of the civil-rights movement and the acrimonious schism in American politics it provoked, the rise of a counterculture centered around rock and roll, drugs, and sneering opposition to middle-class norms, and the emergence of the New Left, all brought into journalism a new and coruscatingly skeptical attitude—often a coruscatingly hostile attitude—toward American government. This process began on the fringes and by the late 1960s and early 70s became the new mainstream.

ONE EARLY marker on the fringe was *Ramparts*. Founded in 1962 as a Catholic literary journal, it quickly veered into New Left politics, chasing conspiracy theories about the assassination of JFK, publishing the diaries of Che Guevara (with an introduction by Fidel Castro), and championing black liberation in some of its less peaceful forms, for example, featuring the prison writings of the Black Panther leader Eldridge Cleaver. In early 1967 *Ramparts* stumbled upon a sensational national security secret that it skillfully deployed to achieve maximum publicity—namely that the Central Intelligence Agency was funding a domestic organization active in European affairs, the National Student Association, and had been doing so since the NSA's inception in 1947.[15]

In channeling money to the NSA in the early fifties, the CIA was responding to the Soviet practice of establishing front groups across Europe seemingly composed of ordinary individuals (which many of them were) interested in promoting peace and progress, but under the control of not-so-ordinary individuals on the staff of Soviet and Eastern bloc intelligence services. To field the side of democracy and freedom in this ideological battle for hearts and minds, the CIA opted to establish front groups of its own, or to funnel support to existing organizations, most of them on Europe's democratic Left, that were already countering the well-funded Soviet propaganda offensive.

The *Ramparts* story opened the sluices. The *New York Times* followed up with revelation upon revelation. While publishing not a word about its own long-standing and intricate history of collaboration with the CIA, it dug further into the subsidies to others and over the following weeks regaled the American public with revelations about one or another organization that had been on the payroll of the spy agency. Dozens of private organizations were left to spiral downward in disarray, rocked by damaged reputations and bitter recriminations as their leaders fractured into two camps: those who had been kept in the dark about the funding and those who knew all along that the CIA was paying the piper.

This was, by any measure, the most significant security leak of the Cold War thus far. The press had seemingly crossed a Rubicon, for here was an operational intelligence program, and its exposure not only damaged American prestige but held the potential of imperiling the well-being of Americans, particularly those traveling behind the Iron Curtain under the auspices of the now tainted organizations, which were suddenly at risk of being perceived as dens of spies.

But whatever harm flowed from the breach (and by the standards of what the press is willing to publish today, the harm was relatively modest) and whatever the quite different motivations of *Ramparts* and the *New York Times* in bringing the CIA subsidies to light, in the end responsibility cannot fairly be laid on the doorstep of the press itself. Here, rather, was a virtually inevitable leak that flowed from the shortcomings of American intelligence, which, notwithstanding its triumphs in the previous decade, was by the 1960s becoming increasingly sclerotic.

The slapdash planning and wishful thinking that lay behind the Bay of Pigs invasion plan was already a warning sign of severe trouble inside the agency. Coincidentally, just as the final touches were being added to that abortive plan, the CIA was also considering a fundamental revision to its program of funding private organizations, with the idea of weaning them from dependency on agency cash, a step strongly urged in 1960 by a commission Eisenhower had charged with reviewing overseas information programs.[16] But here, too, as in the Bay of Pigs, the CIA's leadership failed, a victim of its own complacency. Indeed, in this period it stepped up some of its private funding activities and branched out into new areas, failing to notice that the climate inside the United States was changing, and failing to notice that the climate inside the agency was changing, too. The Cold War consensus was shattering, and even loyalists inside the organization were no longer quite so loyal—or loyal at all.

If a Halberstam on the outside could undergo a political conversion, so could CIA insiders who shared the same milieu, whose children were going to the same schools and listening to the same music, and who were no less exposed to the cultural forces roiling the country. Indeed, as the historian Hugh Wilford has observed, it was in this period that "a new dissident mood" spread into the agency.[17] In this atmosphere, the idea that a program requiring the covert cooperation of dozens if not hundreds of private individuals would not leak out was preposterous. Yet the CIA, supposedly the eyes and ears of the nation, was taken by surprise.

Even at the beginning of the program in the early fifties, there were some who believed breaches were inevitable. The then-trade-union official Arnold Beichman disapproved of the subsidies "not so much for moral reasons as because I felt certain that someday the whole tawdry business would be exposed."[18] The CIA convinced itself otherwise. Indeed, it was so overconfident that its tradecraft badly slipped; it used the same funding conduits—primarily an outfit it set up called the Fairfield Foundation—for all of the organizations on its dole. Thus when the National Student Association was exposed by *Ramparts*, journalists found it an easy task to figure out which other groups were at the other end of the funnel. In short the CIA set itself up for failure of the kind that, after its golden age of the 1950s, would become ever more familiar.

The Johnson administration was caught unawares by the flap, learning of the *Ramparts* article only a week before its appearance. Its meek response was to establish a committee of inquiry that was intended, if not to sweep the matter under the rug, at least to tamp the story down. The CIA's reaction was far more vigorous than that of the White House, but one thing it did not include was any reflection about the difficulties of keeping this particular kind of program secret. Rather it followed a template that was to be drawn upon again over the remainder of the decade by the CIA and later, in the Nixon years, by the White House. It attempted to plug the leaks by investigating and intimidating the perpetrators, in this case, by compiling dossiers on the people in and around *Ramparts*, and by exploiting IRS tax records to find a channel of financial pressure on the magazine and its advertisers.

From the point of view of the government's long-run interest in preserving national security secrets, this reflexive response brought about the worst of all possible worlds, vindicating the press's contention that it had every right and even a positive obligation to disclose whatever it could about a governmental body behaving in rogue-like fashion. The CIA's own actions thus put a first nail in the coffin of legitimate secrecy at a moment when, as today, the United States was at war and secrecy in matters of national security really counted. But the *Ramparts* affair was only an appetizer. The main course was soon to be served by Daniel Ellsberg.

CHAPTER 9

UNNECESSARY SECRETS

On the evening of October 1, 1969 I walked out past the
guards' desk at the Rand Corporation in Santa Monica,
carrying a briefcase filled with top secret documents, which
I planned to copy that night. The documents were part of
a 7,000-page top secret study of U.S. decision making in
Vietnam, later known as the Pentagon Papers. The rest of
the study was in a safe in my office. I had decided to copy it
all and make it public, perhaps through Senate hearings or
the press, if necessary. I believed this course, especially the
latter possibility, would probably put me in prison for the
rest of my life.

So begins Daniel Ellsberg's memoir, *Secrets*, which tells the story of
the most consequential leak in American history.[1]

The political and legal extravaganza Ellsberg set in motion
marked a turning point in American attitudes toward secrecy. If
before Ellsberg there was a tacit acceptance of the fact that our government often had justifiable reasons to operate in secret, the Pentagon Papers served to dissolve that recognition, at least among our
elites. The case also gave rise to two opposing narratives reflecting the deep polarization of American society at the height of the

Vietnam war. To one side Ellsberg was no better than a criminal, a disloyal official who betrayed his country and escaped punishment thanks only to Richard Nixon's own illegal behavior. To the other side he was the lone hero who risked his freedom to halt the bloodshed and whose actions were vindicated by both history and the courts. The denouement of the epic Supreme Court battle provoked by Ellsberg's actions was, it is commonly thought, a decisive victory for the First Amendment, one that henceforth left newspapers free to publish whatever they would.

But the opposing portraits of Ellsberg are both caricatures; so too is any interpretation of the Pentagon Papers case that sees it as a vindication of the *New York Times*'s decision to publish the secret papers. Indeed, if before the Pentagon Papers case the Espionage Act was a loaded gun pointed at the press, after the Supreme Court issued its ruling, the gun was fully cocked.

DANIEL ELLSBERG was born in 1931, grew up as a precocious child in Detroit, and then set off to Harvard, where he earned a B.A. in 1952 and then a PhD in economics, his dissertation exploring a conundrum in game theory now known as the Ellsberg Paradox. A self-described "cold-war Democrat," Ellsberg had been confirmed in his anti-Communist convictions by the horrors inflicted on Eastern Europe in the early Cold War. In 1954, putting principle into practice, he enlisted in the marines and spent three-plus years as an infantry officer, rising through the corps to command a rifle company. Returning to Harvard in 1957—with occasional stints at the Rand Corporation, the military-funded think tank in Santa Monica, California—Ellsberg immersed himself in defense policy. In 1964 he took a position in the Pentagon as a special assistant to John T. McNaughton, one of Secretary of Defense Robert S. McNamara's principal point men.

Ellsberg's portfolio was Vietnam. Laboring seventy hours a week in the E-ring of the Pentagon, the cockpit of American military power, he found himself poring through huge stacks of classified documents bearing top-secret stamps like "Eyes Only," "NoDis," "ExDis," and "LimDis." These categories were intended to ensure that documents circulated only to the high-ranking officials on their distribution lists. In practice, however, the system had grown lax and they were disseminated to a wider group, including Ellsberg, whose name was not on most of the lists. To combat such laxity and to ensure that a document would reach only the principals for whom it was intended, ad hoc intensifiers were employed, like "Literally Eyes Only of the Secretary" or "Literally Eyes Only of the President." But informal pressures overcame the formal rules, and these ultrasecret documents also wound up on Ellsberg's desk. Before long he had as complete a picture of developments in Vietnam as anyone in the U.S. government.

After a time Ellsberg decided to seek an assignment in Vietnam, which in 1965 he found. Serving there in a number of different civilian advisory positions over the next two years, he became immersed in a very different way—up close and personal—in the intricacies of the war. Together with the legendary counterinsurgency expert John Paul Vann, he risked his life touring every province of the South, gaining full exposure to the myriad problems of America's increasingly troubled and bloody Southeast Asian venture.

Leaving Vietnam in 1967 following a bout of hepatitis, Ellsberg returned to Rand, where he expected to put down on paper everything he had learned about the war. His pessimistic assessment of the "irrevocability of stalemate" led him to conclude that the United States had no choice but to exit from the conflict. But even as he was moving in one direction, becoming increasingly opposed to a continued American presence in Vietnam, Lyndon Johnson was moving in another. To salvage the South Vietnamese position, a top-secret plan devised by Gens. Earl Wheeler, chairman of the Joint Chiefs of Staff, and William Westmoreland, America's commanding officer in Vietnam, proposed adding 206,000 troops to the 500,000 already in country; the administration was poised to intensify the conflict dramatically.

As this plan was moving forward, a wrench was tossed into the administration's deliberations by a leak to the *New York Times* disclosing the 206,000 figure and the debate surrounding it within the military and the administration. The story generated intense opposition to the move in Congress, and Johnson, for the first time, had to take such opposition into account. If the *Times* story did not forestall his war plans, it complicated their public management. Ellsberg was not responsible for that leak. But after having obtained and digested Wheeler's report in late February 1967, he had taken a first step in the direction that would eventually make him notorious. Operating in parallel with the unknown leaker, he had arranged to meet with Bobby Kennedy, then the junior senator from New York, and conveyed the relevant memos to him. "This was the first time I can recall," writes Ellsberg, "ever showing a classified document to somebody outside the executive branch, not to mention a top-secret document intended for the eyes of the president."[2]

Ellsberg did not conceive of his meeting with Kennedy to be the scene of a leak; rather it was merely "informing a former and probably future high executive official." But the visible effects of the *New York Times* story on Johnson's decision making planted a seed in his mind: It led, in Ellsberg's telling, to an epiphany. Up to this point, he writes, "I had never questioned the assumption of many students of presidential power that secrecy is vital to preserve a president's range of options," and "I had instinctively accepted the ethos of my profession, the idea that leaking was always inherently bad, treacherous, or at best an unhelpful thing to do." But now, in the aftermath of the Wheeler-plan leak, he came to conclude that "I had been wrong" and that "leaking could be a patriotic and constructive act."[3]

Having put his toe in the water with RFK, Ellsberg now dived into the deep end, embarking on a plan to funnel out "a leak a day of a closely held secret." His idea was less to inform the public than to rattle the administration. "I hoped to convey to readers in the White House that the *Times*'s reporters were working directly from a high-level document they had acquired from a source within the administration."[4] A series of top-secret documents Ellsberg passed to Neil Sheehan of the *New York Times* wound up on the front page of the paper. The administration was indeed rattled, as a memo that appeared on the desk of Johnson's new secretary of defense, Clark Clifford, attests:

> The figures on enemy strength contained in the *New York Times* this morning are precisely the same as those in the last two columns of the attached table, Top Secret, Noforn [not to be shown to foreign nationals]. The CIA figures are from a March 1 memorandum prepared as part of the ongoing review of the situation in Vietnam. This document, copy attached, is classified secret. The last column of the table was added to demonstrate the accuracy of the figures Mr. Sheehan quotes from the NIE [National Intelligence Estimate]. This document is classified Top Secret. Somewhere in the government there has obviously been a horrendous security violation.[5]

Ellsberg continued his covert campaign for a time, watching its consequences unfold and all the while moving steadily toward the counterculture and away from the war-fighting culture of the Pentagon of which he had been such a paragon. Leaving a particularly deep mark on him was an encounter with a disciple of Mahatma Gandhi: "Her name was Janaki," writes Ellsberg, "She was from South India, the region of Madras. The red dust on her forehead was the 'footprint of God.' " Next to her, and to many others like her in the antiwar movement whom he began to seek out, Ellsberg increasingly felt himself in a moral shadow. His political transgressions as a cog in the war machine merged with his personal transgressions. "[Janaki] ate no meat and wore nothing from animals that had been slaughtered. I had, as it happened, a new leather briefcase, which I liked very much. 'It's beautiful," she said at one point. 'What was it?' "[6]

The shadow lengthened. As the war progressed, as Ellsberg's ties to the radical Left deepened, and as his attitude toward his past defense work shifted, his psyche began to unravel. Attending an antiwar gathering in Oakland, California, Ellsberg found himself shaken to the core as he listened to a speech recounting how members of the War Resisters League were committing civil disobedience and going to jail.

> I began to sob silently, grimacing under the tears, shoulders shaking. Janaki was to talk next, but I couldn't stay. I got up—I was sitting in the very last row in the amphitheater—and made my way down the back corridor till I came to a men's room. I went inside and turned on the light. It was a small room, with two sinks. I staggered over to the wall and slid down to the tile floor. I began to sob convulsively, uncontrollably. I wasn't silent anymore. My sobbing sounded like laughing, at other times like moaning. My chest was heaving. I had to gasp for breath . . .
>
> After about an hour I stopped sobbing. I stared blankly at the sinks across from me, thinking, not crying exhausted, breathing deeply. Finally I got up and washed my face. I gripped the sink and stared at the mirror. Then I sat down on the floor again to think some more. I cried again, a couple of times more, briefly, not so violently. What I had just heard . . . had put the question in my mind, What could I do, what should I be doing, to help end the war now that I was ready to go to prison for it?[7]

Ellsberg did mentally get ready for a stay in prison, but he did not resign from his position at Rand. Retaining his security clearance and his access to the flow of top-secret information about developments in the war, he cast about for a way to use his unique position to maximum effect. He had begun reading in this period the top-secret *History of U.S. Decision-Making on Vietnam Policy*. This remarkable study had been commissioned by McNamara in 1967 to generate a complete record, via analyses that were "encyclopedic and objective," of the steps and missteps, including his own, that had led the United States into what he himself had plainly recognized was a quagmire. A team directed by Leslie Gelb, later to join the *Times* as a reporter, editor, and columnist, produced three thousand pages of highly classified analysis of key decisions in the war accompanied by four thousand pages of documents, all of them also highly classified. The entire collection weighed sixty pounds and was bound together in forty-seven volumes.

Ellsberg had participated in the writing of one portion of the study, and what he found in the rest of the enormous trove of secrets only confirmed and deepened his by-now-radical views. The Pentagon Papers, as he saw them now, constituted "documentation of crimes: war crimes, crimes against the peace, mass murder."[8] "In terms of the UN charter and our own avowed ideals, [Vietnam] was a war of foreign aggression, American aggression."[9] It was immoral to deliberately prolong the killing "by a single additional day, or bomb, or death."[10] Ellsberg became determined to put the entire study on the record, with the expectation that it would open the public's eyes to the evil and help bring it to an end.

Removing sections of the study from the classified-documents safe in his office and surreptitiously, over a period of days, smuggling them out past the guards at Rand, he completed the massive job of photocopying the thousands of papers with the help of Anthony Russo, a Rand colleague who had also grown disillusioned with the war. He then set about to find the best way to put the classified collection forward. He approached Senator William Fulbright, chairman of the Foreign Relations Committee, but after prolonged discussions the foray came to naught. An approach to Senator George McGovern, sympathetic but fearful of jeopardizing his presidential aspirations, likewise went nowhere. The same with Senator Charles Mathias of Maryland. Finally, after months of frustration, Ellsberg made his fateful decision to turn the documents, by now copied into two full sets, over to Neil Sheehan of the *Times*.

———

"VIETNAM ARCHIVE: Pentagon Study Traces 3 Decades of Growing U.S. Involvement" was the headline that appeared over the lead story in the *New York Times* on Sunday, June 13, 1971, followed by six pages of related articles, along with excerpts from the Pentagon Papers themselves. Thus began the first installment in a projected series that day by day would lay out everything of importance in the McNamara studies. American journalism had arrived at a watershed. In the middle of a war the nation's premier newspaper had begun publishing top-secret documents obtained via an unexampled breach of security. The question mark now dangling over the newspaper was how the government would react. There was little doubt inside the *Times* that a response would be both quick in coming and draconian. In this they were nine-tenths right.

The initial reaction of the Nixon administration was, at least on that first day, impassive to the point of indifference. Attorney General John Mitchell read the *Times* that morning but did not bother summoning his internal security deputy, Robert Mardian, back from a trip to California. Nixon picked up the paper and noticed the front-page left-hand-column photograph of himself with his daughter Tricia at her wedding in the Rose Garden. The story on the right by Neil Sheehan seemed to escape his attention. The White House audio tapes make it evident that Nixon had either not read the story or that its importance had not registered. That changed only that Sunday afternoon when it came up in a phone conversation with Alexander Haig. Reviewing Vietnam casualty figures, Nixon prodded his military adviser with a revealing question: "Nothing else of interest in the world today?"[11]

Haig then proceeded to tell Nixon about the leak, calling it "a devastating—uh, security breach, of—of the greatest magnitude of anything I've seen." An hour later, talking with Secretary of State William Rogers, Nixon preferred to talk about Tricia's wedding before bringing up the leak, noting that the disclosed documents, from what he could tell, were likely to be far more embarrassing to his predecessors than they were to him: "And it's—uh, it's ver -it's hard on Johnson; it's hard on Kennedy; it's hard on [then–U.S. Ambassador to South Vietnam Henry Cabot] Lodge."[12]

Later in the afternoon, in a telephone conversation, Henry Kissinger at first suggested to Nixon that the impact of the leak would, in at least some respects, be benign or perhaps even beneficial: "In public opinion, it actually, if anything, will help us a little bit, because this is a gold mine of showing how the previous administration got us in there," and "it just shows massive mismanagement of how we got there, and it [unclear] pins it all on Kennedy and Johnson . . . they have nothing from our administration, so actually—I've read this stuff—we come out pretty well in it."[13]

But if the breach was not deemed politically damaging, both Kissinger and Nixon expressed alarm about its foreign policy ramifications. "It hurts us with Hanoi," said Kissinger, "because it just shows how far our demoralization has gone." Contemplating this point, Nixon grew livid, declaring "It's—it's treasonable, there's no question—it's actionable, I'm absolutely certain that this violates all sorts of security laws." Still, at least initially, Nixon was emphatically against taking action against the newspaper. The following evening he told his chief domestic adviser, John Ehrlichman, "Hell, I wouldn't prosecute the *Times*. My view is to prosecute the Goddamn pricks that gave it to 'em."[14] A mere six minutes later, on the telephone with Mitchell in a fateful conversation, Nixon reversed course.

"On consideration, we had only two choices," Nixon was later to write in his memoirs. "We could do nothing, or we could move for an injunction that would prevent the *New York Times* from continuing publication. Policy argued for moving against the *Times*; politics argued against it."[15] In his memoirs Henry Kissinger likewise emphasized the statesmanship of the president's approach, writing that Nixon had "rejected a partisan response. He took the view that the failure to resist such massive, and illegal, disclosures of classified information would open the floodgates, undermining the processes of government and the confidence of other nations." And this was not, Kissinger adds, an abstract notion: "We were at that very moment on the eve of my secret trip to Beijing," and China would inevitably regard the breach as a mark of American untrustworthiness.[16]

These summaries are an accurate reflection of how the denizens of the White House eventually came, as they looked back, to justify their course of action against the *Times*. But as descriptions of how the momentous decision to move against the paper was actually taken they are wholly deficient. The audio tape of Nixon's critical conversation on the phone with Mitchell reveals not statesmanlike "consideration" of "choices," but a cloud of garbled communication, with Mitchell taking the lead:

> MITCHELL: Hello, Mr. President.
>
> NIXON: What is your advice on that—uh, *Times* thing John? Uh—you w—you would like to do it?
>
> MITCHELL: Uh—I would believe so Mr. President, otherwise we will look a little foolish in not following through on our—uh, legal obligations, and—uh.
>
> NIXON: Has this ever been done before?
>
> MITCHELL: Uh—publication like this, or.
>
> NIXON: No [stammering] has the government ever done this to a paper before?
>
> MITCHELL: Oh yes—advising them of their—yes, we've done this before.
>
> NIXON: Have we—alright.
>
> MITCHELL: Yes sir. Uh, I would think that.
>
> NIXON: How—how do you go about it—you do it sort of low key?
>
> MITCHELL: Low key—you call them, and then—uh, send a telegram to confirm it.
>
> NIXON: Uh-huh, uh-huh—say that we're just—uh, we're examining the situation, and we just simply are putting you on notice.

MITCHELL: [Unclear] we're putting them on notice
that they're violating a statute, because we have a
communication from [Secretary of Defense] Mel Laird
as to the nature of the documents, and they fall within
a statute. Now, I don't know whether you've—you've
been—noticed it, but this thing was—uh, Mel is working.

NIXON: Henry [Kissinger]—Henry's on the other—I just—
he just walked in—I'll put him on the other line—go
ahead.

MITCHELL: Uh, Mel—uh, had a pretty good go up there
before the committee today on [the leak], and it's all
over town, and all over everything, and I think we'd
look a little silly if we just didn't take this low-key action
of advising them about the publication.

NIXON: Did Mel—did Mel take a fairly—uh, hard line on
it?

MITCHELL: Uh, yes, he—hahaha—gave a legal opinion,
and it was a violation of the law, which uh, of course
puts us at where we have to get to.

NIXON: Well look—look—as far as the *Times* is concerned,
hell they're our enemies—I think we just oughta do it.[17]

The "low-key action" that Nixon was asking Mitchell to take
against his "enemies" at the *Times* was of course not low key at all
and neither was it, as Mitchell incorrectly informed Nixon, something that the federal government had ever done before. Indeed it
is less than clear from the transcript of this and other conversations
whether Nixon even grasped that his attorney general, as a consequence of this discussion, would be asking for an injunction in the
courts to halt the presses. Thus did the Nixon administration in
impromptu fashion embark on an unprecedented course, pitting the
imperative of national security against the principle of freedom of
the press in an epic court battle. If Ellsberg was seeking maximum
publicity for his revelations, Nixon granted him his wish and more.

On Monday evening, June 14, the Justice Department duly noti-
fied the *Times* by telephone and a telegram to Arthur Ochs Sulzberger over Mitchell's signature:

> I have been advised by the Secretary of Defense that the
> material published in the *New York Times* on June 13, 14,
> 1971 captioned "Key Tests from Pentagon's Vietnam Study"
> contains information relating to the national defense of the
> United States and bears a top secret classification.
>
> As such, publication of this information is directly
> prohibited by the provisions of the Espionage law, Title 18,
> United States Code, Section 793.
>
> Moreover, further publication of information of this
> character will cause irreparable injury to the defense
> interests of the United States.
>
> Accordingly, I respectfully request that you publish no
> further information of this character and advise me that you
> have made arrangements for the return of these documents
> to the Department of Defense.[18]

Tuesday's papers had already hit the presses and they carried the
third installment of the series. That same day, Alexander Bickel, the
Yale constitutional scholar representing the *Times*, argued against
the injunction in a Manhattan federal court. Judge Murray Gurfein,
a Nixon appointee hearing his very first case as a judge, granted
the government the temporary restraining order it was seeking. On
Wednesday the paper ceased publishing the documents, reporting on its front page that it had been blocked by the government.
Other newspapers, beginning with the *Washington Post*, which had
obtained portions of the secret papers on their own from Ellsberg,
stepped in and began publishing, leading to parallel court proceedings in other jurisdictions.

With newspapers frozen by court injunctions for the first time
in our history, the matter rapidly moved up the rungs of the judicial

system. The Supreme Court heard oral argument on June 26. On June 30 it issued its landmark ruling in *The New York Times Co. v. United States*. In a six-to-three decision that produced nine separate opinions and a brief order, the Court removed the stays on publication and permitted the presses to roll once again.

The Court's ruling was greeted with euphoria in newsrooms across the country. At the *Times* a brief moment of "silent disbelief" was followed by "a great deal of hugging, handclapping and jumping up and down," one reporter there recorded. "It's a glorious day. We won it. We've all won it. We've won the right to print," were the words of A. M. Rosenthal, the paper's managing editor. "We are extremely gratified," announced Katherine Graham, publisher of the *Post*, "not only from the point of view of newspapers . . . but gratified from the point of view of government, good government, and the public's right to know."[19] But what was lost amid the celebrations, at least in many quarters, was the fact that the Court's ruling hardly issued the press a permit to publish leaked classified national defense information at its own discretion. Quite the contrary.

THE ISSUE BEFORE the Court in the *New York Times* case was prior restraint. Such a remedy, the majority held, is only available in extraordinary circumstances in which the government can demonstrate "grave and irreparable danger" to the public interest. Justice Brennan had emphatically stated, in his concurring opinion rejecting the government's request for such a restraint, that anything not meeting such a standard was insufficient: "The First Amendment tolerates absolutely no prior judicial restraints of the press predicated upon surmise or conjecture that untoward consequences may result."[20] The consequences had to be definite, the kind of near-certain calamity that met the threshold established by the Supreme Court four decades earlier in *Near v. Minnesota*, when it ruled that "no one would question but that a government might prevent actual obstruction to its recruiting service or the publication of the sailing dates of transports or the number and location of troops."[21] The material in the Pentagon Papers, however sensitive, was not of this acutely dangerous nature, or at least the government had failed to prove that it was, and there was no statute on the books indicating that Congress ever intended to enjoin publication of this less damaging sort.

But if prior restraint was truly an extraordinary remedy, inapplicable in this instance, prosecution *after* publication, the Court made plain, was something else again. On this point, a majority of the justices, four—or perhaps five if we add the vague formulation offered by Justice Thurgood Marshall—can be counted as concurring with Justice Byron White that if a case were to be brought against the *New York Times* under statutes forbidding the publication of military secrets, the matter might end quite differently.

Reviewing the legislative history of the Espionage Act, White noted that Congress "appeared to have little doubt that newspapers would be subject to criminal prosecution if they insisted on publishing information of the type that Congress had itself determined should not be revealed." White accompanied this observation with a warning to the *New York Times* and the other newspapers in the case that they were far from off the hook. National Defense Information, he stated, is protected from disclosures via publication by a variety of statutes, and "if any of the material here at issue is of this nature, the newspapers are presumably now on full notice of the position of the United States, and must face the consequences if they publish. I would have no difficulty in sustaining convictions under these sections [of the relevant statutes] on facts that would not justify . . . the imposition of a prior restraint."[22] In other words the presses of the *New York Times* could now roll, but the editors of the newspaper had already opened themselves up to criminal prosecution.

In the wake of the opinion, John Mitchell echoed this point, pledging to prosecute anyone who had violated the law—precisely, he said, as a majority of the Justices of the Supreme Court had deemed appropriate. In the event, however, the newspapers that published the Pentagon Papers were not indicted. The administration did ask Whitney North Seymour, Jr., the U.S. attorney in the Southern District of New York, to file charges against the *Times*, but Seymour demurred, believing it a lost cause as a New York jury would never vote to convict.[23]

That demurral was perhaps the trigger for the Watergate follies. Nixon, stymied and dismayed by the fact that Ellsberg and whoever else was in on what he believed was a conspiracy against his administration were getting away with it, embarked on another course. He established the "special investigations unit" to stanch further leaks. The illegal antics of the "plumbers," as they called themselves, which included a break-in at the office of Daniel Ellsberg's psychiatrist, were to figure prominently in the scandal that brought down his presidency.

The *Times* was not pursued any further by the Justice Department, but Ellsberg (along with Russo) was charged under the Espionage Act, and also for theft and conspiracy—the first indictment of a leaker in American history. After a manhunt that lasted several weeks, he turned himself in to the authorities on June 28, 1971. The trial did not commence until January 1973. Ellsberg stoutly maintained his innocence, insisting that "Congress had never passed any law that provided criminal sanctions against what I had done: copying and giving official 'classified' information without authorization to newspapers, to Congress, and to what our constitutional principles regard as our 'sovereign public.' "[24] This was far fetched. But whatever the contentions of Ellsberg and his attorneys, the issue in this instance was left formally unresolved. The charges against him and his codefendant were tossed out two months into the trial, when the activities of the plumbers came to light.

Ellsberg would seem to have achieved everything he had ever dreamed of. He would not be going to jail for the 115 years that he had calculated would be his maximum sentence. The Pentagon Papers were out, showing the "murder and the lying machine" for what they were. He had acquired international renown, appearing on prime-time network television, was in heavy demand as a speaker at antiwar rallies, and becoming in all respects a darling of the Left. But he remained deeply disappointed. The storm of controversy he created revolved not around the secrets he had disclosed but rather the legal and political issues raised by Nixon's war against the *Times*. "Mainstream interviewers and other commentators listened to me and treated me with respect. But neither these people nor the public at large could take seriously the warning I was trying to convey." It was nearly all for naught, from Ellsberg's point of view, for the Vietnam War raged on.

ELLSBERG'S disappointment returns us to the central issues raised by his case and the light it sheds on our current predicament in dealing with national security secrecy. To begin with, one reason the actual content of the Pentagon Papers did not particularly resonate in discussion of the war—and would probably have been rapidly forgotten by the public had Nixon not attempted to suppress their publication—was that, in contrast to leaks published by the *New York Times* and other news outlets over the last few years, no current operational secrets were disclosed. Indeed not a single one of the seven thousand pages of the McNamara studies that Ellsberg gave to the *Times* in 1971 was less than three years old. "It is all history," noted Justice William O. Douglas in his concurring opinion. "None of it is more recent than 1968." In fact, a significant portion of the Pentagon Papers dealt with developments during the Eisenhower and Truman administrations.

Although Ellsberg leaked with abandon, there were red lines that he had declined to cross. Even today, as radical as ever, he readily acknowledges that there are certain kinds of materials, "such as diplomatic negotiations, certain intelligence sources and methods, or various time-sensitive military-operational secrets, that warrant . . . strict secrecy."[25] Neil Sheehan, for his part, made an effort to assure that the documents in the collection would not compromise U.S.

codes. In other words, although they were classified top secret, the *Times* made at least a limited effort to assure itself that the revelations in the Pentagon Papers would not in themselves jeopardize national security in any immediate way and/or put American or South Vietnamese lives at risk.

Of course, as we have seen, the Nixon administration had a very different view of the matter. It contended vociferously that "irreparable harm" would follow disclosure of the documents. Yet demonstrating to the courts what exactly the harm would be turned out to be an impossible chore. In Gurfein's court, one of the government's critical witnesses on the matter of damage was Vice Adm. Francis J. Blouin. In cross-examination in open court he averred that "it would be a disaster to publish all of these other documents, let alone the ones that have already been published" and added that "any intelligence organization will derive a great deal of benefit from the articles that have already been published and there is even more juicy material in the other volumes."[26]

To explore the "juicy material" the court then held a closed session in which the admiral was pressed to elaborate. Floyd Abrams, representing the *Times* along with Bickel, recounts how

> it quickly became clear that [Blouin's] objections were so
> far-reaching and would affect so much of what routinely
> was published in the press that the government's reliance
> on his testimony asserting that particular portions of
> the Pentagon Papers could not be published was all but
> impossible. He referred to material that it "would be
> just better not to make public." He regretted that our
> withdrawal plans from Vietnam had been announced
> publicly by President Nixon, and concluded ruefully: "We
> just about live by the open book." . . . More generally, as
> he reviewed articles already published in the *Times*, he
> said "each article gives me the shivers." When the Court
> suggested to Blouin that much of what he objected to

seeing published was in fact public knowledge, having been
repeatedly revealed not only in numerous news reports but
in memoirs and other books, the admiral could only reply:
"I deplore much of what I read."[27]

Other government witnesses in higher courts were no less hapless
when it came to explaining harm. In his memoirs Nixon acknowledges that perhaps more than 95 percent of the material in the Pentagon Papers could have been declassified in 1971 without doing
harm, but that "we were all still worried about the other percent—
even if it were only 1 percent."[28] Solicitor General Erwin Griswold,
who argued the case for the government, pointed in court to eleven
specific items that would cause "great and irreparable harm to the
security of the United States," which he enumerated in a secret legal
brief. But writing in the *Washington Post* fifteen years later, he conceded, "I have never seen any trace of a threat to the national security
from the publication. Indeed, I have never seen it even suggested
that there was such an actual threat."[29]

THE PENTAGON PAPERS case presents a conundrum. The most
celebrated leaker in American history revealed what appear in retrospect to be unnecessary secrets. In attempting to check the flow,
the Nixon administration nonetheless persuaded seven Supreme
Court Justices that their dissemination would cause serious damage
to our national security, with Justice Harry Blackmun holding open
the possibility that their publication would lead to the prolongation
of the war and "the death of soldiers, the destruction of alliances,
the greatly increased difficulty of negotiation with our enemies, the
inability of diplomats to negotiate."[30] But none of these dire prospects came to pass. On its face history would seem to confirm the
standard narrative in which Ellsberg is the heroic whistle-blower and
the *Times*, along with the other newspapers that stepped forward to
publish the Pentagon Papers, were heroic as well, bravely carrying

out what Justice Hugo Black called in his opinion the press's paramount duty "to prevent any part of the government from deceiving the people and sending them off to distant lands to die of foreign fevers and foreign shot and shell."

Black's words are stirring, but they are not in fact the last judgment. If in retrospect it is clear that the release of the information contained in the Pentagon Papers did not pose any sort of tangible threat to American security, this does not mean that the breach did not cause any damage at all. The principal harm—not to be dismissed as trivial but also not requiring the sledgehammer treatment of a prior restraint in the courts or, for that matter, prosecution of any of the newspapers after the fact—appears to have been diplomatic embarrassment and a vivid demonstration to American allies and adversaries alike that the U.S. government was having severe difficulty keeping its secrets secret.

Both those forms of damage are no doubt ones that an open society, if it is to remain open, must accept. "The security of the Nation is not at the ramparts alone," wrote Judge Gurfein memorably as he removed the government's injunction on the *Times*. "Security also lies in the value of our free institutions. A cantankerous press, an obstinate press, an ubiquitous press must be suffered by those in authority in order to preserve the even greater values of freedom of expression and the right of the people to know."[31]

Yet even if one accepts Gurfein's latitudinarian view of the role of the press, there is another form of harm caused by Ellsberg's leak to which it is necessary to call attention. It was spelled out by Lyndon Johnson in a communication that was delivered to Nixon the day after the Pentagon Papers first appeared in the *Times*. As Kissinger is recorded saying on the White House tapes, "[former national security adviser Walt] Rostow called on behalf of Johnson. And he said that it is Johnson's strong view that this is an attack on the whole integrity of government. That if you—that if whole file cabinets can be stolen and then made available to the press, you can't have orderly government anymore."[32]

Johnson had obvious and powerful self-serving motives to want to keep the Pentagon Papers under wraps; they portrayed his conduct of the war in a deeply unflattering light. Yet whatever concern for his own place in history undergirded his message to Nixon, he was nonetheless touching here on one of the essential questions raised by Ellsberg's conduct. However much one might or might not sympathize with Ellsberg's motives, and however one might appraise the harm their disclosure wrought on American foreign policy, the fact is that at root Ellsberg's leak was an assault not only on orderly government but—in a polity that has an elected president and elected representatives—an assault on democratic self-governance itself.

For better or worse the American people in those years had elected Kennedy, Johnson, and Nixon; they had acted at the ballot box to make their leadership and policy preferences clear, including policies about secrecy. Yet here was a bureaucrat at the midlevel of officialdom, elected by no one and representing no one, entrusted with secrets he had pledged to the American people to protect, who was now abusing that trust to foist his own views on a government chosen by the people.

Ellsberg and his defenders maintain in his justification that the American people were being massively lied to by these presidents and that he brought those lies to light. But one must ask if in the main the revelations in the forty-seven volumes of the Pentagon Papers dramatically altered the picture of policy that Americans already had. Mel Gurtov was a Rand analyst who had contributed to the Pentagon Papers and who testified at Ellsberg's trial on his behalf. The main direction of his testimony, as Gurtov would later recollect, was to underscore that "all of the important information was *already* in the public domain." The secret materials, Gurtov continued, "merely lent further credence to what had already been said in the press and in academic studies."[33] In other words instead of painting a radically new picture, the Pentagon Papers merely put forward in detail something that by 1971 the American people already well knew: namely, that as the war was going badly in the

1960s, the Kennedy and Johnson administrations, in their attempt to retain public support for an intervention that they deemed critical to U.S. security, painted it as going well.

Ellsberg and his supporters, who came to view the American intervention in Vietnam as a war crime, call this bald lying. In fact, to those with a less fevered view of America's tragic effort to prevent South Vietnam from falling under Communist rule, it can just as easily be called leadership—leadership that in this instance failed. In this connection one has only to recollect the genuine bald lying with which Attorney General Francis Biddle contended in a formal opinion that Roosevelt's decision to provide destroyers to Great Britain in 1940 was not a violation of the law. Few complain about that momentous act of statesmanship today.

CAN ELLSBERG nevertheless be said to have been somehow, in defying our elected leaders, representing the general will of the American people? It is indisputable that over the course of the late 1960s and early 1970s a steadily growing percentage of Americans came to believe that the American entrance into Vietnam was a mistake. But opinion about how to walk the cat back from that mistake was another matter. As late as 1968, with more than half a million troops in Vietnam, a Gallup poll showed that only 23 percent of Americans identified themselves as "doves"; 61 percent called themselves "hawks."[34] In the period between September 1968 and September 1970, sentiment swung sharply against the war, with the percentage of Americans favoring withdrawal rising from 19 percent to a majority of 55 percent.[35] In a May 1971 poll, on the eve of the Pentagon Papers revelations, a solid majority of Americans—68 percent—favored pulling out of Vietnam by the end of the year.

But that is not the end of the matter. The same respondents in May 1971, when asked if they would favor an immediate withdrawal "if it threatened the lives or safety of United States POWs held by North Vietnam," changed their minds; under those conditions only a mere 11 percent favored pulling out.[36] In other words withdrawal of the kind Ellsberg and his compatriots in the antiwar movement were proposing—a withdrawal that would have meant leaving our captive servicemen to an unnamed fate—was overwhelmingly rejected by the American people. What is more the only poll that ultimately counts in a democracy takes place on election day. In 1972, with the American people having had more than a year to absorb whatever lessons were contained in the Pentagon Papers, George McGovern, the candidate favoring immediate withdrawal from Vietnam, was trounced by Nixon in one of the greatest landslides of American history.

Ellsberg defends his departure from the norms of our democracy by calling it an honorable act of civil disobedience. He came to embrace Gandhian principles of nonviolence, and he also fell under the influence, as he recounts, of Henry David Thoreau's essay, "On the Duty of Civil Disobedience." He came to believe, as Thoreau did, that "obedience to leaders in an unjust cause was itself a choice, a wrong choice." He came to regard the Pentagon Papers as "the U.S. equivalent of the Nuremberg war-crimes documents."[37] He maintained that in resisting a war that was "naked of any shred of legitimacy from the beginning," the "best thing that the best young men can do with their lives is to go to prison."[38]

It was of course every bit Ellsberg's right as a citizen to reach any conclusion he wished about Vietnam. It was also undeniably every bit his right as a human being to follow his conscience and break signed confidentiality agreements, flout laws punishing the disclosure of sensitive national defense information, and disclose each and every secret that he knew about the war. Such conduct is the essence of civil disobedience. But with civil disobedience must come consequences, and these Ellsberg assiduously sought to avoid.

"Under a government which imprisons unjustly," wrote Thoreau, "the true place for a just man is also a prison." But Ellsberg was not merely a leaker, he was an *anonymous* leaker. As often as he declares in his memoir that he was prepared to risk life in prison in pursuit of his principles, in actual fact he took numerous steps to avoid going to jail. Only on the way to surrender to the authorities did Ellsberg publicly declare that "I acted of course at my own jeopardy, and I'm ready to answer to all the consequences of my decisions."[39] But that was a last-minute pose of heroism in the face of inevitable arrest; in actual fact he had been dodging the legal consequences of his decisions for years. To halt what he regarded as deception by the U.S. government, he had engaged in his own extensive deception that included lying on numerous occasions to longtime colleagues and friends. After the Pentagon Papers came out in the *Times*, he went "underground"—his word—dodging the FBI by moving from one location to the next and communicating via randomly chosen phone booths. Ellsberg asserts that his leaking was "a patriotic and constructive act."[40] In fact, it was civil disobedience without accountability and, as such, not a contribution to the "sovereign public" but an assault upon it.

Ellsberg must of course be given a measure of credit for, before turning the Pentagon Papers over to Neil Sheehan, having approached a number of U.S. senators and asked them to put forward the revelations that he believed would bend the river of history. Senators, after all, have authority vested in them by the electorate. Under our Constitution they can say whatever they wish on the floor of the Senate, and that includes disclosing sensitive classified information, without facing criminal prosecution (although they could well be subjected to sanctions by the Senate itself). But the senators whom Ellsberg importuned all declined to help, and they did so for reasons that are significant.

In January 1971, when Ellsberg turned to him, George McGovern was embarking on another run for the presidency. However sympathetic he was to Ellsberg's cause, he recognized that dropping classified military and intelligence documents into the public domain would hardly have helped him gain votes in the political center. In other words, by rejecting Ellsberg's request he was attempting, as any successful candidate must in a democracy, to reflect and to follow the will of the American public as he perceived it. Senator Fulbright, after an initial bout of enthusiasm, also demurred for reasons that were explained to Ellsberg by one of Fulbright's aides: "If Fulbright leaked the papers or went ahead and distributed or published them, he could be charged with having jeopardized the ability to get classified material from the executive, not only for the [Foreign Relations] committee or himself but for the entire Senate."[41]

To put it another way Fulbright declined to follow Ellsberg's bidding because he did not want to violate the rules by which a representative body in our democracy properly handles secrets, and he did not want to live with the consequences of violating those rules, which would not have been personal but institutional: a diminution of cooperation among the branches of government, a diminution of Congress's ability to oversee the executive branch, and a blow to democratic self-government at a moment when it was already under strain.

McGovern and Fulbright chose to remain inside the democratic order. Ellsberg in the end chose to act outside of it. Even if one inescapably finds something admirable in the tenacity with which he pursued his goal, given the cloak of anonymity behind which he hid it is also fair to call him a rogue. He had taken the law into his own hands and was prepared to do so again, which is precisely why he deserved to be stopped and punished. "There was nothing paranoid in the suspicion of President Nixon and Henry Kissinger that I might well put out further classified documents that would threaten their Vietnam policy," explains Ellsberg in his memoirs.[42] In the face of such a declaration it would seem unarguable that a democratic society had every right—even an obligation—to prevent him from striking again.

YET IF ELLSBERG was a lawbreaker and a transgressor of democratic norms, he was by no means the only or the worst in the rogue's gallery of those years of crisis. That honor must be awarded to Richard Nixon. One can readily sympathize with the agony Nixon was suffering as he attempted to end a war he had not chosen to start while being relentlessly hammered by a liberal establishment that only a few years earlier had been avid cheerleaders for the intervention. But this hardly can excuse his abdication of his basic responsibility to observe the law. His decision to go after the *Times* for publishing the Pentagon Papers—if "decision" is the right word for his grunted acquiescence to Mitchell's suggestions in their fateful telephone exchange—appears in retrospect to have been the height of irresponsibility: Draconian action was taken without any deliberation at all.

Nixon's subsequent actions in response to the leak brought him to naked criminality of a sort that, in its malicious intentions and appalling consequences, dwarfed whatever Ellsberg had done. Indeed, it was neither Ellsberg's revelations nor the antiwar movement as a whole that fatally undercut the American effort to safeguard South Vietnam. Rather the undercutting was done by Nixon himself as he secretly worked the levers of government bodies from the IRS to the CIA to the plumbers in unlawful ways. His petty calculations in response to the Ellsberg leak, which segued seamlessly into the illegal decisions of the Watergate affair, led to the collapse of presidential authority and paved the way for the fall of South Vietnam and Cambodia to brutal Communist regimes, with dire consequences for millions.

If our country has had an especially unhappy history wrestling with secrets over the succeeding four decades, Richard Nixon is the major reason why. No other president in American history has given secrecy such a bad name.

CHAPTER 10

ELLSBERG'S EPIGONES

"I'VE LEARNED," SAID the *New York Times* reporter Hedrick Smith the day after the first installment of the Pentagon Papers was published, "that never again will I trust any source in the government."[1] Here in this one sentence was one of the more doleful legacies of Nixon's presidency. For Smith had arrived at this point of unshakable skepticism before the truly massive lying by government in the Watergate scandal had even begun. By the time Nixon's presidency was over, a pervasive suspicion of those in power had taken hold of the country. In 1958, 24 percent of the population felt "you cannot trust the government to do right." By 1973 the percentage had more than doubled and has remained elevated ever since.[2]

The journalistic profession was particularly colored by the cynicism. And by that same time a new breed of superstar reporter became the model that journalists and aspiring journalists and generations of journalists not yet born longed to become. Out were ink-stained wretches. In were dashing investigative reporters like Carl Bernstein and Bob Woodward, garnering renown, best-selling books, glamorous depictions in feature films like *All the President's Men*, all gained while ostensibly safeguarding the public interest. It was a heady brew that proved impossible to resist.

There was also a political backdrop to the change: the shifting political biases of the press. We can readily dismiss the often-drawn caricature of left-wing journalists insidiously toiling to undermine U.S. policy via slanted reporting. In fact press bias is most often something more subtle, with journalists in the 1960s and 1970s swimming in the same "adversary culture"—to use Lionel Trilling's phrase—as everyone else, absorbing a new set of presuppositions fostered by the antiwar movement and forgetting (what the younger among them never knew) the old presuppositions of the Cold War.

By the time the Pentagon Papers broke, the journalistic profession was also in the midst of a profound social transformation. "One's impression is that twenty years and more ago," observed Daniel Patrick Moynihan in *Commentary* in 1971, "the preponderance of the 'working press' (as it liked to call itself) was surprisingly close in origins and attitudes to working people generally. They were not Ivy Leaguers. They now are or soon will be. Journalism has become, if not an elite profession, a profession attractive to elites."[3]

With elite status came the elite's preferences and politics, which in the Vietnam era was very much that of the counterculture. The press, Moynihan continued, was growing "more and more influenced by attitudes genuinely hostile to American society and American government."[4] In a private memorandum Moynihan provided to President Nixon in late 1970, he wrote that the *New York Times* "has a newsroom still predominantly made up of old time liberal Democrats who can be counted on to report a story in a straightforward manner, but every time one of these goes and is replaced by a new recruit from the *Harvard Crimson* or whatever, the Maoist faction on W. 43rd Street gets one more vote. No one else applies."[5]

Moynihan was engaging in his beloved Irish hyperbole, but the valid underlying point is that a fundamental change of outlook was under way and by the time the 1970s were over, the notion of the "patriotic press" was dead and buried. In its place was a new kind of journalism hell bent on demystifying, deconstructing, and, on more than a few occasions, denigrating the U.S. government, especially its conduct of intelligence and foreign affairs.

The climate was such that government itself, particularly Congress, was also drawn into the act, engaging in periodic bouts of self-revelation extending into self-flagellation, as segments of the nation's elite turned against practices that only a few years earlier failed to raise eyebrows. The adversary culture penetrated the executive branch, too. The Pentagon Papers and the Watergate scandal spawned a new and compelling bureaucratic archetype of their own: the government official as intrepid whistle-blower. Indeed Ellsberg was to leaking what Elvis Presley was to rock and roll, and before long a whole series of imitators were vying for attention. Ever since the Nixon presidency the two new archetypes—the rock-star leaker and the rock-star reporter—have operated in tandem, turning the disclosure of secrets from a cottage industry into mass production and pushing it toward hitherto-unthinkable extremes.

The journalist Seymour Hersh was one such rock-star reporter. He began his career as a partisan, a press secretary in 1968 to the antiwar presidential candidate Eugene McCarthy, and a partisan he remained. Nonetheless that same year he was hired by the *New York Times* and soon broke the story of the My Lai massacre, in which hundreds of civilians were slaughtered in a South Vietnamese hamlet in the aftermath of the Tet Offensive. In late 1974 Hersh carried off another spectacular journalistic coup, with a front-page banner headline over his story in the *Times*: "Huge CIA Operation Reported in U.S. Against Antiwar Forces, Other Dissidents in Nixon Years."[6] This article was a trigger for the Church and Pike Committee hearings that brought to light even more abuses, including much of the material known as the "Family Jewels," the report ordered by CIA director James R. Schlesinger and drafted by his deputy (and soon to be director), William Colby, summarizing all activities engaged in by the agency conducted outside of its legal charter in the period from March 1959 to May 1973.

Here, in the lurid disclosures of collaboration with the Mafia in assassination plots on Fidel Castro, experimentation with LSD on unwitting subjects, and domestic surveillance, were more CIA-self-inflicted wounds, with salt openly poured in them by the congressional hearings. The cumulative effect was severe damage to the CIA's standing with the public. In an atmosphere of rampant suspicion of government, secrecy came to be seen, in Colby's words, "not as a tool necessary for the practice of intelligence, but as a device by which intelligence could hide its bungles and mask its wicked activities."[7] Falling under intense scrutiny, the agency dissolved its clandestine mystique and became, for better or worse, the most transparent intelligence service in the history of the world.

IT WAS IN and around this season of self-revelation that the first of a series of Ellsberg epigones appeared and helped accelerate the dissolution. Victor Marchetti was a CIA operative who quit the agency in late 1969 and embarked on a career of exposing its inner workings, appearing frequently on television and radio shows, giving interviews to the press and authoring articles highly critical of his former employer for publications like the *Nation*. He also wrote (with John D. Marks, a former State Department intelligence official) a book, *The CIA and the Cult of Intelligence*, that laid bare many of the secrets with which he had become acquainted over the course of a career that spanned a decade and a half and encompassed a wide variety of assignments, including a stint at the CIA's pinnacle as executive assistant to CIA director Richard Helms, where he had access to the agency's most sensitive intelligence.[8] The manuscript detailed operations and activities of the agency in locations ranging from Indochina to Angola, with portions touching on the very thing that the CIA held most dear: intelligence sources and methods.

But before Marchetti's book could be published, he ran headlong into a wall. As a condition of employment at the CIA back in 1955, he had signed a secrecy agreement that read in part:

> I do solemnly swear that I will never divulge, publish or
> reveal either by word, conduct, or by any other means, any
> classified information, intelligence or knowledge except
> in the performance of my official duties and in accordance
> with the laws of the United States, unless specifically
> authorized in writing, in each case, by the Director of
> Central Intelligence or his authorized representatives.

Upon retiring from the agency in 1969—in case he had forgotten what he had signed a decade and a half earlier—Marchetti was asked to swear to an oath, which he also did, reiterating the promises he had made at the beginning of his agency career.

Getting wind of the news that Marchetti had signed a contract to write a book, the CIA first contemplated prosecuting Marchetti under the espionage statutes. But the likelihood that even more secrets would spill out led it in another direction. It sought to enforce the secrecy agreements Marchetti had signed, obtaining a temporary restraining order and sending federal marshals to his door to notify him that he was forbidden to show his manuscript to anyone, including his publisher, until the CIA had examined it first.

Here, once again, in other words, was another governmental attempt at imposing a prior restraint. But the circumstances differed markedly from the Pentagon Papers case. The government was not seeking to block Marchetti's publisher, Alfred A. Knopf, as it had sought to block Ellsberg's, the *New York Times*. Rather it was pursuing Marchetti himself, not in his capacity as a writer, it maintained, but as an ex–government employee with a web of contractual obligations to his former employer.

Challenging the injunction in the court of appeals, Marchetti contended that the government, having failed to meet the very heavy burden of proving he would cause irreparable harm to the nation, was imposing a "forbidden prior restraint upon freedom of the press." But the court did not agree. While concurring with Marchetti that the First Amendment limits the extent to which the United States can impose secrecy constraints on its employees, it only precludes barring them from discussing *un*classified or previously disclosed material. *Active* secrets were something else.

Citizens like Marchetti, continued the court, "have the right to criticize the conduct of our foreign affairs." But at the same time the government has a "right to secrecy." Indeed it has a "duty to strive for internal secrecy about the conduct of governmental affairs in areas in which disclosure may reasonably be thought to be inconsistent with the national interest."[9] As far as Marchetti's book manuscript was concerned, this meant, said the court, that the CIA had to act promptly to approve or disapprove any material that he presented for clearance, and he would be entitled to have a judge review the agency's decisions.

That is precisely what transpired. CIA security experts combing through the draft that Marchetti now submitted found 339 separate passages they wanted to excise, amounting to between 15 and 20 percent of the book. A second court battle ensued over this censorship, and the CIA partially backed down. In the end, the published version of *The CIA and the Cult of Intelligence* contained only 168 elisions, which Knopf indicated by displaying blank lines where the CIA had been successful in suppressing information and bold text to indicate where the agency had retreated.

But the outcome hardly satisfied civil libertarians. Indeed they were outraged that the Supreme Court had declined to hear an appeal by Marchetti and strike down the CIA's right of prepublication review. "The Supreme Court's refusal to intervene against the CIA's extensive censorship," wrote Tom Wicker in his *Times* op-ed column, "validates one of the most extraordinary prior restraints in American history." The decision "greatly enhances the ability of the Government to classify and withhold information from the public"; it will exert a "chilling effect" on government employees and former employees "who may wish to come forward with classified or 'classifiable' information they consider vital to the public interest."[10]

That "chilling effect" on government employees, of course, was to Wicker a very bad thing. But Wicker's judgment here was itself a remarkable novelty. Not many years earlier, the notion that disaffected CIA operatives should be protected from the legal consequences of breaking their oaths and disclosing classified information at their own discretion would have been almost universally regarded as perverse, a complete reversal of the proper order of things. Here was yet another marker showing how much the culture had changed. But the imperatives of statecraft did not change with it, and neither did the law.

THE SUPREME COURT declined to consider Marchetti's appeal, but soon a similar case, with a twist, made its way into the hallowed chambers. Frank W. Snepp III was a rapidly rising star at the CIA. During his eight years in the agency, most of them spent in Vietnam, he worked as a debriefer of agents, an interrogator of captured Viet Cong guerrillas, and a top analyst of North Vietnamese strategy. Passionately engaged in the effort to salvage the American and South Vietnamese position, Snepp was in Saigon through the war's final days. He was among the last CIA officers to depart the American Embassy roof via helicopter when Saigon fell on April 29, 1975, and was horrified by the failure, as the United States rushed to evacuate its own personnel, to rescue its many Vietnamese friends, who were certain to pay a stiff price for their cooperation with our war effort once the South fell into Communist hands.

The picture of the American Embassy in its final days, Snepp was later to write, "was a kaleidoscope of fractured nightmares . . . an agent flinging himself suicidally against the bolted gates . . . batons smashing fingers locked around the grillwork [*sic*] . . . a Vietnamese mother being hoisted over the parapet by well-meaning guards oblivious that her child has just been swept away by the mobs below."[11] Among those forsaken and left behind was Snepp's own Vietnamese lover, who then took her own life along with that of their infant son.

This disastrous final chapter of the war was the subject of Snepp's scathing portrait of America's betrayal in *Decent Interval*, published by Random House in 1977 to wide acclaim.[12] Like Marchetti, Snepp had signed various secrecy agreements with the agency when he joined in 1968. But unlike Marchetti, who ultimately submitted his manuscript for CIA review, Snepp went in another direction. He had signed a promise not to publish any information drawn from his CIA employment "without specific prior approval by the Agency"[13] and then broke his word. Even while telling his former supervisors in the agency that he would be submitting the manuscript to them for review, he was planning to do otherwise, employing the clandestine tradecraft of espionage to accomplish his goal.

To arrange meetings with his editor at Random House, he used Bernadette Longford, his literary agent's secretary (and another of his lovers), as a "cutout." Whenever "a face-to-face was required, she'd call [the agent's] office and direct him to a random pay phone to pick up precise instructions. Street-corner rendezvous were out . . . due to the threat of surveillance. All our meetings would be confined to a handful of vest-pocket parks in midtown Manhattan, and depending on the time of day and where the shadows were longest, Bernie would make the choice for us, always reserving the decision to the last minute to minimize the risk of our being discovered."[14] When *Decent Interval* was published, fifteen thousand copies were shipped to bookstores, not one of which had ordered it in advance because its existence had been so tightly guarded. A letter from Random House explaining the circumstances followed.

These methods did not succeed in keeping the CIA in the dark, for Snepp's own "friends" within the agency with whom he remained in touch were reporting on him. As it had done with both Marchetti and Ellsberg, the agency pressed the Justice Department to impose a prior restraint on Snepp, complete with an order to seize all copies of *Decent Interval*. But the Justice Department, now staffed by more liberal Carter appointees, declined to take a step certain to excite the wrath of the press. But they did agree to seek sanctions against Snepp for violating his agreements.

On the surface the case was just an ordinary breach of contract: Snepp had made a promise that he would submit his book to pre-publication review, which he had baldly violated. Where the case became extraordinary, and rubbed uncomfortably against the First Amendment, was the government's contention, taken up by the Supreme Court in response to Snepp's appeal of lower court deci-sions, that even if *no* classified information was revealed by the book (a contention to which the government had agreed for the purposes of litigation), it still had "caused the United States irreparable harm and loss." The CIA's position was that a former intelligence agent's publication of unreviewed material was detrimental simply because it was unreviewed. The problem was not the information itself, which might or might not be sensitive, but the demonstration to foreign countries and foreign individuals that a process vital to their own security had disintegrated.

This was the gravamen of testimony in federal court by Adm. Stansfield Turner, Jimmy Carter's CIA director. The breakdown of orderly procedures governing the publication of secrets had led "a number of sources," complained Turner, to "discontinue work with us. We have had more sources tell us that they are very nervous about continuing work with us. We have had very strong complaints from a number of foreign intelligence services with whom we con-duct liaison, who have questioned whether they should continue exchanging information with us, for fear it will not remain secret."[15]

This argument held sway, and the court found that Snepp had "willfully, deliberately and surreptitiously breached his position of trust with the CIA." He had also "deliberately misled CIA offi-cials into believing that he would submit the book for prepublication clearance." The potential damage from such conduct was clear:

> When a former agent relies on his own judgment about
> what information is detrimental, he may reveal information

that the CIA—with its broader understanding of what may expose classified information and confidential sources—could have identified as harmful. In addition to receiving intelligence from domestically based or controlled sources, the CIA obtains information from the intelligence services of friendly nations and from agents operating in foreign countries. The continued availability of these foreign sources depends upon the CIA's ability to guarantee the security of information that might compromise them and even endanger the personal safety of foreign agents.[16]

In the face of Snepp's intentional transgression, the court imposed the remedy sought by the government: Snepp was forced "to disgorge the benefits of his faithlessness." He had to surrender to the government his $120,000 advance and all subsequent royalties from his book. He was also permanently enjoined from distributing any of his writings about his years in the CIA unless they were screened in advance.

MARCHETTI AND SNEPP were both strong judicial victories for secrecy; indeed, after the Snepp case came to a close, Admiral Turner threw a champagne reception for the government lawyers who had run the show. But was the Snepp case also, if not a Pyrrhic victory, something close? For even as it strengthened the rule of law by protecting the integrity of the entire secrecy system, did it not also serve to undermine the very thing that a secrecy system in an open society depends upon most: the confidence of the people living under its strictures?

A strong case can be made—and Snepp made it in a second book, *Irreparable Harm*—that the CIA was itself abusing the secrecy system, leaking classified documents to favored journalists even as it was seeking to muzzle him and pursuing only those leakers who were causing it embarrassment while letting others, more politically palatable, violate the rules with impunity. Thus he pointed to a whole series of works by low- and high-ranking agency officers that appeared in this period that, like his own, were not cleared by the CIA yet did not result in litigation, let alone the forfeiture of royalties. Indeed, when Miles Copeland, another ex-CIA man, published *Without Cloak or Dagger* in 1974, he boasted in his preface of his circumvention of agency censorship: "I have been associated with intelligence agencies long enough to realize how futile it would be for one such as myself to request official permission to publish even the most antiseptic book. So I have been my own censor, and if I have included cases and information that have until now been held under tight security wraps, it is because I cannot accept the reasons for their continued secrecy."[17] Neither Copeland nor his publisher, Simon & Schuster, suffered an iota of juridical discomfort from the transgression. If the CIA's selective pursuit of leakers did not blow a hole in the court cases against Marchetti and Snepp, it did blow a hole in the sense of justice that has to underpin law if it is to be respected and observed.

Still, even if the CIA's behavior must be regarded dimly, this hardly obviates the need for secrecy itself—and a consistently enforced system of rules and laws to preserve secrecy—for the successful conduct of intelligence. And it certainly does not vindicate Snepp's decision to violate his oath. As he himself acknowledges, "I made no attempt at a reasoned defense, only an honest one"—namely that "if the Agency could officially leak to the press to whitewash its role in Vietnam, it had forfeited the right to censor me in the name of national security."[18] Sympathize as much as one might with Snepp's position, he was taking the law into his own hands, a position always difficult to admire, and made even more difficult in this instance by the former CIA agent's melodramatic self-justification, as he puffed himself up into a victim of "McCarthyism" fending off law-enforcement officials as "terrifying" as if they were wearing "swastikas" on their "epaulets."[19]

At the end of the day, even if the CIA was undercutting itself by acting inconsistently, Admiral Turner was right in contending that the "logical extension of the Ellsberg-Snepp syndrome is that any of our 210 million citizens is entitled to decide what should not be classified information,"[20] a condition that would lead to mayhem. Attorney General Griffin Bell was also right in calling attention to the fact that "several hundred other agents recently had been discharged in a purge of the CIA's clandestine service. If Snepp was allowed to flout the secrecy provisions, other ex-agents were likely to follow his lead"[21] and a flood of secrets would be unleashed.

GRIFFIN BELL was not speculating idly. For the flood of secrets from ex-agents was in fact already under way. Marchetti and Snepp, whatever their transgressions, had in the end chosen to play by the rules: Marchetti submitted his book for review, and Snepp obeyed the court and duly surrendered his profits. Philip Agee, yet a third Ellsberg epigone, was something else, a renegade who got away with treason.

Agee was born of prosperity and privilege in Florida. Educated in a Jesuit high school and graduating from Notre Dame in 1956, he joined the CIA the following year. Three years of paramilitary training followed before he was dispatched to Ecuador, Uruguay, and Mexico to work undercover in various capacities. In the course of his work he fell in love with Angela Camargo Seixas, a Brazilian student activist who had been arrested and tortured by the authorities, and worshipped at the altar of Che Guevara.

By this point Agee's political conversion was well under way, and in 1968 he quit the agency. Agee told the story of his left turn in his 1975 book, *Inside the Company: CIA Diary*, in which he lamented his choice of careers: "I became the servant of the capitalism I rejected. I became one of its secret policemen. The CIA, after all, is nothing more than the secret police of American capitalism, plugging up leaks in the political dam night and day so that shareholders of U.S. companies operating in poor countries can continue enjoying the rip-off."[22] To unplug the political dam his book came garlanded with a twenty-two-page list identifying by name and position approximately 250 CIA officers and foreign agents working undercover for the United States.

To avoid meeting the fate that befell Marchetti's book, Agee published his abroad, in Great Britain, where he had fled fearing prosecution in the United States. His fears were not ungrounded. In London the year before his exposé came out, he had announced the start of "a campaign to fight the United States CIA wherever it is operating" and declared his intent "to expose CIA officers and agents and to take the measures necessary to drive them out of the countries where they are operating."[23] His modus operandi was to select a particular country, travel there, use his connections and insider knowledge to ferret out undercover CIA operatives, and then recruit and train local sympathizers to do the same.

Among those whom Agee's followers identified was Richard Welch, the CIA station chief in Athens, who had worked under diplomatic cover as the embassy's first secretary. A few weeks later Welch was shot down on his front doorstep by three masked gunmen belonging to November 17, the Greek terrorist group. Another such outrage occurred in Jamaica, where an American Embassy official was subjected to an armed attack immediately following his identification as a CIA official by Agee's associate and "fellow journalist" Louis Wolf, editor of a publication, the *Covert Action Information Bulletin*, dedicated to outing CIA agents.

Pressure brought to bear by the CIA led to Agee's expulsion from residence in Britain, France, Italy, and the Netherlands, and he ended up settling in Cuba, where he received generous assistance in his writing career from the Cuban intelligence service, which was all too happy to help.[24] His passport was revoked in 1979, an action Agee litigated from afar all the way to the Supreme Court. But remarkably Agee was never brought to justice for actions that went well beyond a violation of trust and entered into what George H. W. Bush was later to call outright treason. Not that the Ford administration, in the aftermath of Welch's murder, declined to give the matter serious consideration. Indeed in early 1977 Richard Thornburgh, Ford's attorney general, had warned Agee that he was the subject of a criminal investigation, and that if he returned to the United States he might face prosecution for having illegally divulged classified information.

But no sooner did Jimmy Carter assume office than the idea was dropped. The ostensible reason for the decision, according to Benjamin Civiletti, the new head of Justice's criminal division, was that after a lengthy investigation "no grounds for prosecution had been found."[25] A CIA spokesman chimed in, declaring quite implausibly, but fishing for support in Congress for tough new antileak legislation, that "we don't have laws protecting classified information."[26] But this was bunk.

It is true that if Agee had been indicted, successfully extradited to the United States, and put on trial for violations of the Espionage Act, a conviction would not have been assured. He would no doubt have insisted to the jury, as the *Times* summarized his position at the time, "that he was providing a public service in alerting citizens to the type of clandestine activity that the agency was undertaking and that many of the operations he wrote about had been either illegal or improper."[27] But the elements of an offense under the Espionage Act, including Agee's disclosure of sensitive information with the all important "reason to believe" that the information could be used to the injury of the United States, were plainly there. Indeed, numerous statements by Agee had demonstrated precisely that state of mind.

One reason the Carter administration declined to prosecute might be something that we tend to forget—namely the extraordinarily sympathetic reception Agee's actions received, at least initially.* Typical was a celebratory review of *Inside the Company* in the

---

*The intelligence expert Thomas Powers offers another explanation. He suggests that Agee would have been "a prime candidate for prosecution under the espionage laws if it weren't for the legal tangle the agency had created for itself when it planned or carried out 'illegal acts' against him." See Thomas Powers, "The Enemy of the Agency," *New York Times*, August 2, 1987, 7.

Times, which, without saying a word—critical or otherwise—about the peril in which the author had placed his fellow Americans, declared that the book's "most valuable purpose is that of exposure, with Mr. Agee playing the 'whistle-blower' who brings heretofore secret information into the light of public revelation" and that its "greatest service is informing . . . public opinion in convincing and disturbing detail" about the misdeeds of the CIA.[28]

The author of yet another *Times* book review from those years, referring to the works of Marchetti, Snepp, and Agee, opined that "so far we have had three defectors from the Central Intelligence Agency, and by my calculation we need 300 more."[29] The problem, as the reviewer saw it, was that "to root out the undergrowth in our democracy will require that at least that many former CIA officers come forward to write about their secret activities since 1947." Investigative journalists alone, continued the reviewer, would not suffice to reveal all the transgressions of the U.S. government, for "even a Seymour Hersh or a Jack Anderson cannot expose enough of what we need to know."

To be fair, by the close of the 1970s, after American diplomats were taken hostage by Islamic revolutionaries in Iran and rumors began to circulate that Agee would travel to Tehran to take part in their trial as an "expert witness," attitudes at the paper became slightly more ambivalent. While a *Times* editorial could still be found lambasting the State Department for its "lawless revocation" of Agee's passport[30] (the Supreme Court was shortly to rule that the revocation was in fact entirely lawful), a subsequent editorial denounced Agee for bringing "discredit on those who want to expose CIA misdeeds," like the *Times* itself.[31]

By this point, of course, the CIA and many in Congress were in an uproar over Agee's malefactions; the tally of CIA officers exposed by him had reached more than one thousand. The result was legislation, the Intelligence Identities Protection Act, which provided prison terms of up to ten years for government employees who revealed the identities of American spies living under cover.

In a provision aimed at Agee's acolyte Louis Wolf, it also punished anyone outside the government, including journalists, who identified agents as part of a "pattern of activities" that would "impair or impede" U.S. intelligence operations.

The *New York Times*, siding with civil liberties organizations, including the ACLU, volubly opposed the bill, calling it a "dumb defense of intelligence" and worse, "legislative folly . . . forbidden by the Constitution."[32] The bill passed both houses by overwhelming margins and was signed into law by Ronald Reagan in 1982. Along with atomic secrets and communications intelligence, the identity of CIA operatives was now one of the three realms to enjoy a special level of legal protection. The new law had an immediate impact on Agee. Fearing the long arm of American law, he ceased his campaign of disclosure and switched careers, opening a travel agency in Cuba that he operated until his death in 2008.

THE Intelligence Identities Protection Act had solved one set of problems; but even as the government was wrestling with Agee, another very different kind of security lapse was thrust to the fore. The campaign against secrecy launched by Daniel Ellsberg was to reach its reductio ad absurdum: disclosure for the sake of disclosure, and of the most potentially damaging sort of all: publication of a detailed recipe for building a thermonuclear bomb. The logic of revelation became: If it can be said, it must be said, and if it is known by some, it must be known by all. In early 1979 three men on the fringes of the far Left—Erwin Knoll, Samuel Day, Jr., and Howard Morland—set this particular boulder rolling into the valley.

Knoll was the editor of the *Progressive*, a Wisconsin-based radical magazine founded in 1909 that stands steadfastly, as it has long advertised itself, "against militarism, the concentration of power in corporate hands, and the disenfranchisement of the citizenry." A refugee from Austria, with a journalistic career that included stints at the *Washington Post* and the Newhouse News Service, Knoll was an adherent of a pacifism so absolute that he regarded even armed resistance to Adolf Hitler as an impermissible evil. Day, the *Progressive*'s managing editor, who was soon to spend time in prison for trespassing on ICBM silos in Missouri, was of a similar political stripe. When in July 1976 Israel rescued its citizens from the Palestinian and German terrorists who were holding them hostage in Entebbe, Uganda,* Day was one of the few people in the United States to denounce their action.[33] Morland, then thirty-six years old, was a talented freelance journalist and former air force captain who, following a path welltrodden in those years, had become a passionate antinuclear activist.

Together the three embarked on a project to express opposition to American nuclear-weapons policy and demolish our secrecy system in one blow. The method was to be the publication of an article in the *Progressive* called "The H-bomb Secret: To Know How Is to Ask Why." Its opening paragraph began: "What you are about to learn is a secret—a secret that the United States and four other nations, the makers of hydrogen weapons, have gone to extraordinary lengths to protect."[34]

Written by Morland for the April 1979 issue of the publication, and assembled from disparate *un*classified sources, the article was a feat of prodigious research, ingenious deduction, and studied deception. It was drawn from sources including obscure and not-so-obscure publications around the world, and interviews with leading nuclear scientists, some of them conducted under false pretenses,

---

*On June 27, 1976, Air France Flight 139 originating in Tel Aviv, carrying 248 passengers and a crew of 12, was hijacked by two Palestinians from the Popular Front for the Liberation of Palestine and two Germans from the German Revolutionary Cells and diverted to Benghazi, Libya, and from there to Entebbe Airport in Uganda. There the terrorists separated the Jewish passengers and the crew and released everyone else. They then threatened to kill the 105 remaining hostages one by one until their demands were met. On July 4, 1976, Israeli commandos flew more than 2,300 miles across Africa to launch a rescue raid. One Israeli commando and three hostages were killed in the firefight, and one hostage who had been hospitalized in Kampala was subsequently murdered by the Ugandan government. All the other hostages were rescued.

with Morland representing himself as writing about strategic-arms negotiations.[35]

The finished article was replete with detailed explanations of every aspect of H-bomb design, from the plastic foam used to separate various components to the elements forming its explosive core. A typical passage read:

> Only the heavier isotopes of hydrogen serve as fuel in a hydrogen weapon. Hydrogen-2 and hydrogen-3, known respectively as deuterium and tritium, are the fuel which explodes with the force of many trainloads of TNT. Tritium is expensive and highly radioactive. For practical reasons, most of the tritium is stored in the weapon as lithium-6, a less expensive, non-radioactive material which is converted instantly to tritium once the fusion process begins. Conveniently, lithium-6 bonds chemically with deuterium to make a gray powder, called lithium-6 deuteride, that is much easier to manage than either pure deuterium or tritium in gaseous form, although it must be kept dry.[36]

The most important uncovered secret at the heart of the essay was an intricate description, complete with diagrams, of "the coupling mechanism that enables an ordinary fission bomb—the kind that destroyed Hiroshima—to trigger the far deadlier energy of hydrogen fusion." Conceiving of such a mechanism had been the achievement of Edward Teller and Stanislaw Ulam in 1951, following years pondering one of the most difficult riddles of physics, and had been kept highly classified by the U.S. government ever since. "The H-bomb Secret," Morland assured readers, would not enable an individual to build a hydrogen bomb in his garage—"Have no fear; that would be far beyond your capability," he wrote in a flippant tone. But it would enable a person to build such a device, he continued, if he or she had "the resources of at least a medium-sized government."[37]

It was precisely this self-admitted possibility—that a medium-size government would draw on Morland's article to guide it in constructing an H-bomb, a weapon *thousands* of times more destructive than the bombs dropped on Hiroshima and Nagasaki—that was to turn the *Progressive* case into a First Amendment battle royal.

AFTER Morland's article was completed in early February, the editors of the *Progressive* sent it to six nuclear weapons experts for review. Some of them were disquieted—worried, as one of them put it, that it risked giving a "broad hint" in H-bomb design to countries aspiring to build one. One of the readers, a graduate student at MIT, passed a copy along to George Rathjens, a professor on the political science faculty, and also the outgoing director of the Federation of American Scientists, a left-of-center organization of leading scientists highly active in support of arms-control agreements.

Rathjens was deeply troubled by what he read and telephoned the editors of the *Progressive* to urge them not to publish. "I have the impression that the information could be used very mischievously, with possibly catastrophic effect," he told them.[38] The editors were not deterred from moving forward. Neither, after the conversation, was Rathjens deterred from taking action of his own. Without the editors' permission, and over their objections, he turned over his copy to the Department of Energy, declaring the step "a matter of conscience."[39]

Nothing happened. The editors of the *Progressive*, distressed at first by Rathjens's decision to inform the government, were now distressed by the government's silence. They began to wonder, in the words of Samuel Day, "whether our blockbuster might be a dud."[40] To find out, and to augment their provocation, they sent a communication of their own to the Department of Energy: "I enclose a copy of some material—entitled 'How a Hydrogen Bomb Works'— which has been submitted for publication in the *Progressive*. Since this is a subject on which the Department of Energy has authoritative information, we would appreciate your verifying the accuracy of the material."[41]

The letter was delayed eight days by a freak snowstorm. The editors sent a second copy, which promptly arrived, but just days before the magazine was scheduled to go into print. Department of Energy officials were greatly alarmed, and the matter rapidly ascended the bureaucratic hierarchy to the desk of James Schlesinger, the secretary of energy himself.

The department decided to try to warn the *Progressive* off publication. The agency's general counsel telephoned the editors and informed them that the article contained "restricted data" as defined by the Atomic Energy Act, and asked them to refrain from publishing it. He offered to have the department work with them to recast those classified portions—all of them concerning technical matters—that would assist foreign nations in the development of thermonuclear technology. If the *Progressive* would not agree, he informed them, then the government would have no choice but to seek an injunction to stop publication.

The following day a delegation of Energy Department and Justice Department officials flew to Madison to make the same plea in person. In their meeting they emphasized that data in the article offered shortcuts that might save another country two to five years in developing a thermonuclear weapon.[42] The editors of the *Progressive* refused to budge. They expressed their determination to publish the article exactly as it stood unless they were served with a restraining order by a court—which is exactly what they wanted and exactly what they got. The *Progressive* editors were flushed with excitement as the meeting adjourned. Said Knoll to his colleagues: "I love it."[43] Morland, for his part, saw himself following the path of one of his heroes and standing on the precipice of fame: "Wouldn't I be able to have more influence, give more talks, write more articles, if I had some notoriety, like Daniel Ellsberg?"[44]

That same afternoon Attorney General Griffin Bell dispatched a memorandum to Jimmy Carter alerting him to the danger and seeking permission to take legal action. "The potentially grave consequences to the security of the U.S. and the world itself resulting from disclosure of the data are obvious and frightening," it read. On the cover page Carter wrote: "Good move; proceed," and the administration swung into action.[45] Invoking the secrecy provisions of the Atomic Energy Act, the Justice Department asked Federal District Judge Robert W. Warren of Milwaukee to block publication. A temporary restraining order was duly issued on March 9, and the judge ordered hearings on a preliminary injunction to begin within ten days.

In making its case the government put before the court the by-now well-established postulate that "national preservation and self-interest permit the retention and classification of government secrets." But it also added a relatively novel element—the "mosaic theory"—to deal with the fact that Morland's article had been constructed entirely from open sources. The mosaic theory, as it has been defined in an obscure corner of American law—the statutes governing naval record keeping—is "[t]he concept that apparently harmless pieces of information when assembled together could reveal a damaging picture."[46] In treating with the *Progressive*, the government maintained that it was authorized to classify and censor such materials in instances "when drawn together, synthesized and collated, such information acquires the character of presenting immediate, direct and irreparable harm to the interests of the United States."[47]

The harm alleged in this particular instance was no small matter. Three cabinet secretaries, Secretary of State Cyrus Vance, Secretary of Defense Harold Brown (a former director of the Lawrence Livermore Laboratory), and Secretary of Energy Schlesinger, had signed separate affidavits warning the court that dissemination of Morland's article heightened the danger of thermonuclear proliferation in a way that would irreparably impair American security.

Morland denied any and all of this, insisting that the information in his article, if it was not already in the public domain, "should be put there . . . so that ordinary citizens may have informed opinions about nuclear weapons."[48] Knoll, for his part, declared himself "totally convinced that publication of the article will be of substantial benefit to the United States" and that the government was engaged in "an attempt to assert incredibly broad powers of secrecy and censorship."[49]

But publishing plans for the construction of an H-bomb was not exactly a popular proposition, and even longtime civil libertarians blanched. Here indeed was a bridge too far even for the *New York Times*, which in an initial editorial opined that, given the stakes in this case, "a week or two of enforced restraint for a monthly journal seems a tolerable price."[50] The *Washington Post*, for its part, deemed the Morland article "John Mitchell's dream case—the one the Nixon administration was never lucky enough to get: a real First Amendment loser."[51]

Affidavits taking both sides of the case were filed by a variety of experts and interested parties, including not only cabinet secretaries but the American Civil Liberties Union, the Federation of American Scientists, and leading physicists, including Hans Bethe, a Nobel laureate who headed the Theoretical Division of the wartime bomb-making effort at Los Alamos and then went on to collaborate intimately with Teller and Ulam in developing the "super," a hydrogen bomb.

Bethe was by the 1970s a fervent advocate of arms control, having pushed for a ban on atmospheric testing of nuclear weapons and antiballistic missiles, favoring nuclear weapons reduction treaties with the USSR, and was shortly to become a ferocious critic of Reagan's Strategic Defense Initiative. He vociferously opposed allowing the *Progressive* article into print, maintaining that "the design and operational concepts described in the manuscript are not expressed or revealed in the public literature nor do I believe they are known to scientists not associated with the government weapons programs."[52]

Warren was to lean heavily on Bethe's affidavit in reaching a decision. The judge also declared himself "greatly impressed" by a contribution filed by Jeremy Stone, submitted on behalf of the Federation of American Scientists, an organization, Warren noted, "with half of America's Nobel laureates in its ranks." Stone's brief implored the *Progressive* to negotiate with the government and reconsider its decision to publish the technical details of the weapon's construction, which would imperil not only the cause of nuclear nonproliferation, but also, by raising a case in which security was so starkly pitted against liberty, the First Amendment itself.

In issuing a preliminary injunction on March 26, Warren to a considerable extent mirrored Stone's brief. The *Progressive*, he wrote, "does not really require the objected-to material in order to ventilate its views on government secrecy and the hydrogen bomb," and, "this Court can find no plausible reason why the public needs to know the technical details about hydrogen bomb construction to carry on an informed debate on this issue." Publication of such details "will result in direct, immediate and irreparable damage to the United States by accelerating the capacity of certain non-thermonuclear nations to manufacture thermonuclear weapons." Indeed, it "could pave the way for thermonuclear annihilation for us all. In that event, our right to life is extinguished and the right to publish becomes moot."[53] The *Progressive*'s refusal to agree to mediation or to redact the sensitive technical portions left him little choice, said Warren, but to issue a prior restraint. Such an injunction, given the national security issues at stake, outweighed the First Amendment rights of the defendants.[54]

WARREN's ruling would seem at first glance to be unassailable. However, it turned out to be anything but. For over the next months, as the injunction traversed the court system, eventually coming before a panel of three federal judges sitting in Chicago, thread after thread was pulled out of the government's case until the entire garment finally unraveled.

A first issue that came in for close examination was whether the secrets at the core of the article were actually secrets at all. For one thing the allegedly ultrasensitive diagrams in Morland's article turned out to have been drawn from an article in the *Encyclopedia Americana* authored by none other than Edward Teller, available already for ten years for the entire world to see. An investigator for the ACLU then found *UCRL-4725*—a highly detailed report on the H-bomb from the University of California Radiation Laboratory—sitting on an open shelf at the Los Alamos Scientific Laboratory public library, a facility visited by numerous foreign visitors. The government immediately removed this and another equally sensitive document from the collection, asserting that they had been released in error. But the diagrams in the *Encyclopedia Americana* became the subject of ridicule and were difficult to explain away.

Once again the government asserted that it was the sum of the information in the article, rather than its parts, that made it dangerous; it was a compilation that would help would-be proliferators steer clear of dead ends, saving them years of research. But damage had been done to its case, not least in the court of public opinion. Newspapers that had initially expressed a measure of sympathy for its position switched allegiance. The *Times* was now branding the government's pursuit of the *Progressive* "lame in both logic and law" and a case "against the national interest—against free speech and free inquiry." On the available evidence, the editorial continued, "the government has failed to prove a sure, grave, direct, immediate and irreparable harm to our nation—the only conceivable justification for censorship."[55]

By the end of the summer the government suffered even more devastating blows when a flurry of other publications—generated from information disseminated by a self-described nuclear weapons "hobbyist"—put all the central findings of Morland's article into the public domain. After a few vain attempts to put fingers in the dikes, with the Justice Department seeking an injunction against one newspaper only to see the same nuclear secrets flow out in others, the government finally let burst the dam. On September 17, four days after oral arguments before the court of appeals got under way, the case was formally dropped. The *Progressive* then published the

Morland article in full in its November 1979 issue. After six months, the second court-imposed prior restraint on publication in American history had come to an end.

WAS THE Carter administration wrong in seeking to suppress Morland's article? From the legal point of view—if we assume that what the article claimed for itself was true, namely, that it could aid a medium-size power in acquiring the hydrogen bomb—then the Department of Energy was on more than solid ground in arguing that "immediate, clear, and irreparable harm" would ensue. The threshold for imposing an *initial* temporary restraining order had clearly been met. Facing a deadline of only days set for them by the editors of the *Progressive*, Energy Department officials hardly had time to make a definitive appraisal of the scientific issues in dispute before letting drop the guillotine. Under the circumstances imposed upon them by the magazine, seeking a temporary restraining order while the security implications could be sorted out seems entirely reasonable. The alternative—of allowing the *Progressive* to open a Pandora's box of nuclear secrets and simply trusting there would be no harm—would have been a gross abdication of responsibility.

But having gained the temporary restraining order, and in seeking to make it permanent, the Carter administration fell into a trap. For the outcome of the proceedings the Justice Department set in motion was a calamity: the worst of all possible worlds. Not only was the article published in the end, but it was given maximum publicity. And the publicity was only the beginning of the damage. To block the article the Department of Energy was forced to compound the harm by affirming in open court that in its essentials Morland had gotten the design of a hydrogen bomb *right*. The Morland article "provides a more comprehensive, *accurate*, and detailed summary of the overall construction and operation of a thermonuclear weapon than any publication to date in the public literature," read the affidavit of the primary technical witness brought in by the government.[56]

This declaration, and several others like it, had an unintended and most untoward result. After the article finally came out, foreign scientists who ordinarily would have paid not the slightest attention to the work of a thirty-six-year-old college graduate scantily educated in physics, whose work appeared in an obscure left-wing periodical, now had excellent reason to subject it to intensive scrutiny. And insofar as there were errors in the bomb design put forward in the *Progressive* article, the litigation ultimately exposed these as well, enabling Morland to publish an erratum in the next issue of the *Progressive*, thereby offering additional assistance to aspiring thermonuclear powers.

With the benefit of hindsight no doubt a far more prudent course for the Department of Energy would have been to have a spokesman say "No comment" and leave Morland's article to dangle forever in obscurity. But no government has the benefit of hindsight. Senior American physicists across the political spectrum, including staunch political liberals like Bethe, were warning of the danger in what the magazine was doing. Kosta Tsipis, another physicist of liberal persuasion, wrote in his affidavit that "the total time necessary for another nation to arrive at a successful device could be foreshortened by the information made available by the article."[57] The brilliant physicist Freeman Dyson predicted that "millions of people would suffer" as a consequence of the *Progressive*'s self-indulgence.[58] Even Daniel Ellsberg, the master leaker and a man, by this juncture, wholly of the radical Left, was opposed, believing that Morland had crossed the line, and pronouncing that, "yes, nuclear weapons design information should be kept secret."[59]

Even more outspoken was Jeremy Stone. Speaking to the American Society of Newspaper Editors, he maintained that the arguments in favor of publishing technical details of such weapons was nothing but "malarkey," comparable to saying "that a study of the environmental implications of the automobile industry required the public to know how the spark plugs are inserted."[60] As for the *Progressive*'s contention that the article would deal a blow to the secrecy system, this, said Stone, was an "increasingly bizarre" stance. The public was already aware of excessive secrecy and should be made further aware of it, "[but] it is hardly going to be aroused by this particular case." Indeed, if anything, the public "*wants* the government to be excessively prudent in hanging onto the secret of the most destructive weapons known to mankind."[61]

To be sure, reputable scientists could be found on the other side of this dispute, and some opponents of publication, like Freeman Dyson, were later to change their mind. Still, was the dissemination of the design plans of hydrogen bombs not a matter where extreme caution should reign? Even today the controversy over the harm done to the cause of nuclear nonproliferation by the *Progressive* article remains unresolved.

Morland himself, recently reflecting on his handiwork, asserts in self-justification that the number of acknowledged thermonuclear nations in 1979—the United States, Russia, Britain, France, and China—remains unchanged three decades later, while in the early 1990s Belarus and Ukraine returned to Russia the thermonuclear weapons that were deployed on their territory when the USSR collapsed. "Thus, on balance," he writes, "the thermonuclear world has shrunk slightly, despite publication of the *Progressive*'s article." The passage of time "has shown the government's affiants to be wrong about the announced danger."[62]

But who could have predicted this outcome with confidence in 1979? In any event, were the government's predictions of danger truly wrong? When the *Progressive* article came out, one notable fact already known and brought before the court was that India had recently initiated work on developing a thermonuclear weapon.[63] Its subsequent progress was slow; in 1998 it tested a first such device in the Rajasthan desert.[64] Many Western analysts believe that the test was a failure but Indian officials insist that their measurements of the subterranean blast gave "unambiguous evidence of fusion energy release."[65] To this day the Indian thermonuclear project continues.

Did the *Progressive* article play any part in encouraging India's generals and scientists to intensify their pursuit of the super? Did it speed their progress and guide them around some of the many blind alleys inevitably entailed in such an endeavor? Even if the probability of an affirmative answer to such questions is low, was the gratuitous publication of *technical* details in the *Progressive* worth even a small risk? What were the benefits? As Warren observed in his ruling, without the restricted technical data, precisely the same case against nuclear secrecy and nuclear weapons policy could have been made.

Morland has an answer. Fears about the spread of atomic weapons technology, he says, arise "largely because of an unconscious racism" in the minds of people who "feel that nuclear information is safe only so long as it does not fall into the hands of Third World people who do not share our civilized values."[66] But this is puerile. Fears of nuclear proliferation are not motivated by racism but by an all-too-legitimate concern over what the spread of atomic and hydrogen bombs into unstable regions of the world—places like North Korea and Pakistan—will imply for the fate of millions.

"The Constitution allows the press to be irresponsible, but not to the extent that it may pose a threat to thousands of lives," noted James Schlesinger in a speech on the occasion of the twenty-fifth anniversary of the *Progressive* case.[67] In that respect, he continued, the controversy provoked by the magazine raised the "central issues for a free society: the balance between freedom and order and, at core, whether or not a free society can protect itself." That was a pertinent question in 1979. It is an urgent question today.

CHAPTER 11

BLACK-LETTER LAW

T HE BOOKENDS OF the 1970s were put in place by Daniel Ellsberg at one side of the decade and Philip Agee and the *Progressive* at the other. If national security secrecy in America today has
a distinct shape it was cast in those ten years. We live in a world
created by those particular tellers of secrets and by the government
officials who, for better or worse, and with better and worse methods, attempted to rein them in.

The experience of Richard Nixon and Watergate left journalism stamped with a deep and abiding cynicism about government.
Even if the mainstream press had looked askance at Agee and only
defended the *Progressive* with a skeptical reluctance, the norms of
what kinds of secrets it was considered acceptable to reveal were radically expanded. Within journalism, to use Daniel Patrick Moynihan's famous formulation, deviancy had been defined downward.

On the other side of the equation, government exerted a new
assertiveness in seeking to control information. This was not only
a reaction to the excesses of the 1970s but, more significantly, was
the result of a pronounced shift in the political winds. The election of Ronald Reagan in 1980 brought to power an administration
determined to prosecute the Cold War from an offensive posture.
Intelligence was one of its significant tools, and the cloak of secrecy

became the garment of choice. A special unit was set up within the FBI to track down leakers within government and permitted to employ court-approved wiretaps and administer polygraph tests to suspects. But this was secrecy's death rattle sounding yet again. The thirty years since then have repeatedly witnessed the two intersecting trajectories of government and the media coming into collision. With minor variations the story line is almost always dismally familiar: the press learning of some secret, the government scrambling to contain it, and the secret, in the end, coming out.

A typical high-profile instance came in 1985 when the *Washington Post* got wind of Operation Ivy Bells, a joint Navy-NSA program to tap an underwater Soviet communications cable in the Sea of Okhotsk. The paper immediately faced the fierce determination of the Reagan administration to block publication. An *operational* intelligence gathering program was at issue. And nothing could have been more sensitive. Even Ben Bradlee, the executive editor of the *Post*, initially considered the story "appalling" and could see "no useful social purpose whatever in publishing news of our new intelligence capability."[1] But then, when it was learned that the Soviets had already uncovered and removed the interception device in 1981, the *Post* reversed field and began preparations to run the story.

But similar U.S. intelligence programs were targeting Russian cables elsewhere, in the Barents Sea and the Mediterranean. Third countries, like China, might also have had their undersea communications lines targeted, although this was something the U.S. government would never say. The stakes were so high that William Casey, Reagan's CIA director, threatened the *Post* with prosecution under the Comint statute. The editors of the *Washington Post*, to their credit, paused to hear and weigh the government's contentions. But then, as in the *Progressive* case, the whack-a-mole phenomenon set in. Try as the U.S. government did to knock down the story in one outlet, it popped up in another. On May 19, 1985, NBC News broadcast a story about "a top-secret underwater eavesdropping operation by American submarines inside Soviet harbors." The

Washington Post, safely coming in second, followed suit. The secret was out. Intelligence sources and methods involving ongoing operations were almost certainly compromised. Adversaries were able to guard against future such endeavors. "No useful social purpose" had been served, but NBC News had its scoop.

Set-piece battles like this between the press and the government punctuated the 1980s and continue to the present day. But the most important development of the post-Ellsberg, pre-9/11 era received relatively scant attention from the press, for as far as leaks are concerned, it was a freak event, a bizarre anomaly, with—from the point of view of the press—a horrid set of facts involving a highly unsympathetic leaker.

SAMUEL LORING MORISON was the grandson of the great naval historian Samuel Eliot Morison. He acquired from his grandfather an unquenchable passion for all things naval, and claimed ownership of the largest collection of boat photographs in the world. Pursuing his passion single-mindedly, Morison gained employment in 1974 as an analyst in U.S. naval intelligence, assigned to study Soviet amphibious vessels and hospital ships at a facility in Suitland, Maryland, where he toiled in a "vaulted area" closed to all persons without a top-secret clearance.[2] He himself had been given the clearance of "Top-Secret-Sensitive Compartmented Information," granting him access to the most closely held secrets of the U.S. government. While holding down this job, Morison was also freelancing for the British annual *Jane's Fighting Ships* and its sister publication, *Jane's Defence Weekly*.

Although Morison had received permission for the freelancing, he had signed a formal agreement that he would not supply classified information or extract unclassified data from classified data and pass it on. By 1984 the arrangement with *Jane's* brought Morison into conflict with his superiors, and he decided to seek a full-time position with the publication. To enhance his employment prospects, he began to provide a regular stream of information to Derek Wood, an editor at *Jane's*, beginning with secret material concerning an explosion that had occurred at the Soviet naval base in Severomorsk, along with information about other accidental blasts in other locations in the USSR and the Eastern bloc.

As his relationship with *Jane's* deepened, Morison one day saw three photographs of the Soviet Union's first nuclear-powered aircraft carrier on the desk of one his colleagues. They had been taken by the KH-11 reconnaissance satellite and bore a stamp of "Secret." On their borders they also had a "Warning Notice: Intelligence Sources or Methods Involved." Unobserved, Morison scooped up the photographs, smuggled them out of the facility, and brought them home, where he cut off the security-classification stamps and the warning notices on the border. He then mailed them off to Derek Wood.

Wood paid Morison three hundred dollars and then published the photos a few days later in *Jane's* and also distributed them to various news agencies, including the *Washington Post*. Naval officials immediately recognized the images in the *Post* and began to investigate, quickly discovering that the photographs were missing from the Suitland facility and presumably stolen. Morison, an obvious suspect given his ties to *Jane's*, was among those questioned. He stoutly denied ever seeing the photographs, let alone stealing them. Indeed, he suggested that two of his colleagues were more likely suspects and should be interrogated.

But on the ribbon of his office typewriter, investigators found a record of extensive correspondence with *Jane's*, including the secret materials about Severomorsk. Then Morison's fingerprints were found on the purloined photographs, which investigators had retrieved from a compliant *Jane's*, anxious not to jeopardize the ties with the U.S. Navy upon which its success as a publication hinged. Even as the pit in which he was trapped was growing deeper, Morison gloated in a phone conversation with Wood that the photographs would never be traced to him. Federal investigators were tapping the line.

Arrested and charged with violations of the espionage statutes and theft of government property, Morison at first persevered in his protestations of innocence. However, in the course of interrogations, investigators speculated aloud about his motive, asking him whether he had perhaps felt that publicizing the photos would bring sorely needed attention to the ongoing Soviet naval buildup. Morison jumped at the suggestion that he had acted to perform a public service and finally admitted to having appropriated the photographs. He continued, however, to deny sending the material about Severomorsk. His prevarications did not turn out well for him. The incriminating typewriter ribbon was only part of the evidence. A search of his home turned up secret intelligence reports about the blast in an envelope marked "For Derek Wood only."

Morison went to trial in October 1985. His attorneys called witnesses who testified that the information provided to *Jane's* did not harm the United States. The government asserted otherwise. The case went to a jury, and Morison was found guilty on all counts. Facing a maximum term of forty years in prison, he was sentenced to two. After serving out his sentence, he was later granted a presidential pardon, along with 139 others, on Bill Clinton's last day in office.

But along the way Morison appealed his conviction. In response to arguments put forward by Morison's attorneys and a flurry of amicus briefs from the press, the court took up a gamut of critical issues. There was much to resolve; remarkably enough Morison's conviction was the first successful prosecution of a leaker in American history.

A relatively minor argument in Morison's arsenal was the question of selective prosecution. Morison contended that in the nearly seven decades since the passage of the Espionage Act, the government had only sought to prosecute one other individual for leaking: Daniel Ellsberg. But the court summarily rejected this line of reasoning. "It is unquestionably true," it ruled, "that the prosecutions [of leakers] generally under the Espionage Act . . . have not been great," but this was hardly because the statute was not intended to reach such cases. Rather the principal reason for the dearth of prosecutions is that "violations under the Act are not easily established. The violators act with the intention of concealing their conduct. They try, as the defendant did in this case, to leave few trails."[3] In other words the major reason why Morison had faced prosecution when so many other leakers had continued unmolested was that he had been singularly inept at maintaining his anonymity. Indeed he had not merely left trails—he had left blinking neon signs—pointing nowhere but to himself.

A more substantial argument put forward by Morison was that the provisions of the law under which he was convicted were vague and overbroad and therefore constitutionally invalid. The conduct in which he had engaged, he maintained, did not fall under the prohibitions of the Espionage Act, which was only designed to punish "classic spying" in which national security secrets were transmitted to foreign agents with intent to injure the United States. He had provided the secret materials not to an enemy intelligence service like the KGB but "to a recognized international naval news organization," and with no harm to the country intended.

But the appeals court found this a distinction without a difference. The relevant provisions of the law, it noted, apply not merely to spies, however that word might be defined, but to "whoever" willfully communicates, delivers, or transmits National Defense Information to a person not entitled to receive it. "The language of the . . . statutes," pronounced the court, "includes no limitations to spies or to 'an agent of a foreign government' . . . and they declare no exemption in favor of one who leaks to the press. It covers 'anyone.'" And contrary to Morison's claim, there was nothing vague about this provision: "It is difficult to conceive of any language more definite and clear." Congress had chosen not to distinguish between leaks to the press and surreptitious conveyance of information to foreign agents for reasons that were readily grasped:

> the danger to the United States is just as great when this
> information is released to the press as when it is released to

an agent of a foreign government. The fear in releasing this type of information is that it gives other nations information concerning the intelligence gathering capabilities of the United States. That fear is realized whether the information is released to the world at large or whether it is released only to specific spies.[4]

Morison also maintained that because the *recipient* of the secret information he distributed was a publication, not an agent of a foreign power, the prosecution violated the First Amendment. But the appeals court held that the legislative record leading to the passage of the Espionage Act contained "no evidence whatsoever" that it was exempting a governmental employee from its restrictions "simply because he transmitted it to a representative of the press." A remaining question was whether Congress itself, in passing the antileak provision of the Espionage Act, had trampled on the First Amendment.

Here the court found of particular relevance the Supreme Court's landmark 1972 decision in *Branzburg v. Hayes*. That ruling brought together a number of then-recent cases in which reporters witnessed behavior that appeared to be illegal. All three were summoned to testify before grand juries. All three, citing the First Amendment, declined to answer questions about their confidential sources. All three were held in contempt and appealed, unsuccessfully, to the Supreme Court.

Like Morison, the appellants in *Branzburg* were claiming, on First Amendment grounds, to be exempt from the requirement to observe the criminal law. Portions of the decision in that case were singularly pertinent to the set of facts that arose in *Morison*: "Although stealing documents . . . could provide newsworthy information," wrote Byron White for the Court,

neither reporter nor source is immune from conviction for such conduct, whatever the impact on the flow of news.

. . . The [First] Amendment does not reach so far as to override the interest of the public in ensuring that neither reporter nor source is invading the rights of other citizens through reprehensible conduct forbidden to all other persons. To assert the contrary proposition is to answer it, since it involves in its very statement the contention that the freedom of the press is the freedom to do wrong with impunity and implies the right to frustrate and defeat the discharge of those governmental duties upon the performance of which the freedom of all, including that of the press, depends. . . . It suffices to say that, however complete is the right of the press to state public things and discuss them, that right, as every other right enjoyed in human society, is subject to the restraints which separate right from wrong-doing.[5]

Thus, by unmistakable implication, not only was a government employee like Morison forbidden to violate statutes governing the control of secret information, but so, too, were journalists. The freedom of the press, in White's unequivocal words, is not "the freedom to do wrong with impunity" and neither—in words singled out by the appeals court in *Morison*—does the First Amendment "confer a license on either the reporter or his news source to violate valid criminal laws."

THE *MORISON* DECISION thus bears directly on the position of the press when it traffics in secret materials. By confirming that leaking of national security secrets is a criminal offense, it suggests that journalists who receive material from leakers are also engaging in crime as either suborners or coconspirators. The author of the *Morison* decision, Circuit Judge Donald Russell, attempted to elide this by stating that "we do not perceive any First Amendment rights to be implicated here." But this flat declaration scanted the fact that journalism, as we know it today, depends heavily on the flow of secret information from confidential sources within government.

This scanting did not sit well with J. Harvie Wilkinson, one of Russell's colleagues on the three-judge panel. Wilkinson took full cognizance of the infringement on the First Amendment, noting that "criminal restraints on the disclosure of information threaten the ability of the press to scrutinize and report on government activity." Even constitutional government, he continued, has a tendency "to withhold reports of disquieting developments and to manage news in a fashion most favorable to itself." What is more, public debate "is diminished without access to unfiltered facts" and "the First Amendment interest in informed popular debate does not simply vanish at the invocation of the words 'national security.'" Indeed, continued Wilkinson,

> National security is . . . not government security from
> informed criticism. No decisions are more serious than
> those touching on peace and war; none are more certain
> to affect every member of society. Elections turn on
> the conduct of foreign affairs and strategies of national
> defense, and the dangers of secretive government have
> been well documented. Morison claims he released satellite
> photographs revealing construction of the first Soviet
> nuclear carrier in order to alert the public to the dimensions
> of a Soviet naval buildup. Although this claim is open to
> serious question, the undeniable effect of the disclosure was
> to enhance public knowledge and interest in the projection
> of Soviet sea power such as that revealed in the satellite
> photos.[6]

Yet even as Wilkinson openly acknowledged the benefits to the public flowing from Morison's conduct, he endorsed his conviction. He stated flatly that Russell's "analysis of the relevant statutes, instructions, and evidentiary rulings is both careful and correct."

Endangered by Morison's conduct was "a public interest that is no less important" than the free flow of information, namely, "the security of sensitive government operations." When this security is freely breached, the public is placed at risk.

> When the identities of our intelligence agents are known, they may be killed. When our electronic surveillance capabilities are revealed, countermeasures can be taken to circumvent them. When other nations fear that confidences exchanged at the bargaining table will only become embarrassments in the press, our diplomats are left helpless. When terrorists are advised of our intelligence, they can avoid apprehension and escape retribution. . . .The type of information leaked by Morison may cause widespread damage by hampering the effectiveness of expensive surveillance systems which would otherwise be expected to provide years of reliable information not obtainable by any other means.[7]

The problem at the core of *Morison*, as Wilkinson identified it, was thus the abiding tension between the flow of "the information needed for a democracy to function, and . . . leaks that imperil the environment of physical security which a functioning democracy requires." The question is "how a responsible balance may be achieved" between these antagonistic forces. The answer supplied by Wilkinson is that where the protection of national security secrets is concerned, the courts must be deferential to the executive. Such deference, he acknowledged, has indisputable costs. It means that "years may pass before the basis of portentous decisions becomes known. The public cannot call officials to account on the basis of material of whose existence and content it is unaware. What is more, classification decisions may well have been made by bureaucrats far down the line, whose public accountability may be quite indirect."[8]

Nonetheless, the alternative of not stanching the flow of national security secrets would be worse; indeed, its consequences for the public "would be grave":

> To reverse Morison's conviction on the general ground
> that it chills press access would be tantamount to a
> judicial declaration that the government may never
> use criminal penalties to secure the confidentiality of
> intelligence information. Rather than enhancing the
> operation of democracy, as Morison suggests, this course
> would install every government worker with access to
> classified information as a veritable satrap. Vital decisions
> and expensive programs set into motion by elected
> representatives would be subject to summary derailment at
> the pleasure of one disgruntled employee.[9]

It was these considerations that led to Morison's conviction, making him the first leaker ever punished by an American court. This in itself is a remarkable testament to the open nature of our society. Despite the laws on the books and despite the provocations offered by a long string of previous offenders, criminal sanctions were sought previously only in rare instances and never before successfully. When the Supreme Court declined in 1988 to hear Morison's further appeal, the circuit court's ruling became enshrined as the law of the land. So it will remain until the Supreme Court takes an occasion to visit the issue. As things stand now, if a jury finds, as did the *Morison* jury, that leaked material is "potentially damaging to the United States," the actions of a leaker are illegal and can be punished by fines and/or imprisonment. What had been gray became, finally, after seven decades, black-letter law.

CHAPTER 12

A WAR ON THE PRESS?

THE SUPREME COURT'S decision to let *Morison* stand was greeted with a hue and cry in the news media and among civil libertarians; the same hue and cry, almost to the word, that followed *Marchetti* and *Snepp*. To Anthony Lewis, *Morison* was "the most dangerous judicial blow in many years to the Madisonian system—the American system—of government accountable to the people."[1] To Morton Halperin of the American Civil Liberties Union, the case opened the way for the Espionage Act to be used against the press and "poses a very severe threat to the First Amendment."[2]

But *Morison* has been on the books now for more than twenty years, and the fears of those like Lewis and Halperin have not exactly come to pass. The flow of leaks into the press continued throughout the remaining years of the Cold War under Reagan and George H. W. Bush, and then under Clinton, too, in the peaceful interlude between the collapse of the Soviet Union and the destruction of the World Trade Center. In the years since September 11 the leaking has continued apace and, remarkably, despite the war on terrorism and multiplying security threats, even accelerated. One can point to dozens of significant breaches of secrecy that, thanks to reporters seeking out disgruntled bureaucrats and inducing them to tell what they know, have entered the political bloodstream and altered the debate.

If the press is in severe difficulty today, that is primarily a result of bleeding red balance sheets, not the heavy hand of the U.S. government. It is an enormous stretch to contend either that the press is impeded by law enforcement in any appreciable way from doing its job or that the American people are left by it ill informed.

This, however, has not been the view of the media and its defenders in the period after September 11, particularly during the Bush years. According to Floyd Abrams, testifying before Congress in 2005, in his four decades representing the media the work of reporting had "never been as seriously threatened as it is today."[3] To Norman Pearlstine, the former editor in chief of Time Inc. and now the top newsman at Bloomberg, today's situation "chills essential news-gathering and reporting."[4] William Safire, the longtime conservative columnist for the *New York Times*, asserted that "the fundamental right of Americans, through our free press, to penetrate and criticize the workings of our government is under attack as never before."[5] Nicholas Kristof, the *Times* columnist, concurred, saying, "we're seeing a broad assault on freedom of the press that would appall us if it were happening in Kazakhstan."[6]

"Under attack as never before"? "Kazakhstan"? Time after time exaggeration bordering on hysteria is the characteristic reaction from the media to threats to the perceived interests of news gatherers. During the George W. Bush years the hysteria exploded in a kind of paroxysm. Yet if one compares the Bush administration's treatment of civil liberties to the genuine depredations that occurred during wartime over America's past hundred years—World War I (the Sedition Act and all that followed from it), World War II (the internment of Japanese Americans), the Korean War (McCarthyism), Vietnam (Watergate)—it can be argued that its reaction to September 11 was a remarkable demonstration of maturity and restraint. But whatever one's assessment, let us give Abrams, Pearlstine, and company their due. Their words may be heated, but none of them is a hothead or extremist, and they do have some evidence to back them up.

Thus the federal government has sought in a number of high-profile cases to subpoena journalists and compel them, on pain of contempt citations, to disgorge their confidential sources, that is, the identity of the leakers in the government who have provided them with information. By undermining the pledge of absolute confidentiality that journalists give to sources within the government, this practice, say advocates for the media, threatens to choke off the flow of information on which the public depends. The most notorious such case of recent years began as an investigation into a leak about the CIA. It ended with the *Times* reporter Judith Miller sentenced to eighteen months of incarceration for refusing to obey a subpoena and testify before a grand jury. She held out for eighty-five days in a federal jail until she changed her mind and agreed to talk.

In roughly the same period the FBI and the Justice Department embarked on what ranks as the most radical antileak prosecution in American history, deploying the Espionage Act to prosecute three men, Lawrence Franklin, a Defense Department employee, and Keith Weissman and Steven Rosen, lobbyists with AIPAC. In 2006 Franklin pleaded guilty in a Virginia federal courthouse to charges that had included (before some of them were dropped in a plea bargain) conveying national defense information to the two AIPAC men, to journalists, and to an Israeli diplomat. He was sentenced to twelve years and six months in prison (subsequently reduced to house arrest and community service). The AIPAC lobbyists in turn were indicted for having received classified national defense information from Franklin and then passing it on to journalists and also to an Israeli diplomat. Thus arose the first instance ever in which the Espionage Act was deployed to prosecute private individuals rather than government employees for mishandling secrets, a most ominous development from the perspective of the press, for the lobbyists had been indicted for engaging in activity that journalists engage in every day of the week.

Both the Miller and the AIPAC cases therefore elicited entirely predictable professions of dread and horror in the press. But both, for different reasons, are much less troubling in the broader scale of things than they might initially appear. Thus, to begin with the Miller saga, it was in almost all respects an outlier, and certainly not indicative of a pattern that journalists, eagerly bestowing on themselves martyrdom status, proclaim is naked repression.

Precisely to avoid running into conflicts over First Amendment rights, the Justice Department has long observed internal guidelines that sharply limit the circumstances in which subpoenas are issued to journalists. Historically such subpoenas have been few and far between: The Justice Department has issued approximately a dozen over the last two decades. But the investigation that landed Judith Miller in prison was exceptional in a crucial way. It was not run by the Justice Department. Her incarceration was the handiwork of Patrick Fitzgerald, a special prosecutor appointed to investigate the misdeeds not of the press but those of the Bush administration itself. Whatever one thinks of Miller's imprisonment, it is impossible to lay responsibility for it at the White House doorstep. Indeed it was voices in the media, including Judith Miller's employer, the *New York Times*, that were initially cheering on Fitzgerald.

Fitzgerald was attempting to determine who in the government, possibly in violation of the Intelligence Identities Protection Act, had revealed that Valerie Plame was an undercover officer at the CIA. In pursuing his investigation via Judith Miller, Fitzgerald was relying on the Supreme Court's ruling in *Branzburg*. That case had made it plain that when crimes are being investigated, and journalists possess information about the crime, they are in many (but not all) circumstances obliged to obey subpoenas, including those that ask them to reveal their confidential sources. "We cannot seriously entertain the notion that the First Amendment protects a newsman's agreement to conceal the criminal conduct of his source, or evidence thereof, on the theory that it is better to write about crime than to do something about it," was Justice White's pithy formulation.[7]

Journalists may loathe the *Branzburg* decision, and they have long been seeking passage of a federal "shield law" that would effectively overturn it and exempt themselves from being called to testify in both civil and criminal proceedings. But at the time Miller was incarcerated, Congress, like successive Congresses before it, had considered passage of a shield law only to reject it. The American people, in other words, acting through their elected representatives, had had ample opportunity to establish a testimonial privilege for journalists and declined to do so.

In *Branzburg*, Justice White had spelled out the primary objection. "It is obvious," he wrote for the Court, "that agreements to conceal information relevant to commission of crime have very little to recommend them from the standpoint of public policy." Historically, White pointed out, citizens not only are forbidden to conceal a crime, they have a positive "duty to raise the 'hue and cry' and report felonies to the authorities." Concealment, even of a crime in which one is oneself not a participant, is itself a crime—misprision of a felony—punishable by a statute enacted by the very first Congress and still on the books. Covering up a crime, wrote White, "deserves no encomium, and we decline to afford it First Amendment protection by denigrating the duty of a citizen, whether reporter or informer, to respond to grand-jury subpoena and answer relevant questions put to him."[8] Judith Miller declined to respond to such a subpoena and was cited for contempt. From the legal point of view this was right and proper, for she was being contemptuous of a grand-jury process that is the cornerstone of our criminal laws.

But even if right and proper, whether the incarceration of Miller was wise and prudent is something else. As a special prosecutor Fitzgerald was free of the obligation specified in the Justice Department's guidelines to obtain the attorney general's permission before subpoenaing a journalist. Given the uproar such a step was certain to cause, it is extremely doubtful that Attorney General John Ashcroft would have issued one on his own and then thrown Miller into jail as Fitzgerald did. As a special prosecutor beholden to no one, Fitzgerald was completely insulated from the costs of such a step. Ashcroft was not. Fitzgerald, unlike Ashcroft, was also under no obligation to balance investigative purposes with respect for the First Amendment.

Indeed the course of action on which Fitzgerald embarked revealed him to be a classic runaway special prosecutor. As almost all special prosecutors have historically done, Fitzgerald sought to expand his investigative purview beyond its initial mandate. Thus when Fitzgerald issued his subpoena to Judith Miller, the identity of the official who had first disclosed Plame's identity to the press was already known to him; it was Richard Armitage, the number two man at the Department of State.* But by this time Fitzgerald was after something else: a perjury charge against I. Lewis "Scooter" Libby, Vice President Cheney's chief of staff, who he believed had provided false statements to federal investigators tracking down the leak.

Perjury is a serious offense, yet once again it is questionable whether the Justice Department, as opposed to an independent special prosecutor, would have taken the step of tossing a reporter into jail when the underlying crime that gave rise to the perjury had been solved or shown (as was probably the case here) not to have been a crime at all. Fitzgerald was no doubt acting within the law, but whether he was acting heedlessly within it is another matter. He did indeed succeed in extracting the information he was seeking from Miller and gaining a conviction of Libby, but the revulsion he provoked along the way will if anything make the incarceration of reporters less rather than more frequent. The problem exposed by the Judith Miller case is not a general fragility of freedom of the

---

*Also striking, and bearing on whether Fitzgerald was acting as a loose cannon, is the considerable doubt that exists about whether Plame's CIA status was actually "undercover" at the time the leak investigation began. Her CIA affiliation was already known in Washington cocktail circles, and even her own memoir, *Fair Game*, acknowledges that the Soviet double agent Aldrich Ames had probably provided her identity (along with those of one hundred or so other CIA operatives) to the KGB back in 1994. It had to be assumed by CIA management that these had been sold (for favors or cash or both) to the intelligence services of other countries around the globe. The fact that Fitzgerald never indicted Armitage, Libby, or anyone else for disclosing Plame's CIA employment suggests that it was clear to him, probably from almost the inception of the investigation, that no violation of the Intelligence Identity Protection Act had been committed.

press; rather it is a special-prosecutor law that throws by the wayside the formal and informal checks and balances of our judicial system.

THE AIPAC AFFAIR presents another kind of anomaly—"a very odd case" is what T. S. Ellis III, the presiding judge, called it.[9] Given its abortive outcome—just weeks before the trial was set to commence, prosecutors withdrew the charges with their tails between their legs—it is hardly something the Justice Department is likely to repeat with anything remotely resembling its particular set of facts.

It is necessary here, of course, to separate discussion of the charges against Lawrence Franklin, a civil servant who had signed an agreement to protect national security secrets, from those leveled against the two AIPAC men. Although all three were indicted for taking part in the same alleged conspiracy, they played very different roles and were subject to very different obligations.

To begin with Franklin, his motives in consorting with the AIPAC lobbyists conformed in most ways to the typical leak scenario in which a bureaucrat funnels information to those outside government in an effort to shape policy. In this instance Franklin hoped, by providing information to AIPAC, to call attention circuitously to a threat to the United States from Iran that he believed Bush's National Security Council was underestimating.

But as Ellis noted in sentencing him, Franklin also had another motive as well, "personal ambition"; he was seeking to enlist AIPAC's help in getting a transfer from the obscurity of the Iran desk at the Pentagon to a coveted slot at the NSC.[10] The fact that in the course of the investigation thirty-seven secret and thirty-eight top-secret documents were found in his home in blatant violation of security regulations only dug him deeper into a hole.* One can certainly raise

---

*With five children, a disabled wife, and a home in West Virginia far from the Pentagon, Franklin contends that his purpose in bringing the classified documents home was simply to work on them. The government has never alleged that he disseminated any of them to unauthorized persons.

legitimate questions about the murky circumstances that prompted the FBI to investigate AIPAC in the first place, an investigation in which Franklin was ensnared. But the fact is that what law enforcement uncovered in the course of that investigation made his prosecution virtually inevitable.

Yet it is doubtful that the conviction of Franklin, and of Morison before him, has made other would-be leakers particularly reticent about disclosing classified information to journalists. Between September 2001 and February 2008, the FBI investigated eighty-five reported leaks of classified intelligence information to the media. Not one of these cases (apart from the AIPAC matter) even reached prosecution, let alone resulted in a guilty verdict.[11] The risks involved in leaking remain extraordinarily low. Morison and Franklin's greatest mistake was to get caught, a rarity given that leak investigations are so notoriously unproductive. In addition to Morison and Franklin, there has been only one other conviction for leaking classified data. In late 2009, Shamai Liebowitz, an Israeli-American attorney working on contract as a translator for the FBI, pleaded guilty to charges of passing government documents bearing a "secret" classification to a blogger. Three successful prosecutions for leaking classified information over the course of the last thirty years—indeed, three such cases in total over the entire sweep of American history—does not exactly constitute a reign of terror.*

ONE CAN go further in another direction. If the prosecutions of Morison, Franklin, and Liebowitz have had a deterrent effect, however modest, that would not be a bad but a good thing. "The press is free to do battle against secrecy," Justice Potter Stewart once said

---

*A case can be made for including a fourth, rather obscure case, that of Jonathan Randal, a former Drug Enforcement Administration analyst based in Atlanta who in 2002 pleaded guilty to charges of stealing government documents and providing them to the *Times* of London. Unlike Morison, Franklin, and Liebowitz, the documents in question were unclassified but "sensitive," involving a narcotics investigation. Randal was sentenced to a year in prison.

in an address to the Yale Law School. "But the press cannot expect from the Constitution any guarantee that it will succeed. There is no constitutional right to have access to particular government information, or to require openness from the bureaucracy."[12] The idea that information pertaining to national defense can be protected by criminal law is hardly an affront to freedom of speech and democratic governance. Our entire history, if it is told honestly, makes that plain.

The prosecution of the two AIPAC men, in contrast to the Franklin and Judith Miller cases, was in many respects a genuinely disturbing development, but also even more exceptional and certainly more instructive. The origins of the investigation into the two lobbyists are still shrouded in obscurity; there is no evidence that the Bush White House was behind it; indeed, the investigative phase of the case predated it. And if anything, like the Judith Miller–Valerie Plame–Scooter Libby affair, the indictment of the three men is something that the Bush administration—which enjoyed warm relations with the State of Israel and with AIPAC itself—would have been more than happy to see disappear.

Although no definitive account of the case's origins has emerged, the most common theory bruited about traces the initial investigation to a group of agents in the FBI, led by a counterintelligence official by the name of David Szady. Szady and some of his colleagues remained convinced, long after the 1985 arrest of Jonathan Pollard on espionage charges, that Israel was continuing to spy on the United States. A second Pollard, or a second and a third, was thought to be participating in the spy effort. A second Pollard was indeed eventually uncovered. In 2008 an eighty-five-year-old former army employee, Ben-Ami Kadish, pleaded guilty to having two decades earlier stolen classified documents from the Picatinny Arsenal in Dover, New Jersey, and passing them to an Israeli agent.

But not a scintilla of evidence has ever surfaced that AIPAC has had any sort of espionage relationship with Israel. What has surfaced instead is blatant evidence of anti-Semitism within the FBI. In particular, before the AIPAC case came along, Szady was reportedly involved in a prolonged investigation into the loyalty of a Jewish CIA staff attorney by the name of Adam Ciralsky that ended by hounding him out of the spy agency.[13] Only eight days after Ciralsky began to work at the agency, CIA and FBI counterintelligence officials began to draw up a "master list" of his "Jewish activities" since the age of fifteen, such as visits to Israel as a teenager and his service as a counselor at the day camp of a Milwaukee Jewish Community Center.[14] Official documents from the case speak of Ciralsky's "rich Jewish friends" and describe him as a "rich Jewish employee." One memo declares: "From my experience with rich Jewish friends from college, I would fully expect Adam's wealthy daddy to support Israeli political/social causes."[15] A subsequent review of the investigation led CIA director George Tenet to regret publicly "that some of the language used by some of the investigators in this case was insensitive, unprofessional and highly inappropriate."[16]

The crude thinking of the FBI and CIA on display here, and the actions prompted by such thinking, might well explain in whole or in part how the AIPAC investigation got off the ground. Whatever the genesis of the case, beginning in 1999 or perhaps even earlier, the FBI had placed a number of lobbyists for the organization under surveillance. Two of them, Steven Rosen, AIPAC's director of foreign policy issues, and Keith Weissman, the lobby's senior Middle East analyst, were observed interacting with Israeli diplomats. In one conversation overheard by the FBI, Rosen told an Israeli official that he "overheard an extremely sensitive piece of intelligence" concerning terrorist activities in Central Asia.[17] Further surveillance over the next few years revealed many more meetings of the AIPAC men with both Israeli and U.S. officials, in some of which, according to the indictment, classified information was discussed.

One such American official was Franklin. In August 2002 the FBI began to listen in on Rosen and Weissman discussing Iran on the telephone with him. In early 2003 agents observed them meeting him for breakfast at a restaurant in Arlington, Virginia. The conversation was somehow recorded and, according to the indictment, "Franklin disclosed to Rosen and Weissman national defense information relating to a classified draft internal United States government policy document concerning a Middle Eastern country."[18] Shortly thereafter they met again for breakfast, this time at Union Station, where, according to the charge sheet, "the three men moved from one restaurant to another and then finished the meeting in an empty restaurant, in order to find a quiet place and avoid having anyone overhear their conversation about the classified draft internal United States government policy document concerning a Middle Eastern country."[19]

On a subsequent day Franklin faxed to Rosen's office what the indictment describes "as a document he had typed himself" that contained "information which appeared in the classified appendix to the classified draft internal policy document" that they had previously discussed. Some of the information provided by Franklin was then passed by the AIPAC men to Israeli diplomats. More meetings and telephone conversations ensued as Rosen and Weissman worked to keep the Pentagon secrets flowing. Thus according to the indictment, after one meeting Rosen "specifically noted the information Franklin had identified was highly classified" and said to Weissman, "this channel is one to keep wide open insofar as possible." Weissman explained "that he was taking Franklin to a baseball game." Rosen replied, " 'Smart guy. That's the thing to do.' " "On or about June 30, 2003," continues the indictment, "Weissman and Franklin, together, attended a major league baseball game in Baltimore, Maryland."[20]

In June 2004, as the relationship between Franklin and the AIPAC men was deepening, the FBI swept in and raided Franklin's home, where it found the previously mentioned trove of classified documents. Caught in a gross security violation, Franklin agreed to cooperate with the FBI in further investigation of Rosen and Weissman. Later in the month, with Franklin now wearing a wire, the three met again and Franklin, at the behest of the FBI, dangled before the AIPAC men a fake classified document containing what he described as highly secret information: "Agency stuff," he called it, and told Weissman he could get into trouble for having it. Weissman declined to take the bait, but the gist of the document was imparted orally. The nature of this "Agency stuff" remains classified, but several reports assert that Franklin told the AIPAC men that Israeli operatives located in Kurdistan were being targeted for assassination by Islamic terrorists. In other words the FBI deliberately had Franklin convey secret information that they knew the AIPAC men would pass on to Israeli diplomats. Lives, after all, were on the line.

That is precisely what transpired. Not long thereafter, in late August 2004, the FBI raided Rosen's office, copying his personal computer's hard drive. AIPAC offices were searched again in December, and the files and computers of a number of other officers of the lobbying organization were seized. Finally, in August 2005, Rosen and Weissman were arrested, charged under the Espionage Act with "having unauthorized possession of, access to, and control over information relating to the national defense," and conspiring to "willfully communicate, deliver and transmit that information directly and indirectly to a person or persons not entitled to receive it."[21]

The indictment was a sensation, generating controversy not only about alleged Israeli spying but the unprecedented nature of the charges. Rosen and Weissman, after all, were not government employees and had not sworn oaths to protect any classified information they had received. In this respect the charges were a completely novel application of the law, and seemed to collide directly with the First Amendment. "If this indictment is allowed to stand," argued the defendants as they asked the court to toss out the case, a statute "intended to address classic spying will not be applied to erring government officials but now will be applied to private American citizens pursuing First Amendment protected activities."[22]

Beyond this apparent constitutional infringement, there were said to be other problematic aspects of the indictment. Throughout all of Franklin's meetings and discussions with Rosen and Weissman, no classified documents had ever changed hands. The single fax that Franklin had sent to Rosen's office, the government was forced to concede, had been sent unsolicited, did not contain markings indicating it was classified, and was in fact not classified but merely a summary of another classified document. Thus, all the secrets that Rosen and Weissman had allegedly learned had been imparted to them orally. This made it impossible to know, they averred, exactly what information they had received was protected by the classification system.

They also did not know and had no way of knowing, they said in their defense, whether Franklin was authorized by higher-ups in the Pentagon to speak to them. Meeting a government official for breakfast and looking for a quiet place to talk in Union Station or accompanying one to a baseball game in Baltimore is not evidence of a crime, it is routine Washington behavior. Neither, for that matter, is exchanging information. Such interchange is a well-established feature of our system of rule that made it impossible for the AIPAC men to gauge whether Franklin's disclosures were in any way outside of the ordinary flow of information that lubricates the gears of our government.

To demonstrate that nothing nefarious had taken place, the AIPAC defense lawyers proposed (against vociferous government objections) to subpoena a parade of high-ranking Bush administration officials, including Secretary of State Condoleezza Rice, national security adviser Stephen J. Hadley, and more than a dozen others who would testify that they themselves customarily discussed sensitive American foreign policy planning with journalists and lobbyists, including representatives of AIPAC. They also intended (also against vociferous government objections) to call experts on the classification system itself, who would testify that *all* the information received by the defendants was either already in the public domain or otherwise innocuous and improperly treated by the government as secret.

In evaluating these arguments Ellis wrote a series of closely argued opinions that explored with considerable subtlety and erudition the constitutional conundrums wrapped up inside the Espionage Act. One of the most critical issues before him, and the one which, as it happens, touched journalists most directly, was whether the statute could in fact be deployed against private citizens. The defense had argued, as we noted earlier, that to do so would stretch the law "far beyond constitutional limits" and "criminalize speech by persons not employed by government, not responsible for the preservation of classified information, and not involved in the violation of any Executive Order or regulation."[23] Such a reading of the law would not only hit lobbyists, it would muzzle the press. After all, members of the press not only meet with government officials, they "*publish* the information they obtain from these meetings." Indeed, "on many occasions, the media boldly state that they have classified material in their possession as a result of these meetings." What is more, unlike the AIPAC defendants, "reporters actually *solicit* the leaking of classified information and seek to get this information in writing."[24]

Ellis did not buy this defense argument, or at least he did not buy it in whole. He agreed that the interests at stake both for the defendants and, by extension, journalists "are significant and implicate the core values the First Amendment was designed to protect."[25] He also agreed that the statute opened the dangerous possibility that, when turned against private individuals, it could be used as a means of punishing "criticism of incompetence and corruption in the government."[26] But such pitfalls were not the end of story, for along with the perils of the law there were safeguards built into it.

Thus, in passing the Espionage Act, Congress did not merely proscribe the dissemination of secrets; it proscribed the dissemination of only those secrets "in which national security is genuinely at risk." A unilateral assertion by the government that national security had been harmed would hardly suffice to settle the matter in any particular instance. Rather the nature and extent of the harm was a question for a jury to decide. Judgment by jury, wrote Ellis, ensures that "the espionage statute has no applicability to the multitude of leaks that pose no conceivable threat to national security, but threaten only to embarrass one or another high government official."[27] Protecting the First Amendment rights of the defendants even further, the statute explicitly demands that the prosecution prove beyond a reasonable doubt that the accused acted with "reason to believe [the disclosure of information] could be used to the injury of the United States." The government would also have to prove, ruled Ellis, that the leaked information itself is potentially injurious to the United States and the accused has to be *aware* that it is potentially injurious.

These multiple safeguards cure the constitutional infirmities that would otherwise be present in the statute. The alternative—the contention of the defense that the law could not apply to private citizens—would lead to an absurdity. The logical end point of the defendants' line of reasoning, wrote Ellis, is that "once a government secret has been leaked to the general public and the first line of defense thereby breached, the government has no recourse but to sit back and watch as the threat to the national security caused by the first disclosure multiplies with every subsequent disclosure." This position, Ellis ruled, "cannot be sustained." On the contrary, "both common sense and the relevant precedent point persuasively to the conclusion that the government can punish those outside of the government for the unauthorized receipt and deliberate retransmission of information relating to the national defense."[28]

Ellis's ruling was a serious blow to the defense in that it let the charges against Rosen and Weissman stand; the case was not summarily dismissed as they had hoped. But the ruling was a far more serious blow to the prosecution. For Ellis's reading of the Espionage Act erected a series of hurdles that, at trial, would be immensely difficult for the prosecutors to surmount. Indeed, as the case subsequently unfolded in a series of motions and countermotions, it became increasingly clear that the government would be unable to prove that the secrets at issue in the case were of the proscribed character. It also became clear that there was no evidence indicating that the defendants ever had the requisite "reason to believe" their conduct would injure the United States. Unable to overcome these barriers, in May 2009, after four years of maneuvering and just weeks before the trial was to commence, the Justice Department opted to withdraw the indictment in the face of near certainty it would not prevail at trial.

A misbegotten case had finally come to an ignominious end. Four years of the defendants' lives had been taken from them. Thousands of hours of Justice Department labor were wasted. The political legacy was ugly: From its inception the case had given rise to a cottage industry on the Far Left and Right devoted to exposing the "dual loyalty" of American Jews, who were said to be spying en masse for Israel. Now, in the dismissal of the case, the power of the "Israel Lobby" to manipulate events was said by these same fringe elements to be proved yet again. The only benefit to the public came from T. S. Ellis III, who bequeathed to the nation the most comprehensive and probing explication of the Espionage Act to date.

CHAPTER 13

THE PECULIAR CULMINATION

Along with the Judith Miller–Valerie Plame–Scooter Libby imbroglio, the indictment of the AIPAC men presents a paradox. For even as our government has swung into action in those two cases in which little or no risk of harm to national security was at stake, it has remained conspicuously inert in the face of leaks that were potentially devastating to national security. Thus, for four years, Rosen and Weissman had been suspended in boiling water for trafficking in secrets. If they were finally pulled out, it was because their conduct was shown not to be criminal. This was a happy outcome for the AIPAC defendants, but it raises an obvious question. Are there circumstances under which journalists might be thrust into the cauldron for publishing leaks and *not* pulled out?

In sentencing Lawrence Franklin to prison, Judge Ellis was explicit about the reach of the espionage statutes, leaving no doubt that reporters and editors and authors of books fall within its ambit. "Where you ran afoul," he said to Franklin from the bench,

> is arrogating to yourself the decision whether to comply
> with the law, even though you thought you could bring
> about a benefit. That's not open to Americans. We are

committed to the rule of law. So, all persons who have
authorized possession of classified information, and
persons who have *unauthorized* possession, who come into
possession in an unauthorized way of classified information,
must abide by the law. They have no privilege to estimate
that they can do more good with it. So that applies to
academics, lawyers, *journalists*, professors, whatever. They
are not privileged to disobey the laws, because we are a
country that respects the rule of law.[1]

Ellis, of course, is only a district court judge. Above him sit the
appellate courts and the Supreme Court, which would be certain
to scrutinize closely his rulings should he or another district judge
ever send a journalist to prison for publishing sensitive secrets. But
Ellis has explicated the law like no jurist before him, and higher
courts would be likely to rely heavily on his carefully wrought
determinations. From the understanding of the Espionage Act he
bequeathed us one can offer informed speculation about how the
New York Times would have fared if, say, it had been prosecuted for
publishing the story with which we began, the December 16, 2005,
article revealing the National Security Agency's Terrorist Surveillance Program.

Some of the differences between what the *Times* did and what
the AIPAC defendants did would seem on their face to make a case
against the newspaper far stronger. In the AIPAC case, as we have
seen, all the secrets were imparted orally. This would have created
a measure of doubt in the minds of a jury (notwithstanding some of
the defendants' seemingly self-incriminating statements) about how
aware they were that they had received closely held information. In
the NSA case, on the other hand, there can be little argument over
whether the *Times* knew what it was receiving and disclosing.

The paper's own reporting was unambiguous; the December 16
article explicitly refers to the "classified nature" of the material, as
well as the *Times*'s own hesitations, for precisely that reason, in pub-

lishing it. Eric Lichtblau had called it "perhaps the most classified program in government."[2] James Risen, for his part, had given his book, *State of War*, a subtitle proclaiming it a "secret history," and it contains references to the highly classified nature of the NSA program throughout. Neither the *Times* nor Risen could exactly defend themselves by claiming, as Rosen and Weissman did, that they lacked "fair notice" that the material they received and published was secret.[3] Both had conceded the point in advance when they broadcast the secret nature of the program to the world.

Other comparisons further inculpate the *Times*. In a trial the AIPAC defendants would have asserted that they had no idea whether Franklin was authorized to pass along the material he was providing them. Uncertainty on this score was another reason why they did not have fair notice they were engaging in forbidden conduct. With the *Times* the position is reversed. Risen and Lichtblau themselves asserted that their sources were fearful of breaking the law: "Nearly a dozen current and former officials," they wrote, "were granted anonymity because of the classified nature of the program." Even more damning: In the acknowledgments to his book Risen thanks "the many current and former government officials who cooperated" with him, adding that they did so "sometimes at great personal risk." What was the "great personal risk" if it was not getting nabbed under the espionage statutes like a Morison or a Franklin for leaking? This is an explicit acknowledgment from Risen that he was not only witnessing a crime but taking part in it; in a criminal context "cooperated" can be a synonym for "conspired."

Still, a significant hurdle for the prosecution would be demonstrating to a jury that the *Times* had the requisite state of mind that is a crucial element of the crime. In particular, did its reporters and editors have "reason to believe" that their disclosure "could be used to the injury of the United States"? They would of course deny that they had any such state of mind. Far from believing that the story would damage the United States, they were performing a public service, they would claim, calling attention to malfeasance in government, bringing into public view the Bush administration's illegal breach of FISA.

Prosecutors would have several counters. They would begin by drawing attention to the fact that lawyers at the NSA and the Justice Department had reviewed and approved the program and Congress, too, had been regularly briefed about it and not registered any objections, let alone leveled allegations of illegality. They would point out that in our system of justice it is not for the *Times* to determine what is legal and illegal; that is a matter for grand juries and courts. Mere allegations of illegality do not create any kind of judicial terra firma. They certainly do not provide a basis for committing a crime of one's own.

They would also recount to jurors the numerous warnings about harm to the nation that the newspaper had received from the administration in advance of publication. The White House, after all, as Bill Keller himself had recounted, "argued strongly that writing about this eavesdropping program would give terrorists clues about the vulnerability of their communications and would deprive the government of an effective tool for the protection of the country's security." Merely listening to such warnings, warnings delivered in person by the president and his top intelligence and national security officials, put them on notice. The warnings created, or should have created, in the minds of the *Times*'s editors, a "reason to believe" that injury to the United States "could" ensue. In the end their state of mind would have been a matter for a jury to ponder. It is fair to say that in a prosecution of the *Times* under the Espionage Act, the verdict would, at the very least, have hung in the balance.

Yet there is an additional wrinkle. The Espionage Act is not the only statute that might have been deployed in such a prosecution. As we have seen, in 1950, after the Black Chamber and the *Chicago Tribune* leaks, Congress passed Section 798 of Title 18, the Comint Act. The kind of intelligence protected by the statute was precisely what the NSA wiretapping story of December 16, 2005, was all about. Here is the Comint Act in full, with emphasis added to those words and passages applicable to the conduct of the *New York Times*:

§798. Disclosure of Classified Information

(a) *Whoever* knowingly and willfully communicates, furnishes, transmits, or otherwise makes available to an unauthorized person, or *publishes*, or uses in any manner prejudicial to the safety or interest of the United States or for the benefit of any foreign government to the detriment of the United States *any classified information—*

(1) concerning the nature, preparation, or use of any code, cipher, or cryptographic system of the United States or any foreign government; or

(2) concerning the design, construction, use, maintenance, or repair of any device, apparatus, or appliance used or prepared or planned for use by the United States or any foreign government for cryptographic or communication intelligence purposes; or

(3) *concerning the communication intelligence activities of the United States* or any foreign government;

Or

(4) obtained by the processes of communication intelligence from the communications of any foreign government, knowing the same to have been obtained by such processes—

Shall be fined not more than $10,000 or imprisoned not more than ten years, or both.

(b) As used in this subsection (a) of this section—*The term "classified information" means information which, at the time of a violation of this section, is, for reasons of national security, specifically designated by a United States Government Agency for limited or restricted dissemination or distribution;*

The terms "code," "cipher," and "cryptographic system"

include in their meanings, in addition to their usual meanings, any method of secret writing and any mechanical or electrical device or method used for the purpose of disguising or concealing the contents, significance, or meanings of communications;

The term "foreign government" includes in its meaning any person or persons acting or purporting to act for or on behalf of any faction, party, department, agency, bureau, or military force of or within a foreign country, or for or on behalf of any government or any person or persons purporting to act as a government within a foreign country, whether or not such government is recognized by the United States;

The term "communication intelligence" means all procedures and methods used in the interception of communications and the obtaining of information from such communications by other than the intended recipients;

The term "unauthorized person" means any person who, or agency which, is not authorized to receive information of the categories set forth in subsection (a) of this section, by the President, or by the head of a department or agency of the United States Government which is expressly designated by the President to engage in communication intelligence activities for the United States.

Unlike the murky Espionage Act, this statute is completely unambiguous. It does not, as I noted previously, encompass the broad and amorphous category of "National Defense Information." Rather it narrowly defines the class of protected information. In their treatise on the espionage statutes, Edgar and Schmidt call Section 798 a "model of precise draftsmanship." As they state, "the use of the term 'publishes' makes clear that the prohibition is intended to bar public speech," which clearly includes writing about secrets in a newspaper.

Nor is a motive or a particular state of mind required in order to obtain a conviction. Rather, violation of the statute occurs merely "on knowing engagement of the proscribed conduct, without any additional requirement that the violator be animated by anti-American or pro-foreign motives."[4] In publishing its NSA wiretapping story, the *Times* had clearly run afoul of the Comint Act. Indeed this is something that even some of its defenders, like Morton Halperin, formerly of the ACLU and now at the Open Society Institute, have openly conceded.[5]

The last leg of the *Times*'s defense would be to challenge, on constitutional grounds, the application of either the Espionage Act or the Comint Act to any prosecution of a newspaper. They would assert that any scheme that allows for the punishment of the press is an unconstitutional affront to the First Amendment. As they reproachfully remind their critics, the amendment is unambiguous: "Congress shall make no law . . . abridging the freedom of speech, or of the press." "No law" means "no law," they are wont to repeat.

But the courts have long held, and the press itself has long readily accepted, that these seemingly unequivocal words are fully compatible with legal restrictions on what journalists can and cannot say in print. Statutes forbidding certain kinds of commercial speech and punishing libel, to which virtually no one inside the media ever objects, have long been held to be fully constitutional abridgements of freedom of the press.* And as we have seen, a line of cases from the Pentagon Papers through *Marchetti*, *Snepp*, and *Morison* show that under some circumstances the Supreme Court would uphold laws punishing the publication of secret national defense information.

---

*Congress in recent years has also outlawed certain forms of political speech. The 2002 McCain-Feingold campaign-finance legislation made it a criminal act punishable by up to five years of imprisonment for American citizens, acting independently of a candidate, to pay for a television or radio advertisement that merely mentions the names of candidates in a race for federal office. Interestingly the *New York Times*, for all of its professed devotion to the First Amendment, vigorously supported passage of McCain-Feingold and has subsequently defended it against constitutional challenges. Floyd Abrams, more consistent than his client, has condemned McCain-Feingold as "nothing less than outright suppression of speech of the most odious nature."

———

OF COURSE our exercise in hypothetical prosecution collides directly with historical reality. The fact is that the supposedly secrecy-obsessed Bush administration was presented with a dream case against the *Times* but declined to bring it. Although Attorney General Gonzales hinted, as I recorded in my opening chapter, that the administration was contemplating prosecution, in the end the paper was left unmolested. There is little mystery why this particular dog barked but did not bite.

First if not foremost, the threat of "graymail" hung in the air—the certainty that in any such litigation many more valuable secrets would spill out as the *Times*'s lawyers engaged in discovery proceedings that sought to explore every aspect of the NSA program. But an even larger consideration was the sheer political trauma such a prosecution would have inflicted. If the *Times* had done what it did in 2002 or 2003, when memories of September 11 were still raw and the threat of a follow-on attack seemed imminent, there is little doubt that the Justice Department would have prosecuted the newspaper tooth and nail.

But by early 2006 the fear had attenuated, the Bush administration had been drained of political power by the bloody stalemate in Iraq, and the American public was perhaps more politically polarized than at any juncture since the Vietnam War. In those circumstances the spectacle of FBI agents raiding the nation's premier newspaper, hauling away computers and file cabinets, and frog-marching a shackled Bill Keller into court would have triggered a political earthquake. In declining to take action, the Bush administration was following the well-known maxim: Do not pick a fight with those who buy ink by the barrel.

But if inaction was the prudent approach, it also incurred a cost in the coin of deterrence. For no sooner than it became evident that no legal action would commence did the *Times* strike again, this time even more egregiously. "Bank Data Secretly Reviewed by U.S. to Fight Terror" was the front-page headline on June 22, 2006, of a 3,550-word exposé written by two familiar names, the reporters Eric Lichtblau and James Risen. The paper (followed immediately by the country's other leading dailies) had revealed another clandestine and ultrasensitive counterterrorism program, this one conducted jointly by the CIA and the Treasury Department, focusing on al-Qaeda finances.

The article recounted how, shortly after September 11, the federal agents gained access to the electronic records of a Belgian financial clearinghouse, the Society for Worldwide Interbank Financial Telecommunication (SWIFT), which tracks the approximately $6 trillion in funds that flow among financial institutions around the world. Buried in the huge collection of data were the transactions of al-Qaeda operatives as they moved money from country to country to sustain their infrastructure and prepare attacks.

The 9/11 Commission had castigated the CIA for neglecting to collect and analyze intelligence about terrorist financing. It noted that in the 1990s, the agency's Osama bin Laden unit "had originally been inspired by the idea of studying terrorist financial links" but had not followed through. As a consequence, "few personnel assigned to it had any experience in financial investigations" and "any terrorist-financing intelligence appeared to have been collected collaterally, as a consequence of gathering other intelligence."[6] The commission recommended augmenting such efforts, noting that "information about terrorist money helps us to understand [al-Qaeda] networks, search them out, and disrupt their operations."[7] In initiating the secret operation to tap the SWIFT database, this is precisely what the Bush administration sought to do.

As happened with the NSA story, the White House learned of the *Times*'s impending story in advance and mounted a full-court press to persuade the paper to spike it. On the eve of publication, Secretary of the Treasury John Snow met with Bill Keller to warn him that publication would undermine "a highly successful counterterrorism program" and alert "terrorists to the methods and sources used to track their money trails." John Negroponte, the Director of National Intelligence, telephoned Keller with a similar message.

The 9/11 Commission's cochairmen, former governor of New Jersey Thomas Kean and former U.S. Representative from Indiana Lee Hamilton, one a Democrat, the other a Republican, also weighed in with high *Times* executives. To no avail.

A "disgraceful act" that caused "great harm" to the nation were President Bush's words after the story appeared in the *Times*.[8] The House of Representatives followed suit, passing a resolution condemning the "disclosure and publication" for impairing "the international fight against terrorism" and exposing "Americans to the threat of further terror attacks."[9] But what precisely was the damage? The *Times* categorically asserted that there was none because al Qaeda already knew well from countless reports in the American press that the United States was attempting to track its finances. This was incontrovertible. But also incontrovertible was that al Qaeda's leadership had only a dim idea of the particular monitoring techniques in use and, even more critically, a scant understanding of their reach and scope.

Indeed in the *Times* story itself there was abundant evidence that some leading terrorist operatives did not know how to keep their financial transactions hidden from American intelligence. Lichtblau and Risen reported that the SWIFT monitoring program had already scored notable successes, enabling investigators to apprehend, among others, the most-wanted terrorist in Southeast Asia, Riduan Isamuddin, also known as Hambali, who had organized the 2002 bombing attack in Bali, killing 182 people. Not all Islamic terrorists, it seems, were so well acquainted with U.S. monitoring efforts as the *Times* had asserted. And if senior operatives like Hambali had been sloppy, were lower-level figures likely to have been more careful? But now, with details of the SWIFT program splashed across the pages of papers across the world, the *Times* had changed the rules of the surveillance game, to the detriment of American security.

WHY ON THIS occasion, in the teeth of intense pressure from the White House, did the editors of the *Times* go forward with the story?

Five months earlier, when they published their exclusive about NSA wiretapping, the editors had rejected last-minute pleas from Bush and his advisers by pointing to the debate within the government over the program's legality. However one appraises that decision in light of the hidden motives of the paper, it had at least a surface justification rooted in allegations of government misconduct. But with SWIFT, even such a surface justification was notably absent.

Thus, in an extraordinary "Letter to Readers" explaining the paper's actions, Bill Keller pronounced the *Times* agnostic on the program's legal status, and he readily conceded that "we have not identified any serious abuses of privacy so far."[10] With no allegations of wrongdoing at issue, publishing the SWIFT story, he averred, was a means of protecting the public from *potential* violations of the Bush White House in the realm of personal privacy. "We remain convinced," wrote Keller, "that the administration's extraordinary access to this vast repository of international financial data, however carefully targeted use of it may be, is a matter of public interest."[11]

Eric Lichtblau, for his part, relying on anonymous experts, explained that the SWIFT program was "arguably extralegal," resting on a "largely untested legal theory."[12] But Lichtblau adduced no arguments to demonstrate its illicit character. And he could not adduce such arguments because his anonymous experts, if they existed at all, would have been flatly wrong. The SWIFT program operated under authority that Congress had granted to the president in 1977 when it passed the International Emergency Economic Powers Act. Congress was regularly briefed on the financial monitoring, which was taking place under a valid warrant. "Letter-of-the-law legal," is what Byron Calame, the *Times* own ombudsman, called it, and a program with "a clean record on privacy abuse."[13]

Performing a half pirouette, Lichtblau also claimed that the aim of the SWIFT story "was never to declare the program legal or illegal."[14] Rather it was to "lay out the facts of the program and let people decide for themselves what they thought of it."[15] It was also "above all else an interesting yarn about the administration's extraordinary efforts since 9/11 to stop another attack."[16]

In these two parallel explanations we come to the heart of the matter, or rather two conjoined hearts. For if the SWIFT story was published because it was *"above all else* an interesting yarn," then the paper was engaging in high irresponsibility. It is difficult to conceive of a more frivolous justification for a step with such potentially grave consequences. And if the paper, alternatively, revealed the program because it wanted to "let the people decide for themselves what they thought of it," then it was trampling on the will of the American people themselves.

Along with the public's "right to know," constantly invoked by the press, there is also something rarely spoken about let alone defended: namely the public's right *not* to know. Yet when it comes to certain sensitive subjects in the realm of security, the American people have voluntarily chosen to keep themselves *un*informed about what their elected government is doing in their name. The reason why they choose to keep themselves uninformed is not an enigma. It is obvious. What they know about such matters our adversaries will know as well. If we lay our secrets bare and fight the war on terrorism without the tools of intelligence, we will succumb to another attack. A late convert to this view was none other than the *Times*'s ombudsman himself. Having originally applauded his newspaper for publishing the SWIFT story, four months of digesting letters from outraged readers led to a change of mind: "I don't think the article should have been published,"[17] Calame now wrote in his column. Too late, the damage was done.

CHAPTER 14

NO MATTER THE COST

T HE SWIFT EPISODE, like other episodes before it, raises
fundamental questions about the place of a free press in our
democracy. Journalists have their own distinctive view of that place:
"We have an obligation to cover the government, to offer information about its activities so citizens can make their own decisions.
That's the role of the press in our democracy," wrote Dean Baquet,
the then-editor of the *Los Angeles Times*, after his newspaper published its own version of the SWIFT story. "The founders of the
nation," he continued, "actually gave us that role, and instructed us
to follow it, no matter the cost."[1]

No matter the cost? Upon hearing Baquet's words, the founders
of the nation would have reached for their cudgels, and not only for
the cavalier declaration that the press can do whatever it wishes,
irrespective of what the price tag might be in American interests
or American lives, but also for its thoroughgoing distortion of the
actual system of self-government they erected.

Baquet's understanding of that system, like Keller's, and like
that of so many others in the press, was fashioned during the Vietnam War and the Nixon era, when a good number of today's top
journalists cut their teeth. But it is a false and self-serving understanding rooted in historical myth. Even among the press's most

stalwart defenders—among them dazzling attorneys like Floyd Abrams—there are those who know well that it is a myth. "The First Amendment initially offered little protection to speakers whose views displeased those in power," states Abrams plainly in his recent book, *Speaking Freely.*[2] But Abrams does not appear to have ever explained this straightforward historical fact to his long-time clients at the *New York Times*—or if he did, they were not paying the slightest attention. When Bill Keller expatiates on the unlimited freedoms invested in the press by the "inventors" of this country, he is brazenly revising history. And his revisionism is in the service of a supremely ironical objective: In the name of democracy, he is justifying an assault on democracy.

The assault comes from two directions. On one front are the so-called whistle-blowers, who operate in tandem with journalists and are hailed by them as "heroes" who run "risks" to bring wrongdoing to light. But there are less rosy lenses through which to view such individuals.

Consider the pledge that government employees must sign before being granted access to official secrets. It is set forth in a standard government form titled "Classified Information Nondisclosure Agreement," which includes the following words:

> I have been advised that the unauthorized disclosure, unauthorized retention, or negligent handling of classified information by me could cause damage or irreparable injury to the United States or could be used to advantage by a foreign nation.
>
> I hereby agree that I will never divulge classified information to anyone unless: (a) I have officially verified that the recipient has been properly authorized by the United States Government to receive it; or (b) I have been given prior written notice of authorization from the United States Government Department or Agency (hereinafter Department or Agency) responsible for the classification of

the information or last granting me a security clearance that such disclosure is permitted. . . .

I further understand that I am obligated to comply with laws and regulations that prohibit the unauthorized disclosure of classified information. . . .

I have been advised that any unauthorized disclosure of classified information by me may constitute a violation, or violations, of United States criminal laws. . . .

I understand that all conditions and obligations imposed upon me by this Agreement apply during the time I am granted access to classified information, and at all times thereafter. . . .

I reaffirm that the provisions of the espionage laws, other federal criminal laws and executive orders applicable to the safeguarding of classified information have been made available to me; that I have returned all classified information in my custody; that I will not communicate or transmit classified information to any unauthorized person or organization; that I will promptly report to the Federal Bureau of Investigation any attempt by an unauthorized person to solicit classified information.[3]

Nothing about this promise is unclear. No one who affixes his name to this nondisclosure agreement is compelled to do so; government officials sign it of their own free will.

What is more, officials who uncover illegal conduct in the government are by no means bound by their signature to keep silent and permit violations of law to continue. Congress has enacted "whistleblower protection acts" that offer clear and workable procedures for civil servants to report misdeeds and ensure that their complaints will be duly and properly considered. When classified matters are at issue, these procedures include direct appeals to the Justice Department and to members of the intelligence committees in Congress. They emphatically do not include blowing vital secrets by disclosing them to al Qaeda and the rest of the world via the front pages of the *New York Times*.

Somewhere upward of 2.4 million Americans hold security clearances.[4] A population that size will always contain a significant quotient of individuals disaffected for one or another reason. The power to leak on a confidential basis offers any one of the 2.4 million a megaphone into which he or she can speak while wearing a mask. Often acting from partisan motives or for personal advancement, and almost always under the cover of anonymity, such whistle-blowers are willing to imperil the nation but not their careers.

A case in point is Thomas M. Tamm, a lawyer at the Justice Department who anonymously passed information to the *New York Times* about the NSA surveillance program. Tamm, who publicly acknowledged his covert role *after* he came under investigation, says he acted not only because he objected to the program itself, but because he was "pissed off" at the Bush administration for a range of other policies and was hoping that the appearance of a story in the *Times* would damage Bush's 2004 reelection prospects.[5] Here, then, in the guise of a civil servant, is a "veritable satrap" of the kind that Judge Wilkinson had warned against in *Morison*.[6]

THE SECOND FRONT in the assault on democracy comes from journalists themselves. "When gathering and reporting news," Time Inc.'s Norman Pearlstine stated in congressional testimony not long ago, "journalists act as surrogates for the public."[7] That observation can be true. But when journalists reveal secrets necessary to secure the American people from external enemies, a converse observation can be true. In that event, journalists are not surrogates for the public but usurpers of the public's powers and rights.

Reporters and editors regard themselves as public servants, but they suffer from a tendency to forget that they are private individuals, elected by no one and representing no one. They indefatigably demand openness in government and claim to defend the people's "right to know." But they operate inside private corporations whose employees and officers report ultimately only to shareholders and which are themselves not at all transparent. Indeed, the putative watchdogs of the press, ever on the lookout for the covert operations of government, can themselves be covert operators, with agendas hidden from the public.

Reporters like Eric Lichtblau and James Risen are not, as they proclaim and as they no doubt perceive themselves, disinterested seekers of truth. They may not be the "Maoists" from the *Harvard Crimson* that Moynihan had warned Nixon about, but as leaps out from the pages of their books, they are passionate advocates of a particular stance in our great foreign policy wars. The press plays an indispensable role in our system as a checking force, but its practitioners can and sometimes do wield their power—the power to withhold and disclose and shade and color information—for political ends of their own choosing.

That is not the only point of conflict between the press and the public, for newspapers are also profit-seeking institutions. Every day of the year, journalists delve into the potential and real financial misdeeds and conflicts of interest besetting corporate America. But, curiously, newspapers seldom if ever delve into the potential and real conflicts of interest besetting journalism. Or perhaps not so curiously. For journalists operate inside a market economy in which financial rewards accrue not just to news corporations and their shareholders but also to they themselves. A Pulitzer Prize brings immense prestige in the profession, and a $10,000 check, a sum almost always matched by news organizations with generous raises and/or bonuses. And then of course there is a book market in which "secret histories" like James Risen's can generate hundreds of thousands of dollars in royalties. Lecture fees can add tens of thousands of dollars more. The incentives to cast aside scruples about injury to national security and lay bare vital secrets can be powerful, indeed, irresistible.

No doubt easing the way for conduct inimical to the country, and salving the journalistic conscience, is the fact that the damage done to our security is rarely clear-cut, readily apparent, or directly trace-able at all. By trading on precious secrets, Herbert Yardley reaped fame and fortune in the 1920s and 1930s, claiming all the way to the bank that his revelations were in the public interest. And when his *American Black Chamber* appeared, it was treated by some in the press as nothing more than an interesting yarn, one "interspersed with startling and amusing tidbits," as the *Saturday Evening Post* gushed at the time. The consequences for our country of Yardley's startling and amusing tidbits were not felt for a decade. But when the iron rain came on December 7, 1941, it fell hard.

THE CONSTITUTION is not a suicide pact, said Justice Robert H. Jackson famously. But how should we contend with those who, for reasons not entirely intellectual, treat one provision of the Constitu-tion as if it were, and would follow their absolutist conception of the First Amendment to the death—or, rather, to the deaths of others? From our nation's inception to the present day our legal system has contained the tools to protect the public from those who would do it harm. Laws enabling prosecution of malefactors—fully constitu-tional laws—are on the books. Yet they are not being enforced.

In the midst of the war on terror the supposedly ultrasecretive Bush administration declined to act against the *New York Times* in the face of successive provocations. Barring another murderous strike on our homeland, it is a safe wager that no future adminis-tration will act either. Perfectly understandable reasons (to which I have already adverted), fear of both graymail and great political upheaval, underpin the government's reticence. When in the pages of *Commentary* in 2006 I had called for the Justice Department to prosecute the *New York Times* under the Comint Act, I never for a moment expected it would happen. As I told one interviewer at the time, "Before my essay came out, I would say the chance was zero percent. After the article came out, the odds have risen to .05 per-cent." Instead of tossing Bill Keller and others in jail, my real hope,

I explained, was to have set in motion a "chilling effect" on a press that was placing us all at risk.[8]

There is scant evidence that a chill of any sort has descended, although it is striking how thin-skinned some news organizations, the *Times* in particular, have become in their self-presentation when dealing with secrets. The mere fact that Bill Keller has felt it necessary to publish extraordinary statements defending the paper's decision making in the NSA and SWIFT cases reveals a sense within its editorial offices that public tolerance of its behavior is at risk. But at the same time, there is still no reason to doubt that should the right occasion arise—if not this year than next, if not during this administration then during the next—precious secrets of the kind that do genuine damage to our national security will be once again spilled across the front pages of the *Times* and other newspapers. The question I raised in *Commentary*—under what circumstances can and should journalists be prosecuted for publishing government secrets?—remains in want of an answer.

The case for prosecution rests upon the enormous damage such leaks can inflict. Yet the confusion-inducing paradox here is that unless we are particularly unlucky, demonstrating the damage we have suffered or will suffer from a leak in any particular instance will always be an exercise in indeterminacy. We are contending, after all, not only with our own secrets but with those of our adversaries, who themselves engage in concealment and are never so kind as to tell us how they are countering the policies and capabilities divulged by our press. Our government's inability to describe the damage is thus built in to the problem itself and is then twisted around by the media into an additional rationale for behaving heedlessly. No harm, no foul, are the watchwords they repeat.

Yet we live now in a world in which small groups of remorseless men are plotting to strike our buildings, bridges, tunnels, and subways, and seeking to acquire weapons of mass destruction that they would not hesitate to use against our cities, taking the lives of hundreds of thousands or more. To contend with that grim reality, our national-security apparatus inexorably generates more secrets, and more sensitive secrets, and seemingly exercises weaker control over those same vital secrets than ever before. Since time immemorial it has been a basic precept of warfare that disclosure of plans and capabilities to an adversary comes at one's peril. But leaks also stifle collaboration with our allies—an essential component of counterterrorism—who are loath to share their intelligence with us lest their hard-won secrets become public, costing them precious resources and even lives. This was the legitimate complaint of Admiral Turner when, testifying against Snepp, he stated that "I cannot estimate to you how many potential sources or liaison arrangements have never germinated because people were unwilling to enter into business with us."[9] Not long before September 11 President Clinton, not particularly hawkish in national security matters, echoed the same warning, declaring that leaks "damage our intelligence relationships abroad." They also, he added, "compromise intelligence gathering, jeopardize lives, and increase the threat of terrorism."[10]

Those are costs of great magnitude, but one must additionally weigh in the balance other less dramatic but no less important exactions imposed by leaks. We have already noted the injury to democratic rule when unelected individuals act to override the public's will. With it also comes the destruction of our government's ability to deliberate in an orderly and coherent fashion. In a system in which a single individual burrowed deep inside a bureaucracy can derail entire policies simply by placing a call to a James Risen or a Seymour Hersh, there is constant anxiety that sensitive information will hemorrhage. The consequence is that the most critical decisions taken by the U.S. government must be decided upon by small groups of trusted individuals at the very apex of power. As these decisionmakers guide the ship of state, they are deprived of the enormous pool of expertise available below deck. This is a recipe for dysfunction and paralysis, ensuring that decisions of profound consequence are taken without adequate counsel while some options are altogether foreclosed. The results for our statecraft have all too often spoken for themselves.

With the injury to our security spanning the immediate to the long-term, the case for the relentless prosecution of leakers within government is irrefutable. Yet apprehending leakers has in almost every instance proved fruitless. Given the obstacles in the way of that approach, the case for prosecuting the journalists who operate out in the open would seem to be equally or even more compelling.

YET THERE IS another side to the story that must not be brushed aside. Legal action against the press would have undeniable costs to our democracy and our freedom. We cannot lose sight of facts that we noted at the outset, namely, that our national security system is saddled with pervasive mis- and overclassification that remains entrenched despite universal recognition of its existence and numerous attempts at reform. We face the ineradicable potential for misuse of secrecy to obscure incompetence and to promote illicit ends. Closed doors are incubators for corruption and can enable units of government, as in Watergate and the Iran-Contra affair, to depart from the confines of law. Judge Gurfein's words in the Pentagon Papers case—that a "ubiquitous press must be suffered by those in authority in order to preserve the even greater values of freedom of expression and the right of the people to know"—are potent and must be acknowledged as such.

The public interest in transparency is diametrically opposed to the public interest in secrecy. With the two desiderata set in extreme tension, would it truly make sense for the Justice Department to prosecute the press on each and every occasion when it drops classified information into the public domain? Even to an advocate of more stringent security like myself, such an approach would be absurd, a cure that would drain the lifeblood from democratic discourse and kill the patient.

Fortunately there are far more attractive avenues for finding the proper balance. The Pentagon Papers case is once again a lodestar. The road out of our perplexing dilemma was mapped there in a concurring opinion of uncommon eloquence by Justice Potter Stewart, a devoted friend of the press and protector of the First Amendment.

The Constitution entrusts the executive, Stewart wrote, with "largely unshared power" in the realm of foreign policy and national security. The executive thus also bears "the largely unshared duty to determine and preserve the degree of internal security necessary to exercise that power successfully." Being unshared, "it is an awesome responsibility, requiring judgment and wisdom of a high order." A host of considerations "dictate that a very first principle of that wisdom would be an insistence upon avoiding secrecy for its own sake. For when everything is classified, then nothing is classified, and the system becomes one to be disregarded by the cynical or the careless, and to be manipulated by those intent on self-protection or self-promotion."[11]

In the face of the danger of degeneration into a dense web of self-interested secrecy of the sort Stewart is describing, it becomes impossible to quarrel with him that, in the final analysis, "the only effective restraint upon executive policy and power in the areas of national defense and international affairs may lie in an enlightened citizenry—in an informed and critical public opinion which alone can here protect the values of democratic government." For this reason Stewart concluded that "a press that is alert, aware, and free most vitally serves the basic purpose of the First Amendment. For without an informed and free press there cannot be an enlightened people."

But Stewart was thus placing government secrets between a hammer and an anvil. For even as he saw a central role for an informed and free press, he did not blink from asserting the government's overriding right to control information. He concurred with Justice White's holding that the *Times* could well be criminally liable for publishing secrets. In his own opinion, he stated flatly that "in the area of basic national defense the frequent need for *absolute* secrecy is, of course, self-evident," and "that it is the constitutional duty of the Executive—as a matter of sovereign prerogative . . . to protect the confidentiality necessary to carry out its responsibilities in the fields of international relations and national defense."

The contradiction here is conspicuous. On the one hand Stewart is saying the press must be empowered to keep the American people informed. On the other hand the government must be empowered— indeed it has a "constitutional duty"—to control information. Can this circle be squared?

It can be. The press, one can readily extrapolate from Stewart's opinion, does and should have an essential checking role on the government in the realm of foreign affairs, national defense, and intelligence. That checking role, if it is to be more than a charade, must extend, as it now does, into the inner workings of the U.S. national security apparatus where secrecy is the coin of the realm. But even as the press strives to carry out this function, this does not mean it should be exempt from the strictures of law. What it *does* mean is that in enforcing the law, the executive must exercise "judgment and wisdom of a high order" and seek to punish the publication only of those secrets that truly endanger national security while giving a pass to all lesser infringements. "The hallmark of a truly effective internal security system," wrote Stewart, "would be the maximum possible disclosure, recognizing that secrecy can best be preserved only when credibility is truly maintained." Prosecutorial discretion is a means to bring about that maximum possible disclosure while seeing to it that genuinely important secrets remain secure.

It is right and proper that jaywalkers are not ticketed for crossing little-trafficked roads. It is also right and proper that they are arrested for wandering onto interstate highways. In this respect the Espionage Act, derided by some as incomprehensible, is drawn with precision. The information it safeguards, as Judge Ellis made plain in his rulings in the AIPAC case, is not merely secret—the equivalent of casual jaywalking—it must be "National Defense Information," information that is both closely held *and* harmful to the nation if disclosed.

If prosecutors must exercise discretion in their choice of when to prosecute, so too must editors exercise discretion in their choice of what to publish. If they publish secrets whose disclosure is arguably harmless—say, for example, the still-classified CIA budget for fiscal year 1964—or secrets that conceal abuses, say, for example, the cynical manipulation of information "by those intent on self-protection or self-promotion," they should trust that, if indicted by a wayward government, a jury of twelve citizens would evaluate the government's ill-conceived prosecution and vote to acquit.* On the other hand, if editors disclose a secret vital to our national security—and have no justification for doing so beyond a desire to regale readers with an "interesting yarn" replete with "startling and amusing tidbits" and haul in a Pulitzer Prize along the way—they should also be prepared to face the judgment of a jury of twelve citizens and, if convicted, the full wrath of the law.

Newspaper editors are fully capable of exercising discretion about sensitive matters when they so choose. A dramatic example came to light in 2009 when the *Times* revealed that it had succeeded for a period of six months in suppressing news that one of its reporters, David Rohde, had been kidnapped in Afghanistan by the Taliban. The editors seemed to exercise the art of concealment with greater success than the U.S. government's own secrecy apparatus is often capable of achieving. Neither the *Times* nor its industry competitors, who readily agreed to gag themselves at the *Times*'s request, published a word about the missing journalist until Rohde escaped his captors and made his way to safety. "We hate sitting on a story," explained Bill Keller. "But sometimes we do. I mean, sometimes we do it because the military or another government agency convinces us that, if we publish information, it will put lives at risk."[12]

All honor to Bill Keller for that. But when the lives of *non-*

---

*An acquittal is almost certainly what would have resulted, for example, if the Nixon administration had indicted the *New York Times* for publishing the Pentagon Papers; indeed, as we have seen, it was certainty of an acquittal that led Whitney North Seymour, Jr., to decline even to empanel a grand jury in the case. The same holds for the AIPAC case, where the prosecution's flimsy case crumbled in anticipation of a jury's scorn.

journalists are on the line, such discretion cannot be—and under our current laws is not—a strictly voluntary affair. Despite Keller's claims the *Times* and other leading newspapers have been far from responsible in their handling of secrets. But even if they were models of rectitude, the public would still be left without recourse in the face of other lesser publications that are not such models, or openly disloyal outlets that might in the future come along, publishing the modern-day equivalent of the sailing dates of transports or the movement of troops.

IN ORAL ARGUMENTS in the Pentagon Papers case there was an unforgettable exchange between Justice Stewart and Alexander Bickel, who was arguing the side of the *New York Times*:

Q: Mr. Bickel, it is understandably and inevitably true that in a case like this, particularly when so many of the facts are under seal, it is necessary to speak in abstract terms, but let me give you a hypothetical case. Let us assume that when the members of the Court go back and open up this sealed record we find something there that absolutely convinces us that its disclosure would result in the sentencing to death of one hundred young men whose only offense had been that they were nineteen years old and had low draft numbers. What should we do?

A: Mr. Justice, I wish that there were a statute that covered it.

Q: Well, there is not. We agree, or you submit, and I am asking in this case what should we do?

A: I am addressing a case of which I am as confident as I can be of anything that Your Honor will not find that when you get back to your chambers. It is a hard case. I think it would make bad separation of powers law. But it is almost impossible to resist the inclination not to let the information be published, of course.

Q: As you know, and I am sure you do know, the concern that this Court has term after term with people who have been convicted and sentenced to death, convicted of extremely serious crimes in capital cases, and I am posing you a case where the disclosure of something in these files would result in the deaths of people who are guilty of nothing.

A: You are posing me a case, of course, Mr. Justice, in which that element of my attempted definition which refers to the chain of causation—

Q: I suppose in a great big global picture this is not a national threat. There are at least twenty-five Americans killed in Vietnam every week these days.

A: No sir, but I meant it is a case in which the chain of causation between the act of publication and the feared event, the death of these one hundred young men, is obvious, direct, immediate.

Q: That is what I am assuming in my hypothetical case.

A: I would only say as to that that it is a case in which, in the absence of a statute, I suppose most of us would say—

Q: You would say the Constitution requires that it be published, and that these men must die, is that it?

A: No, I am afraid that my inclinations to humanity overcome the somewhat more abstract devotion to the First Amendment in a case of that sort.[13]

Commenting on this poignant exchange, Floyd Abrams, a lifelong defender of the First Amendment, writes that, "looking back on it, I cannot escape the conclusion that Bickel's response was a required one."[14] Yet in this Abrams is a dissenter in his own house. His view is outside the mainstream of the press today and not shared by the First Amendment's most avid exponents. Even back then the

ACLU took the pains of filing a rare postargument brief disavowing Bickel's reply and insisting that the one hundred young men should perish to keep the Constitution pure. And today Geoffrey Stone would also not permit inclinations to humanity to overcome his abstract devotion to the First Amendment. He too disavows Bickel's concession, saying that the required answer to Stewart's question, "though painful, must be no."[15]

This is not a discussion confined to lawyers: The ACLU and Stone's position has spread infectiously. Bill Keller can be taken at his word when he says that the *Times* will sit on a story when lives are *directly* in jeopardy. But when lives are *indirectly* in jeopardy—and indirect jeopardy is the ways things almost always are outside the rarefied world of courtroom hypotheticals—the unspoken dictum "Publish and let others perish" has become axiomatic in the profession.

Back in 1931, in *Near v. Minnesota*, the Supreme Court took it as a given that "*no one would question* but that a government might prevent . . . the publication of the sailing dates of transports or the number and location of troops [emphasis added]." But today journalists almost certainly *would* question. In 1987 two of our country's most famous newsmen, Peter Jennings of ABC and Mike Wallace of CBS, were asked on a television program if they would warn American troops of an impending ambush. The exact question put to them was: Does a journalist "have some higher duty, either patriotic or human, to do something other than just roll film as soldiers from his own country were being shot?" Wallace's immediate response, echoed by a vacillating Jennings, was: "No. You don't have a higher duty. No. No. You're a reporter!"[16]

This appalling stance and the guileless lack of shame with which it was pronounced is precisely the same stance that underpins the publication of national-defense secrets today. The Fourth Estate has changed beyond recognition since the era when Roosevelt could speak of the "patriotic press," a description that if employed today the press would itself instantly reject. Long gone is the era when a president could come before the press gallery and declare, as John F. Kennedy did in 1961, that "[i]n time of 'clear and present danger,' the courts have held that even the privileged rights of the First Amendment must yield to the public's need for national security" and at the present moment "the danger has never been more clear and its presence has never been more imminent." For such words, an American leader would be greeted with scoffs dipped in acid. Indeed, with a press now wantonly compromising operational counterterrorism programs, things have swung to an extreme without precedent in our history.

Bill Keller and Dean Baquet and journalists like them are claiming unfettered freedom of action with accountability to no one but themselves. They refuse to recognize that the law, even a law seldom or never employed as a coercive instrument, is an expression of the public's will. What they fail to see or will not acknowledge is that the statutes protecting national security secrets are not just a mechanical system of sanctions, but, like all laws in a democracy, a moral guidepost, a code by which the press can be judged by the public and by which the press can judge and police itself.

That self-judging and self-policing is not occurring today. To the contrary, America's premier newspaper is playing the lead part in a drama written during World War II by the diehard isolationist Colonel McCormick. Like McCormick, as they imperil the public, the editors of the *Times* wrap themselves in the mantle of the First Amendment. Like McCormick, they assert, out of a seemingly invincible ignorance, that in publishing whatever they choose no matter the cost, they are carrying out the mandate of the Founding Fathers. In fact things are the other way around; the conduct of the press today raises the question posed by James Schlesinger of whether the free society built by the Founders can defend itself, and not only from external dangers but also from those who would subvert democracy by placing themselves above the law.

ACKNOWLEDGMENTS

Necessary Secrets was written with support from the Lynde and Harry Bradley Foundation, the Smith-Richardson Foundation, the Earhart Foundation, and the Achelis and Bodman Foundations. I am grateful to each for the precious resources they afforded me. I wish to thank in particular Marin Strmecki and Allan Song of Smith Richardson, Montgomery Brown of Earhart, and John Krieger of the Achelis and Bodman Foundations. I owe special thanks to Dianne Sehler of Bradley, who has been a supporter of my work, and steadfast friend, over a period of many years.

The Witherspoon Institute in Princeton has been a wonderful home in which to write a book, providing a place for quiet reflection and congenial discussion with colleagues deeply interested in the fundamental problems and prospects of democratic governance. Luis Tellez, Witherspoon's visionary president, was more generous and welcoming than I ever had reason to expect. Alicia Bryczki, who keeps the trains running on schedule at Witherspoon, has been a delightful colleague and friend. Witherspoon's assistant director, Patrick Hough, has been graciously helpful on many occasions. Sean Quigley, my research assistant during the summer of 2009, provided significant assistance with the notes and fact checking.

Robby George and Brad Wilson of Princeton's James Madison

Program in American Ideals and Institutions opened their institute's doors to me. The friendships I formed with them, and with some of the estimable constitutional scholars, political theorists, and historians who assemble there, exemplify the true meaning of companionship, intellectual and otherwise.

In the spring of 2009, the Hudson Institute in Washington, DC, invited me to join its ranks. I am grateful for the honor and thankful to its executives—Herb London, Grace Terzian, John Walters, Enders Wimbush, and especially my old friend from graduate-school days Ken Weinstein—for the warm welcome and collegial working conditions they have afforded me.

I am indebted to George Freeman, Jill Abramson, and Dean Baquet of the *New York Times*; James Goodale, formerly of the *Times*; Walter Pincus of the *Washington Post*; Floyd Abrams; and Daniel Ellsberg, who, despite our disagreements, engaged with me in courteous discourse that helped sharpen my understanding of the issues.

A number of other friends and colleagues provided assistance and/or wise counsel along the way, including Rié Ando, Max Boot, Peter Field, Lon Jacobs, Neal Kozodoy, Jim Piereson, Richard Samuelson, Maria Sequeira, Bob Turner, Baruch Weiss, James Q. Wilson, and Jie Zhang. Steve Aftergood, the editor of *Secrecy News* and a leading authority on the subject, patiently answered my questions and granted me access to valuable old files. Les Lenkowsky played a vital role in bringing this book to fruition and is owed special thanks. Bill Kristol generously extended himself on many occasions for which I am particularly appreciative.

A dear friend, Wendy McCurdy, made two vital contributions: She came up with the book's title and she put me in touch with Chris Calhoun of Sterling Lord Literistics, whose skillful representation put the manuscript in the hands of W. W. Norton. I am grateful to my superb editor there, Maria Guarnaschelli, for acquiring and then championing the book, and to all at Norton who helped it take shape, especially the indefatigable Melanie Tortoroli, the ultra-

meticulous Sue Llewellyn, and Bill Rusin, who got the Norton loco-
motive into high gear.

I owe a special debt of gratitude to three old friends and one
new one who read the manuscript in advance of publication. Aaron
Friedberg and his wonderful wife, Adrienne, opened their home in
Princeton to me. Throughout, Aaron was an eager sounding board,
a font of incisive criticism, and encourager-in-chief. Kurt Guthe
offered numerous helpful suggestions and plied me with a wealth of
source material from the inexhaustible archive that he carries around
in his head. Sarah May Stern was a tireless reader and trenchant
critic whose reactions led to many improvements, great and small.
I was honored to have received penetrating comments from Jack
Goldsmith, whose own book, *The Terror Presidency*, is a thrilling
testament to personal and intellectual courage.

Finally, my sister, Miriam DiMaio, and her husband, Daniel
DiMaio, both read the manuscript and offered invaluable correc-
tions. I am indebted to them for that and, together with my aunt,
Jeanne Jonas, also for many other things too significant to enumer-
ate here. My late mother and father, Laure and Herman Schoenfeld, must also be thanked for even more important things. They are
sorely missed.

NOTES

PREFACE

1. Sam Tanenhaus, "Correspondence," *New Republic,* May 21, 2007, 7.
2. Herbert Butterfield, *The Whig Interpretation of History* (1931; reprint, New York: W. W. Norton, 1965).
3. Geoffrey R. Stone, *Perilous Times: Free Speech in Wartime: From the Sedition Act of 1798 to the War on Terrorism* (New York: W. W. Norton, 2004).

INTRODUCTION

1. Bush is here being paraphrased by Bill Keller. Eric Lichtblau, *Bush's Law: The Remaking of American Justice* (New York: Pantheon, 2008), 208.
2. Ibid.
3. "Letter From Thomas Jefferson to Colonel Edward Carrington, January 16, 1787, in *Letters and Addresses of Thomas Jefferson,* ed. William B. Parker (New York: Unit Book Publishing Co., 1905), 53.
4. Edward Albert Shils, *The Torment of Secrecy* (New York: Free Press, 1956), 12.
5. Daniel Patrick Moynihan, *Secrecy: The American Experience* (New Haven: Yale, 1998), 214.
6. "Presidential Letter to the Men and Women of the CIA," April 16, 2009, https://www.cia .gov/news-information/press-releases-statements/release-of-doj-opinions.html.
7. "Obama Administration Reverses Promise to Release Torture Photos," statement by ACLU executive director Anthony D. Romero, May 15, 2009, http://72.3.233.244/ safefree/torture/39587prs20090513.html.
8. For an intelligent discussion of recent trends, see William J. Leonard, "The Importance of Basics," remarks at the National Classification Management Society's Annual Training Seminar, June 15, 2004, http://www.fas.org/sgp/isoo/leonard061504.pdf.
9. Mark Lawrence, "Executive Branch Leads the Leakers: Senate Staff Study Challenges Claims That Congress Is to Blame," *Washington Post,* July 28, 1987, A13.
10. "Statement by the President to the House of Representatives," November 4, 2000, http:// www.fas.org/sgp/news/2000/11/wh110400.html.
11. Edward Longaker, *The Presidency and Individual Liberties* (Ithaca: Cornell University Press, 1961), 175.
12. H. H. Gerth and C. Wright Mills, eds., *From Max Weber: Essays in Sociology* (New York: Oxford, 1946), 233.
13. Bill Dedman, "Obama Blocks Access to White House Visitor List," MSNBC, June 16,

2009, http://www.msnbc.msn.com/id/31373407/. Under a torrent of criticism, and facing lawsuits from "public interest" groups, the Obama administration subsequently relaxed the restrictions, disclosing the identities of some visitors but refusing to release the entire log.

CHAPTER 1. WITHOUT FEAR OR FAVOR?

1. Jack Goldsmith, *The Terror Presidency: Law and Judgment Inside the Bush Administration* (New York: W. W. Norton, 2007), 71–72. I am heavily indebted to this memoir for a number of key insights into the Bush presidency.

2. James Risen and Eric Lichtblau, "Bush Let U.S. Spy on Callers Without Courts," *New York Times*, December 16, 2005, A1.

3. Katherine Shrader, "CIA Chief Says Wiretap Disclosure Damaging," Associated Press, February 2, 2006.

4. Representative Jane Harman, press release, December 21, 2005.

5. Shrader, "CIA Chief Says Wiretap Disclosure Damaging."

6. ABC News Transcripts, "Interview with General Michael V. Hayden," ABC News, *This Week*, February 5, 2006.

7. "Bush: Secret Wiretaps Have Disrupted Potential Attacks," CNN, December 20, 2005, http://www.cnn.com/2005/POLITICS/12/19/nsa/.

8. Walter Pincus, "Prosecution of Journalists Is Possible in NSA Leaks," *Washington Post*, May 22, 2006, A04.

9. Lichtblau, *Bush's Law*, 193.

10. Joe Hagan, "The United States of America vs. Bill Keller," *New York Magazine*, September 18, 2006, http://nymag.com/news/media/20334/.

11. Lichtblau, *Bush's Law*, 194–95.

12. "Talk to the Newsroom: Executive Editor Bill Keller."

13. Hagan, "The United States of America vs. Bill Keller."

14. Risen and Lichtblau, "Bush Let U.S. Spy on Callers Without Courts."

15. Bill Keller, "The Public Editor's Journal," *New York Times*, December 16, 2005, http://publiceditor.blogs.nytimes.com/2005/12/31/more-on-the-eavesdropping-article/.

16. Ibid.

17. Byron Calame, "Behind the Eavesdropping Story, A Loud Silence," *New York Times*, January 1, 2006, ibid.

18. Ibid.

19. David S. Kris, *Modernizing the Foreign Intelligence Surveillance Act*, Brookings Institution (2007), 7, http://www.brookings.edu/~/media/Files/rc/papers/2007/1115_nationalsecurity_kris/1115_nationalsecurity_kris.pdf.

20. Gen. Michael V. Hayden, director of Central Intelligence, Testimony Before the Senate Committee on the Judiciary, July 26, 2006, http:www.fas.org/irp/congress/2006_hr/072606hayden.html.

21. Thomas Jefferson to John B. Colvin, September 20, 1810, Jefferson Digital Archive, http://etext.virginia.edu/etcbin/ot2www-singleauthor?specfile=/web/data/jefferson/texts/jefall.o2w&act=text&offset=6448927&textreg=2&query=colvin (emphasis added).

22. United States Department of Justice, "Legal Authorities Supporting the Activities of the National Security Agency Described by the President," January 19, 2006, 1, http://www.fas.org/irp/nsa/doj011906.pdf.

23. House Subcommittee on Legislation of the Permanent Select Committee on Intelligence, *Foreign Intelligence Surveillance Act: Hearings on H.R. 5794, H.R. 9745, H.R. 7308, and H.R. 5632*, 95th Cong., 2nd sess., 1978, 15.

24. Statement of Deputy Attorney General Jamie S. Gorelick, Amending the Foreign Intelligence Surveillance Act: Hearings Before the House Permanent Select Committee on Intelligence, July 14, 1994, 61, 64 (emphasis added).

25. Memorandum from John Yoo, Deputy Assistant Attorney General Office of Legal Counsel, to Timothy Flanagan, Deputy Counsel to the President, "The President's Constitutional Authority to Conduct Military Operations Against Terrorists and Nations Supporting Them," September 25, 2001, cited in Goldsmith, *The Terror Presidency*, 98.

26. See Goldsmith, *The Terror Presidency*, 148–49.

27. Lichtblau, *Bush's Law*, 173.

28. Lichtblau, *Bush's Law*, 167, 171.

29. "Letter from Sen. Jay Rockefeller to Vice President Cheney regarding NSA domestic wiretapping," July 17, 2003, http://www.talkingpointsmemo.com/docs/rock-cheney1 .html.

30. Lichtblau, *Bush's Law*, 202.

31. Ibid., 203.

32. Ibid., 202–03.

33. Ibid., 203.

34. "New York Times Company Policy on Ethics in Journalism" October 2005, B1, "Participation in Public Life," http://www.nytco.com/press/ethics.html.

35. James Risen, *State of War: The Secret History of the CIA and the Bush Administration* (New York: Simon & Schuster, 2006), 1–3.

36. Ibid., 10.

37. Ibid., 36.

38. Ibid., 10.

39. Ibid., 59.

40. Ibid., 5.

41. Ibid., 7.

42. "New York Times Company Policy on Ethics," A6, 69, "Obligations to Our Company."

43. Ibid., 7.

44. Ibid., B3, 103, "Protections Against Financial Conflicts" (emphasis added).

45. Ibid., B6, "Books and Rights to Our Materials."

46. Ibid., 12, "The Nature of This Policy."

47. "Transcript of Goldsmith Awards Ceremony," http://www.hks.harvard.edu/presspol/ goldsmith_awards/Transcripts/2006_goldsmith_awards.pdf.

48. Douglass Cater, Jr., *The Fourth Branch of Government* (Boston: Houghton-Mifflin, 1959), 19.

49. Michael Schudson, *Discovering the News: A Social History of American Newspapers* (New York: Basic Books, 1978), 160.

50. Harvey Mansfield, Jr., "The Media World and Democratic Representation," in *Rhetoric and American Statesmanship*, ed. Glen E. Thurow and Jeffrey D. Wallin (Durham, NC: Carolina Academic Press, 1984), 55–70.

51. Bill Keller, "Letter From Bill Keller on The Times's Banking Records Report," *New York Times*, June 25, 2006, http://www.nytimes.com/2006/06/25/business/media/25keller-letter.html.

CHAPTER 2. SECRETS OF THE FOUNDERS

1. Benjamin Franklin, "An Account of the Supremest Court of Judicature in Pennsylvania, Viz. The Court of the Press, *Federal Gazette*," September 12, 1789, *The Writings of Benjamin Franklin*, vol. 10, ed. Albert Henry Smyth (London: Macmillan, 1907), 39–40.

2. Ibid.

3. Daniel N. Hoffman, *Governmental Secrecy and the Founding Fathers: A Study in Constitutional Controls* (Westport, CT: Greenwood Press, 1981), 14. I have relied extensively on this pathbreaking study throughout my discussion of the founding.

4. Carl J. Friedrich, *The Pathology of Politics: Violence, Betrayal, Corruption, Secrecy, and Propaganda* (New York: Harper & Row, 1973), 177.

5. Hoffman, *Governmental Secrecy and the Founding Fathers*, 13.

6. Madison to W. T. Barry, August 4, 1822, in *The Writings of James Madison*, vol. 9, ed. Gaillard Hunt (New York: G. P. Putnam's Sons, 1900), 103.

7. Jeremy Bentham, *The Works of Jeremy Bentham*, vol. 2 (Edinburgh: Tait, 1838), 315.

8. Ibid.

9. *Journals of the Continental Congress, 1774–1789*, vol. 1 (Washington, DC: U.S. Government Printing Office, 1904), 26.

10. *Secret Journals of the Acts and Proceedings of U. S. Congress, Documents Illustrative of the Formation of the Union of the American States*, vol. 1 (Washington, DC: U.S. Government Printing Office, 1927), 34.

11. "Letter from G. Washington, 8 Miles East of Morris Town," July 26, 1777, CIA Center for the Study of Intelligence, https://www.cia.gov/library/center-for-the-study-of-intelligence/csi-publications/books-and-monographs/intelligence/letter.html.

12. *Organization of Intelligence*, CIA Center for the Study of Intelligence, March 15, 2007, https://www.cia.gov/library/center-for-the-study-of-intelligence/csi-publications/books-and-monographs/intelligence/orgintell.html.

13. Ibid.

14. Hoffman, *Governmental Secrecy and the Founding Fathers*, 14.

15. Ibid., 15.

16. Ibid.

17. Max Farrand, ed., *The Records of the Federal Convention of 1787*, vol. 3 (New Haven: Yale University Press, 1911), 86.

18. Hoffman, *Governmental Secrecy and the Founding Fathers*, 21.

19. Farrand, *The Records of the Federal Convention of 1787*, 333n.

20. Ibid., 479.

21. Ibid.

22. Ibid., 368 (emphasis in original).

23. Hoffman, *Governmental Secrecy and the Founding Fathers*, 22; Farrand, *The Records of the Federal Convention of 1787*, 76.

24. Alexander Hamilton, James Madison, and John Jay, *The Federalist or the New Constitution*, (1788; reprint, New York: Heritage Press, 1943), 433.

25. Ibid.

26. Ibid., 470.

27. Farrand, *The Records of the Federal Convention of 1787*, 47.

28. Hamilton, Madison, and Jay, *The Federalist*, 433.

29. Hoffman, *Governmental Secrecy and the Founding Fathers*, 28.

30. Patrick Henry, *Life, Correspondence, and Speeches*, ed. William Wirt, vol. 3 (New York: Charles Scribner's, 1891), 496.

31. Ibid.

32. Ibid.

33. John Marshall, "On the Federal Constitution," in *The World's Famous Orations*, ed. William Jennings Bryan, vol. 8 (New York: Funk and Wagnall's, 1906), 149.

34. Hoffman, *Governmental Secrecy and the Founding Fathers*, 37.

CHAPTER 3. "HIGHLY DANGEROUS TO THE PUBLICK SAFETY"

1. *New York Times Co. v. Sullivan*, 376 U.S. 254 (1964).

2. Leonard W. Levy, *Emergence of a Free Press* (New York: Oxford University Press, 1985).

3. Ibid., 8.

4. Ibid., 12.

5. Leonard W. Levy, *Origins of the Bill of Rights* (New Haven: Yale University Press, 1999), 111.

6. Levy, *Emergence*, 125.

7. Ibid., 126.

8. Ibid.

9. Zechariah Chafee, Jr., "Freedom of Speech in War Time," *Harvard Law Review* 32 (June 1919), 932–73.

10. Dumas Malone, *Jefferson and His Time*, vol. 3 (Boston: Little Brown, 1962), 393.

11. Levy, *Origins*, 109 (emphasis added).

12. Ibid.

13. Ibid., 109–110 (emphasis added).

14. *Secret Journals*, vol. 1, 34.

15. John Keane, *Tom Paine: A Political Life* (New York: Grove Press, 2003), 178.

16. Thomas Paine, *The Political Works of Thomas Paine* (Chicago and Toronto: Belfords, Clarke, and Co., 1879), 202.

17. Thomas Paine, *The Life and Works of Thomas Paine* (New Rochelle, NY: Thomas Paine National Historical Association, 1928), 80.

18. Hoffman, *Governmental Secrecy and the Founding Fathers*, 182.

19. Edmund Randolph, *A Vindication of Mr. Randolph's Resignation* (Philadelphia: Charles H. Wynne, Printer, 1795), 40.

20. Ibid., 17.

21. Ibid.

22. Hoffman, *Governmental Secrecy and the Founding Fathers*, 203.

23. Ibid., 199.

24. Ibid., 204.

25. Ibid., 209.

26. James Willard Hurst, *The Law of Treason in the United States: Collected Essays* (Westport, CT: Greenwood Press, 1971), 79.

27. Ibid., 75.

28. Ibid., 96.

29. Ibid., 101.

30. Ibid., 102.

31. Ibid.

32. Ibid., 136.

33. Stone, *Perilous Times*, 264.

34. Ibid.

35. Joseph Story, *Commentaries on the Constitution of the United States* (Boston: Hilliard, Gray and Co., 1833), chap. 44, sec. 1874.

CHAPTER 4. CLEAR AND PRESENT DANGER

1. "Secretary Norton Announces New Visitor Plan for Statue of Liberty," National Park Service News Release, March 30, 2004, http://home.nps.gov/applications/release/Detail .cfm?ID=472.

2. Report of the Commission on Protecting and Reducing Government Secrecy, Appendix A (Washington, DC: U.S. Government Printing Office: 1997), A-9, http://www.fas.org/ sgp/library/moynihan/appa2.html.

3. Woodrow Wilson, *The New Freedom: A Call For the Emancipation of the Generous Energies of a People* (New York: Doubleday, Page & Company, 1913), 70.

4. Woodrow Wilson, *The Essential Political Writings*, ed. Ronald J. Pestritto (Lanham, MD: Rowman & Littlefield, 2005), 255.

5. Woodrow Wilson, *President Wilson's Great Speeches and Other History Making Documents* (Chicago: Stanton and Van Vliet, 1917), 204.

6. *Schenck v. United States*, 249 U.S. 47 (1919).

7. Ibid.

8. Ibid.

9. *Frohwerk v. United States*, 249 U.S. 204 (1919).

10. Ibid.

11. Ibid.

12. "Rose Pastor Stokes is Arrested Again," *New York Times* (March 28, 1918), 16.

13. "To Suppress Disloyalists," editorial, *Washington Post* (January 18, 1918), 6.

14. Abraham Lincoln, *Speeches and Writings 1859–1865* (New York: Library of America, 1989), 459–60.

15. J. Cutler Andrews, *The North Reports the Civil War* (Pittsburgh: Pittsburgh Press, 1955), 30.

16. Stone, *Perilous Times*, 152.

17. Ibid.

18. Chafee, "Freedom of Speech in War Time," 948.

19. Ibid., 967.

20. *Abrams v. United States*, 250 U.S. 616 (1919).

21. Wilson, *The New Freedom*, 113.

22. Andrews, *The North Reports the Civil War*, 576.

23. Ibid., 648–49.

24. Ibid.

25. "Net Now Protects Harbor," *New York Times* (February 18, 1917), 13, and "Lay Submarine Net at Narrows to Protect Port," *New York Tribune* (February 18, 1917), 1.

26. Harold Edgar and Benno C. Schmidt, Jr., "The Espionage Statutes and Publication of Defense Information," *Columbia Law Review* 73, no. 5 (May 1973), 930–1087.

27. Ibid., 955.

28. 18 U.S.C. §§ 793, 794.

29. Jonathan Epstein, "German and English Propaganda in World War I" (paper presented at New York Military Affairs Symposium December 1, 2000), http://libraryautomation.com/nymas/propagandapaper.html.

30. Barbara Tuchman, *The Zimmermann Telegram* (New York: Macmillan, 1966), 183.

31. Edgar and Schmidt, "The Espionage Statutes," 936.

CHAPTER 5. THE BLACK CHAMBER

1. Roberta Wohlstetter, *Pearl Harbor: Warning and Decision* (Palo Alto: Stanford University Press, 1962), 375. Unless otherwise indicated, the Japanese intercepts quoted in this chapter are from Wohlstetter. My usage of the terms "codes" and "ciphers" is in the nontechnical sense of any encrypted communication.

2. Ibid.

3. David Kahn. *The Codebreakers: The Comprehensive History of Secret Communication from Ancient Times to the Internet* (New York: Scribner, 1996), 19.

4. David Kahn, *The Reader of Gentlemen's Mail: Herbert O. Yardley and the Birth of American Codebreaking* (New Haven: Yale University Press, 2004). I have relied heavily on Kahn throughout this chapter.

5. Herbert O. Yardley, *The American Black Chamber* (Annapolis: Naval Institute Press, 1931), 20.

6. Ibid., 21.

7. Kahn, *The Reader*, 251.

8. Yardley, *The American Black Chamber*, 269.

9. Ibid., 277.

10. Ibid., 313.

11. Ibid., 312.

12. Ibid., 322.

13. Ibid., 333.

14. Ibid.

15. Ibid., 370.
16. Kahn, *The Reader*, 105.
17. Ibid., 106.
18. Ibid.
19. Ibid.
20. Ibid., 108.
21. Ibid.
22. National Security Agency, "The Many Lives of Herbert O. Yardley," *Cryptologic Spectrum* (Autumn/1981), 12. The article has been declassified by the NSA, but the identity of its author remains a secret.
23. Ibid.
24. Ibid.
25. Ibid., 10.
26. Kahn, *The Reader*, 122–23.
27. Ibid., 125.
28. Ibid., 130.
29. Ladislas Farago, *The Broken Seal: "Operation Magic" and the Secret Road to Pearl Harbor* (New York: Random House, 1967).
30. Kahn, *The Reader*, 241.
31. National Security Agency, "The Many Lives," 25.
32. Ibid., 26.
33. Yardley, *The American Black Chamber*, 332.
34. Ibid., 313.
35. U.S. Army-Naval Communication Intelligence Coordinating Committee, *The Need for New Legislation Against Unauthorized Disclosures of Communication Intelligence Activities Special Report No. 1*, June 9, 1944, 48.
36. National Security Agency, "The Many Lives," 11.
37. Kahn, *The Reader*, 131.
38. Laurence F. Safford (Capt.), "A Brief History of Communications Intelligence in the United States," in *Listening to the Enemy: Key Documents on the Role of Communications Intelligence in the War with Japan*, ed. Ronald H. Spector (Wilmington, DE: Scholarly Resources, Inc., 1988), 8.
39. U.S. Army-Naval Communication Intelligence Coordinating Committee, *The Need for New Legislation*, 49.
40. Ibid.
41. Kahn, *The Reader*, 131.
42. National Security Agency, "The Many Lives," 12.

CHAPTER 6. THE PRICE OF IMPUNITY

1. U.S. Army-Naval Communication Intelligence Coordinating Committee, "The Need for New Legislation," 30.
2. Ibid.
3. Ibid., 31.
4. Clay Blair, Jr., *Silent Victory: The U.S. Submarine War Against Japan* (New York: Bantam, 1975), 424; and Michael Lee Lanning, (Lt. Col.), *Senseless Secrets: The Failures of U.S. Military Intelligence from George Washington to the Present* (New York: Carol Publishing, 1995), 192.
5. Richard Norton Smith, *The Colonel: The Life and Legend of Robert R. McCormick* (New York: Houghton-Mifflin, 1997), 329.
6. Ibid., 322.
7. Ibid., 379.
8. Ibid., 331.

9. Ibid., 409.

10. Ibid., 388.

11. Thomas Fleming, "The Big Leak," *American Heritage* 8, no. 38 (December 1987), http://www.americanheritage.com/articles/magazine/ah/1987/8/1987_8_64.shtml.

12. Smith, *The Colonel*, 417.

13. Fleming, "The Big Leak."

14. Ibid.

15. Ibid.

16. Burton K. Wheeler, *Yankee From the West: The Candid Turbulent Life Story of the Yankee-born U.S. Senator From Montana* (New York: Doubleday, 1962), 32–33.

17. "Hitler Announced to the Reichstag the Declaration of War Against the United States," Monitoring Service of the British Broadcasting Corporation (December 11, 1941), http://www.ibiblio.org/pha/policy/1941/411211b.html.

18. Harvey Asher, "Hitler's Decision to Declare War on the United States Revisited: A Synthesis of the Secondary Literature," *Newsletter of the Society for Historians of American Foreign Relations* (September 2000).

19. Henry F. Schorreck, "The Role of COMINT at the Battle of Midway," Washington, DC, Department of the Navy Historical Center, March 7, 2006, http://www.history.navy.mil/library/online/srh230.htm.

20. Larry J. Frank, "The United States Navy v. the Chicago Tribune," *Historian* 42, no. 2 (February 1980), 297.

21. Dina Goren, "Communications Intelligence and the Freedom of the Press: The *Chicago Tribune*'s Battle of Midway Dispatch and the Breaking of the Japanese Naval Code," *Journal of Contemporary History* 16, no. 4 (October 1981), 675.

22. Ibid., 666.

23. Ibid., 668.

24. Ibid., 671.

25. Frank, "The United States Navy," 299.

26. Goren, "Communications Intelligence," 671.

27. U.S. Army-Naval Communication Intelligence Coordinating Committee, "The Need for New Legislation," 34.

28. Kahn, *Codebreakers*, 591.

CHAPTER 7. THE "PATRIOTIC PRESS"

1. Albert Einstein to Franklin D. Roosevelt, August 2, 1939, http://www.lanl.gov/history/road/pdf/Einstein.pdf.

2. Executive Order no. 8381, *Federal Register* 5 (March 26, 1940), 1147. For a comprehensive history of the American classification system from the colonial era to the present, see Arvin S. Quist, *Security Classification of Information* (September 20, 2002), http://fas.org/sgp/library/quist/index.html.

3. Executive Order no. 9182, *Federal Register* 7 (June 16, 1942), 4468.

4. The history of the security measures put in place in the Manhattan Project is told in Vincent C. Jones, *United States Army in World War II, Special Studies, Manhattan: The Army and the Atomic Bomb* (Washington, DC: Center of Military History, United States Army, 1985).

5. Ibid., 269.

6. Ibid.

7. Ibid., 277.

8. Ibid., 272.

9. Ibid., 271.

10. Ibid., 270–71.

11. Michael S. Sweeney, *Secrets of Victory: The Office of Censorship and the American Press and Radio in World War II* (Chapel Hill: University of North Carolina Press, 2001), 35.

12. Ibid.
13. Jones, *United States Army*, 278.
14. Sweeney, *Secrets of Victory*, 56.
15. Ibid., 143.
16. Jones, *United States Army*, 278.
17. Ibid., 279.
18. Leslie R. Groves, *Now It Can Be Told: The Story of the Manhattan Project* (New York: Harper & Row, 1962), 325.
19. William Leonard Laurence, *Dawn Over Zero: the Story of the Atomic Bomb* (New York: Alfred A. Knopf, 1946), xi.
20. Groves, *Now It Can Be Told*, 326.
21. Ibid.
22. *Presidential Documents: The Speeches, Proclamations and Policies That Have Shaped the Nation From Washington to Clinton*, ed. J. F. Watts and Fred L. Israel (London: Routledge, 1999), 285.
23. Laurence, *Dawn Over Zero*, 224.
24. Erika J. Fischer, *Complete Biographical Encyclopedia of Pulitzer Prize Winners, 1917–2000* (Munich: K. G. Saur, 2002), 192.
25. Amy Goodman and David Goodman, "The Hiroshima Cover-Up," *Baltimore Sun*, August 5, 2005, http://www.commondreams.org/views05/0805-20.htm.
26. Jeremy Bernstein, *Hitler's Uranium Club: The Secret Recordings at Farm Hall* (New York: American Institute of Physics Press, 1995).

CHAPTER 8. TO THE "RAMPARTS"

1. Executive Order 10290, *Federal Register* 16 (September 27, 1951), 9735.
2. U.S. Congress, *Report of the Joint Committee on the Investigation of the Pearl Harbor Attack* (Washington, DC: U.S. Government Printing Office, 1946), 253 (emphasis added).
3. U.S. Army-Naval Communication Intelligence Coordinating Committee, *The Need for New Legislation*, 64–65.
4. Timothy L. Ericson, "Building Our Own 'Iron Curtain': The Emergence of Secrecy in American Government," in *Government Secrecy: Classic and Contemporary Readings*, ed. Susan L. Maret and Jan Goldman (Westport, CT: Greenwood Press, 1999), 146.
5. Quist, *Security Classification of Information*, chap. 4, http://fas.org/sgp/library/quist/chap_4.html.
6. Edgar and Schmidt, "The Espionage Statutes," 1069.
7. George Gallup, "Survey Finds 8 Out of 10 Voters Approve U.S. Help to Korea," *Washington Post*, July 2, 1950, M1.
8. David Halberstam, *The Making of a Quagmire* (New York: McGraw Hill, 1965; reprint, Lanham, MD: Rowman & Littlefield, 2007), 202.
9. "What Price Vietnam?" editorial, *New York Times*, February 10, 1965, 40.
10. Carl Bernstein, "The CIA and the Media," *Rolling Stone*, October 20, 1977, http://www.carlbernstein.com/magazine_cia_and_media.php.
11. Ibid.
12. Harrison Salisbury, *Without Fear or Favor: An Uncompromising Look at the New York Times* (New York: Times Books, 1980), 160.
13. Arthur M. Schlesinger, Jr., *A Thousand Days: John F. Kennedy in the White House* (Boston: Houghton-Mifflin, 1965), 72.
14. John F. Kennedy, "Address Before the American Newspaper Publishers Association," April 27, 1961, http://www.jfklibrary.org/Historical+Resources/Archives/Reference+Desk/Speeches/JFK/003POF03NewspaperPublishers04271961.htm.
15. Sol Stern, "A Short Account of International Student Politics and the Cold War with Particular Reference to the NSA, CIA, etc.," *Ramparts*, March 1967, 29–38.

16. Hugh Wilford, *The Mighty Wurlitzer* (Cambridge: Harvard University Press, 2008), 236.
17. Ibid., 234.
18. Ibid., 87.

CHAPTER 9. UNNECESSARY SECRETS

1. Daniel Ellsberg, *Secrets: A Memoir of Vietnam and the Pentagon Papers* (New York: Penguin, 2003), xi.
2. Ibid., 202.
3. Ibid., 205–6.
4. Ibid., 207.
5. Ibid.
6. Ibid., 212.
7. Ibid., 272.
8. Ibid., 383.
9. Ibid., 255.
10. Ibid., 256.
11. *The Pentagon Papers: Secrets, Lies, and Audio Tapes: Audio Tapes from the Nixon White House*, "Telephone Conversation With Alexander Haig," June 13, 1971, National Security Archive (June 13–15, 1971), http://www.gwu.edu/~nsarchiv/NSAEBB/NSAEBB48/transcript.pdf.
12. Ibid., "Telephone Conversation With William Rogers," June 13, 1971.
13. Ibid., "Telephone Conversation With Henry Kissinger," June 13, 1971.
14. Ibid., "Telephone Conversation With John Ehrlichman," June 14, 1971.
15. Richard Nixon, *The Memoirs of Richard Nixon* (New York: Grosset & Dunlap, 1978), 509.
16. Henry Kissinger, *Years of Upheaval* (New York: Random House, 1987), 116.
17. *The Pentagon Papers: Secrets, Lies*, "Telephone Conversation With John Mitchell," June 14, 1971, http://www.gwu.edu/~nsarchiv/NSAEBB/NSAEBB48/mitchell.pdf.
18. David Rudenstine, *The Day the Presses Stopped: A History of the Pentagon Papers Case* (Berkeley: University of California Press, 1996), 92.
19. Sanford Ungar, *The Paper & the Papers* (New York: Columbia University Press, 1989), 251.
20. *New York Times Co. v. United States*, 403 U.S. 713 (1971).
21. *Near v. Minnesota*, 283 U.S. 697 (1931).
22. *New York Times Co. v. United States*, 403 U.S. 713 (1971).
23. Author's e-mail correspondence with George Freeman, assistant general counsel, *New York Times*, May 5, 2009.
24. Ellsberg, *Secrets*, 429.
25. Ibid., 205.
26. Floyd Abrams, *Speaking Freely: Trials of the First Amendment* (New York: Viking, 2005), 26.
27. Ibid., 26–27.
28. Nixon, *Memoirs*, 509.
29. Erwin Griswold, "Secrets Not Worth Keeping: The Courts and Classified Information," *Washington Post*, February 15, 1989, A2.
30. Blackmun is here approvingly quoting a lower court's determination.
31. *United States v. New York Times Company et. al.*, 71 Civ. 2552 (1971).
32. *The Pentagon Papers: Secrets, Lies*, National Security Archive (June 13–15, 1971), http://www.gwu.edu/~nsarchiv/NSAEBB/NSAEBB48/nixon.html.
33. John Prados and Margaret Pratt Porter, *Inside the Pentagon Papers* (Lawrence: University Press of Kansas, 2004), 27 (emphasis added).
34. "Johnson's Rating on Vietnam Drops," *New York Times*, February 14, 1968, 4.

35. William Lunch and Peter W. Sperlich, "American Public Opinion and the War in Vietnam," *Western Political Quarterly* 32, no. 1 (March 1979), 31.
36. John Mueller, "American Public Opinion and Military Ventures Abroad: Attention, Evaluation, Involvement, Politics, and the Wars of the Bushes" (paper presented at the annual meeting of the American Political Science Association, Philadelphia, 2003), http://psweb.sbs.ohio-state.edu/faculty/jmueller/APSA2003.PDF.
37. Ellsberg, *Secrets*, 391.
38. Ibid., 256.
39. Ibid., 408.
40. Ibid., 206.
41. Ibid., 357.
42. Ibid., 441.

CHAPTER 10. ELLSBERG'S EPIGONES

1. Hedrick Smith, quoted in Harrison Salisbury, *Without Fear or Favor: An Uncompromising Look at the New York Times* (New York: Times Books, 1980), 194.
2. Schudson, *Discovering the News*, 178.
3. Daniel Patrick Moynihan, "The Presidency & the Press," *Commentary*, March 1971, 43.
4. Ibid., 43.
5. Daniel Patrick Moynihan, "Memorandum for the President," November 13, 1970, http://www.nixonlibrary.gov/virtuallibrary/documents/jun09/111370_Moynihan.pdf.
6. Seymour Hersh, "Huge CIA Operation Reported in U.S. Against Antiwar Forces, Other Dissidents in Nixon Years," *New York Times*, December 22, 1974, A1.
7. Colby, *Honorable Men*, 310.
8. Victor Marchetti and John D. Marks, *The CIA and the Cult of Intelligence* (New York: Alfred A. Knopf, 1974).
9. Ibid.
10. Tom Wicker, "A Score for Secrecy," *New York Times*, June 1, 1975, 194.
11. Frank Snepp, *Irreparable Harm: A Firsthand Account of How One Agent Took on the CIA in an Epic Battle Over Free Speech* (New York: Random House, 1999), 32.
12. Frank Snepp, *Decent Interval: An Insider's Account of Saigon's Indecent End* (New York: Random House, 1977).
13. *Snepp v. United States*, 444 U.S. 507 (1980).
14. Snepp, *Irreparable Harm*, 82.
15. *Snepp v. United States*, 444 U.S. 507 (1980).
16. Ibid.
17. Miles Copeland, *Without Cloak or Dagger* (New York: Simon & Schuster, 1974), 13.
18. Snepp, *Irreparable Harm*, 116.
19. Ibid., 163.
20. Stansfield Turner, "The CIA's 'Unequivocal' Right to Prior Review," *Washington Post* (December 7, 1977), A27.
21. Griffin Bell and Ronald J. Ostrow, *Taking Care of the Law* (New York: William Morrow and Co., 1982), 128.
22. Philip Agee, *Inside the Company: CIA Diary* (New York: Simon & Schuster, 1975), 558. The book was soon also published in the United States and elsewhere, and translated into two dozen languages.
23. *Haig v. Agee*, 453 U.S. 280 (1981).
24. Oleg Kalugin, *Spymaster: My Thirty-two Years in Intelligence and Espionage Against the West* (New York: Basic Books, 2009), 219–20.
25. Anthony Marro, "U.S. Won't Charge Ex-Agent Over Book On C.I.A. Operations," *New York Times*, March 21, 1977, 7.
26. Ibid.

27. Ibid.

28. Richard R. Lingeman, "The Unmasking of a Spy," *New York Times*, July 31, 1975, A18.

29. A. J. Langguth, "For More CIA Books," *New York Times*, July 14, 1980, 18.

30. "Getting at the Spy Hunters," editorial, *New York Times*, July 14, 1980, 18.

31. "Trial by Agee," editorial, *New York Times*, January 7, 1980, 18.

32. "A Dumb Defense of Intelligence," editorial, *New York Times*, September 28, 1981, 18.

33. Samuel H. Day, *Crossing the Line: From Editor to Activist to Inmate: A Writer's Journey* (Baltimore: Fortkamp Pub. Co., 1991), 93.

34. Howard Morland, "The H-bomb Secret: To Know How Is to Ask Why," *Progressive*, November 1979, 3.

35. Bill Leuders, *Enemy of the State: The Life of Erwin Knoll* (Monroe, ME: Common Courage Press, 1996), 133.

36. Morland, "H-bomb Secret," 11.

37. Ibid., 3.

38. Day, *Crossing the Line*, 104.

39. Ibid., 106.

40. Ibid., 108.

41. Ibid.

42. Ibid., 118.

43. Ibid., 116.

44. Howard Morland, *The Secret That Exploded* (New York: Random House, 1981), 193.

45. Day, *Crossing the Line*, 120.

46. Availability of Department of the Navy Records and Publication of Department of the Navy Documents Affecting the Public, 32 C.F.R. §701.31 (2005).

47. *United States v. Progressive, Inc., Erwin Knoll, Samuel Day, Jr., and Howard Morland*, 467 F. Supp. 990 (W.D. Wis. 1979).

48. Ibid.

49. Douglas E. Kneeland, "Editor of H-Bomb Article Says U.S. Acts to Stifle Press," *New York Times*, March 14, 1979, 18.

50. "Ban the Bomb—And the Press?," editorial, *New York Times*, March 11, 1979, 20.

51. "John Mitchell's Dream Case," editorial, *Washington Post*, March 11, 1979, C6.

52. *United States v. Progressive, Inc.*

53. Ibid.

54. Ibid.

55. "Public Bombs, and Minds Born Secret," editorial, *New York Times*, March 25, 1979, E18.

56. *United States v. Progressive, Inc.*

57. Alexander De Volpi, *Born Secret: the H-Bomb, the Progressive Case and National Security* (New York: Pergamon, 1981), 68.

58. Howard Morland, "The Holocaust Bomb: A Question of Time," Federation of American Scientists, November 15, 1999 (rev. February 8, 2007), http://www.fas.org/sgp/eprint/morland.html.

59. Morland, *The Secret That Exploded*, 144.

60. Jeremy Stone, "Prior Restraint: How Much to Print About the Hydrogen Bomb," in *Problems of Journalism—Proceedings of the American Society of Newspaper Editors* (New York City: ASNE, 1979), pp. 36–40.

61. Ibid. (emphasis in original).

62. Morland, *Holocaust Bomb*.

63. De Volpi, *Born Secret*, 272.

64. William Webster, *Nuclear and Missile Proliferation,* Hearing Before the Committee on Governmental Affairs, United States Senate (Washington, DC: U.S. Government Printing Office, May 18, 1989), 12; and S. B. Manohar, B. S. Tomar, S. S. Rattan,

V. K. Shukla, V. V. Kulkarni, and Anil Kakodar, "Post Shot Radioactivity Measurements on Samples Extracted from Thermonuclear Test Site," *Bhabha Atomic Research Center (BARC) News Letter*, July 1999, http://www.fas.org/nuke/guide/India/nuke/990700-barc.htm.

65. Press Statement, Atomic Energy Commission, Government of India, September 15, 2009, http://www.dae.gov.in/press/nuctest.htm.

66. Morland, *Secret That Exploded*, 173.

67. James Schlesinger, "Weapons of Mass Destruction, National Security, and a Free Press: Seminal Issues as Viewed Through the Lens of the Progressive Case," *Cardozo Law Review* 26, no. 4 (March 2005), 1347.

CHAPTER 11. BLACK-LETTER LAW

1. Ben Bradlee, *A Good Life: Newspaper and Other Adventures* (New York: Simon & Schuster, 1995), 470.

2. The description of the Morison case that follows is drawn from the trial record, *United States v. Samuel Loring Morison*, 844 F.2d 1057, http://cases.justia.com/us-court-of-appeals/F2/844/1057/79546/1988.

3. Ibid.

4. Ibid.

5. *Branzburg v. Hayes*, 408 U.S. 665 (1972).

6. *United States v. Samuel Loring Morison*.

7. Ibid.

8. Ibid.

9. Ibid.

CHAPTER 12. A WAR ON THE PRESS?

1. Anthony Lewis, "Silence By Law," *New York Times*, April 7, 1988, A27.

2. Stuart Taylor, Jr., "U.S. Court Backs Conviction in Spy Satellite Photos Case," *New York Times*, April 5, 1988, A1.

3. Floyd Abrams, "Testimony Before the Judiciary Committee, United States Senate" (July 20, 2005), http://www.firstamendmentcenter.org/PDF/Abrams.testimony.S.Judic.Com.PDF.

4. Norman Pearlstine, ibid.

5. William Safire, "The Runaway Prosecutor," *New York Times*, September 29, 2004, 18.

6. Nicholas Kristof, "Our Not-So-Free Press," *New York Times*, November 10, 2004, 25.

7. *Branzburg v. Hayes*.

8. Ibid.

9. Sentencing Hearing, *United States v. Lawrence Anthony Franklin*, 1:05 Cr 225 (E.D.VA. January 20, 2006), 16–17, http://www.fas.org/sgp/jud/franklin012006.pdf.

10. Ibid., 22.

11. *Questions For the Record, Current and Projected National Security Threats to the United States*, A Hearing Before the Senate Intelligence Committee (January 11, 2007), 153, http://www.fas.org/irp/congress/2007_hr/threat-qfr.pdf.

12. Potter Stewart, "Or of the Press" (address at Yale Law School, Sesquicentennial Convocation, November 2, 1974).

13. Edwin Black, "Official Heading AIPAC Probe Linked to Anti-Semitism Case," Jewish Telegraphic Agency, Washington, DC, September 20, 2004, http://www.democraticunderground.com/discuss/duboard.php?az=view_all&address=102x844770.

14. Complaint, *Adam J. Ciralsky v. Central Intelligence Agency, et al.* (D.D.C. July 19, 2000), http://antipolygraph.org/litigation/ciralsky/ciralsky-complaint.shtml.

15. John Diamond, "Associated Press Report," April 9, 1999.

16. George Tenet, Letter to Abraham Foxman, April 13, 1999, http://www.adl.org/PresRele/ASUS_12/3365_12.asp#from_cia.

17. Superseding Indictment, *United States v. Lawrence Anthony Franklin, Steven J. Rosen, Keith Weissman*, 1:05 Cr 225 (E.D.VA. August 4, 2005), http://www.fas.org/irp/ops/ci/franklin0805.pdf.

18. Statement of Facts, *United States v. Lawrence Anthony Franklin*, 1:05 Cr 225 (E.D.VA. October 5, 2005) 3, http://www.fas.org/sgp/jud/aipac/franklin_facts.pdf.

19. Ibid., 4.

20. Superseding Indictment, *United States v. Lawrence Anthony Franklin*, 14.

21. Ibid., 6.

22. Memorandum of Law in Support of Steven J. Rosen's and Keith Weissman's Motion to Dismiss, *United States v. Lawrence Anthony Franklin, Steven J. Rosen and Keith Weissman*, 1:05 Cr 225 (E.D.VA. January 19, 2006), 2, http://www.fas.org/sgp/jud/rosen011906.pdf.

23. Ibid., 2–3.

24. Ibid., 9–10 (emphasis added).

25. Memorandum Opinion, *United States v. Steven J. Rosen and Keith Weissman*, 1:05 Cr 225 (E.D.VA. August 9, 2006), 45, http://www.fas.org/sgp/jud/rosen080906.pdf.

26. Ibid., 45. Ellis is citing Wilkinson's concurring opinion in *United States v. Samuel Loring Morison*.

27. Ibid., 56. Ellis is again citing Wilkinson.

28. Ibid., 53.

CHAPTER 13. THE PECULIAR CULMINATION

1. Sentencing Hearing, *United States v. Lawrence Anthony Franklin*, 22 (emphasis added).

2. Lichtblau, *Bush's Law*, 193.

3. Memorandum of Law in Support of Steven J. Rosen's and Keith Weissman's Motion, 20.

4. Edgar and Schmidt, "The Espionage Statutes," 1065.

5. "Reader Letters: The Espionage Act and the 'New York Times,' " *Commentary* 121, no. 6 (June 2006), 3–4.

6. *The 9/11 Commission Report*, National Commission on Terrorist Attacks Upon the United States (Washington, DC: U.S. Government Printing Office, 2004), 185.

7. Ibid., 382.

8. Peter Baker, "Surveillance Disclosure Denounced," *Washington Post*, June 27, 2006, A01.

9. *Congressional Record*, 152 (June 29, 2006), H 4817–H 4827.

10. Keller, "Letter From Bill Keller on The Times's Banking Records Report."

11. Eric Lichtblau and James Risen, "Bank Data Is Sifted by U.S. in Secret to Block Terror," *New York Times*, June 23, 2006, A1.

12. Lichtblau, *Bush's Law*, 253.

13. Byron Calame, "Secrecy, Security, the President and the Press," *New York Times*, July 2, 2006, http://www.nytimes.com/2006/07/02/opinion/02pub-ed.html.

14. Lichtblau, *Bush's Law*, 252.

15. Ibid.

16. Ibid., 252.

17. Byron Calame, "Can 'Magazines' of The Times Subsidize News Coverage?" *New York Times*, October 22, 2006, 12 (emphasis added).

CHAPTER 14. NO MATTER THE COST

1. Dean Baquet, "Why We Exposed the Bank Secret," *Los Angeles Times*, June 27, 2006, http://articles.latimes.com/2006/jun/27/opinion/oe-baquet27.

2. Abrams, *Speaking Freely*, xiii.

3. "Classified Information Nondisclosure Agreement," Standard Form 312. The complete form is available at http://www.fas.org/sgp/isoo/new_sf312.pdf.

4. Steve Aftergood, "More Than 2.4 Million Hold Security Clearances," *Secrecy News*, July 29, 2009, http://www.fas.org/blog/secrecy/2009/07/security_clearances.html.

5. See Michael Isikoff, "The Fed Who Blew the Whistle," *Newsweek*, December 22, 2008, 40. As of this writing Tamm has not been formally charged with a crime. The status of the investigation into the NSA leak remains unknown.

6. *United States v. Samuel Loring Morison.*

7. Pearlstine, "Testimony Before the Judiciary Committee."

8. Scott Sherman, "Chilling the Press," *Nation*, 283, no. 3 (July 17–24, 2006), 4.

9. *Snepp v. United States.*

10. "Statement by the President to the House of Representatives."

11. *New York Times Co. v. United States* (emphasis added).

12. Bill Keller, "After Reporters' Escape From Taliban, Media Weigh Ethical Questions," *Jim Lehrer NewsHour*, June 22, 2009, http://www.pbs.org/newshour/bb/asia/jan-june09/escapetaliban_06-22.html.

13. *New York Times Co. v. United States*, oral arguments, http://www.gwu.edu/~nsarchiv/NSAEBB/NSAEBB48/argument.pdf, 45–47.

14. Abrams, *Speaking Freely*, 44.

15. Stone, *Perilous Times*, 318.

16. James Fallows, "Why Americans Hate the Media," *Atlantic* 277, no. 7 (February 1996), 144–58.

INDEX

ABOUT THE AUTHOR

Gabriel Schoenfeld is a Senior Fellow at the Hudson Institute in Washington, DC, and a resident scholar at the Witherspoon Institute in Princeton, New Jersey. His essays on national security and modern history have appeared in leading publications, including the *New York Times*, *Wall Street Journal*, *Los Angeles Times*, *Washington Post*, *Weekly Standard*, *New Republic*, *Atlantic*, *National Interest*, and *Bulletin of the Atomic Scientists*. From 1994 to 2008 he was senior editor at *Commentary*. His previous book, *The Return of Anti-Semitism*, was published by Encounter in 2004.

Before joining *Commentary*, Schoenfeld was a Senior Fellow at the Center for Strategic and International Studies in Washington, DC, where he founded the research bulletin *Soviet Prospects*. Schoenfeld was an IREX Scholar at Moscow State University, holds a PhD from Harvard University's Department of Government, and is a United States Chess Federation master. The father of three daughters, Schoenfeld lives in New York City.